The Apple Grower

The
Apple Grower

A GUIDE FOR THE
ORGANIC ORCHARDIST

Michael Phillips

CHELSEA GREEN PUBLISHING COMPANY
WHITE RIVER JUNCTION, VERMONT
TOTNES, ENGLAND

To my

DAD

I so wish you could still be here

to help pick the apples

For more information about Acres U.S.A., or to receive a free sample issue
or catalog, call 1-800-355-5313, or visit www.acresusa.com.

Chelsea Green Publishing Company
Post Office Box 428
White River Junction, Vermont 05001

(800) 639–4099
www.chelseagreen.com

Designed by Christopher Kuntze.

Printed in the United States.
First printing, 1998.
01   00   99   2   3   4   5

Library of Congress Cataloging-in-Publication Data

Phillips, Michael, 1957–
The apple grower : a guide for the organic orchardist / Michael Phillips.
    p.   cm.
Includes bibliographical references (p. 232) and index.
ISBN 1–890132–04–7
1. Apples—United States.   2. Organic farming—United States.
3. Apples.   4. Organic farming.   I. Title.
SB363.2.U6P48   1998
634'.1184–dc21   98–3631
                                CIP

Contents

CHAPTER SEVEN

Spray Options   150

CHAPTER EIGHT

Reaping the Harvest   175

Acknowledgments

A book like this belongs to all who love to grow fruit. From the incredible men and women who met in the 19th century to ponder curculio strategies to the incredible men and women seeking to restore sanity to our food system today. Many more have added their "bit" than I can begin to recount or even suspect.

Yet a few deserve a special personal mention. My fruit-growing horizon has been broadened considerably by these grower friends: John Bunker and Mark Fulford of Fedco Trees, Guy Ames in Arkansas, Don McLean and Chris Edmonds and Brian Caldwell and Hugh Williams in New York, John Bemis and Alan Suprenant in Massachusetts, Jim Gallot in Vermont, and Cynthia Anthony and Steve Page in Maine. A special thanks goes to Margaret Christie for organizing our "Apple Grower to Apple Grower" meetings these past many years. Alan Eaton and Bill Lord of Cooperative Extension here in New Hampshire helped tremendously in teaching this "agricultural expatriate" some fruit growing basics. Paul Sachs of North Country Organics has diligently answered every letter and phone query about the life-giving soil. Lost Nation Orchard itself would not exist if it weren't for my incredible apple partner, David Craxton, and his lovely and creative wife, Andrea. Ken Haedrich nudged me onward in the writer's craft to the point where I tracked down two very generous editors at Chelsea Green: Ben Watson and Jim Schley. More effort has gone into this book than it took to build the stone foundation for our post-and-beam barn . . . showing that hefting words and hefting stones are both about the art of placement. The father of a 1½-year-old daughter with a deadline can't forget the babysitting crew that gave me daytime enough to write: thank you Camilla, Beth, Gene and Nonie, and Mom. And thank you, Gracie, for being such a joyful little booper. Lastly, love to my Nancy for making our life and homestead so wonderful.

This book is an enthusiastic probing of what we know and what we hope to know about orcharding. Future editions are intended to incorporate grower feedback. I deeply appreciate Chelsea

Green Publishing's willingness to push the marketing margins with a detailed fruit grower's manual meant to embrace all. The sustainable path is the only one intelligent humans should be taking in these tenuous times. Every spring when the orchard blooms, we need to remember that hope, too, always begins anew.

SUSANNAH BECKER

Introduction

Apples and other tree fruit have been grown organically for centuries. Conventional chemical methods have only been used during the past hundred years or so, yet most orchard consultants will tell you: *it's impossible to grow fruit organically*. The paradox, however, lies in the economy of these times, not in the orchard itself. Drawing on both the intuitive practices of our great-grandparents' time and the scientific discoveries of today's integrated pest management (IPM) research, a handful of apple growers across the country are producing beautiful organic fruit. Apples like these can be produced only on small farms and in the backyards of people who are intimately involved with their trees.

The Apple Grower is intended to bring the stewards of these orchards—and those who dream of doing the same—together. To share what is known and not known about all aspects of organic fruit production. To state the commercial realities of orchard ventures and look at how the economic context can be changed for the better. To carry on the work of our great-grandparents into the next century. To learn how we can pass on to future generations orchards that are not hazardous to our health.

Many of the threads to the tapestry we're weaving are in place. The basic knowledge about good orchard ground, pruning techniques, the value of thinning, and commonsense harvesting is well established. The debates about rootstocks and varieties, groundcover management, and spray options are good ones. Our brightest threads come from replicated results in controlling apple scab, lepidopterous moths, and apple maggot flies. Yet there are vaguer threads too. We're zeroing in on plum curculio after generations of frustration. Our eyes are opening to the fascinating world of microorganisms and the bigger picture of true soil health. The human thread is perhaps the most ambiguous of all: why do we ask of our orchards what we do?

There are definite answers to some long-standing dilemmas in this book. Equally key is understanding the ways we need to think to overcome further challenges. The depth of detail provided here comes from many sources and it should inspire us as growers to develop additional strategies. Everyone —whether you're struggling to make a living at farming or are a fledgling home orchardist—can contribute to the discussion and draw insights from this book. Knowledge and cooperation are part of our power. The rest lies in the heart and in a deep love for our trees.

I intend no organic snobbery in this, frankly, very organic orcharding book. My respect is high for growers who view thoughtful chemical intervention as a vital economic necessity. We all take a tremendous risk that nature will look kindly on our labors to bring forth the fruits of the earth. And, all the more so, that the consuming public will reward our conscientious work with a respectable living. I have chosen an integrated organic approach to orcharding for reasons you'll find outlined later. Beliefs are a very personal matter, yet we can all learn from each other. We all have good hearts and want to pass on a better world to our children. Let us unite in a sane agriculture and work together to find the right balance with nature and a very out-of-whack modern society.

It's exciting to be embracing the complexity of the fruit orchard—*the* most challenging frontier an organic grower can face—with you. Don't be daunted by the myriad pest dynamics presented in any orcharding book. Your stewardship path will become clearly defined as you identify the particulars of your orchard site. Fortunately, no one has to deal all at once with all the bugs or all the diseases or all the climatic curveballs offered up by nature. Orcharding without the use of synthetic chemicals is daunting, but not undoable. The high quality of today's organic apples would have pleased our great-grandparents immensely. Reviving a small farm economy that values such fruit at its full worth may well be the greater challenge.

Finally, should your journeys ever happen to take you through Lost Nation, do stop by and visit my orchard, which has been the proving ground for most of the ideas and practices outlined in this book. We'll sling some compost, probe out a borer or two, and drink a toast—vintage cider, of course—to the noble apple tree.

The Apple Grower

CHAPTER I

Outlook for Organic Apple Growing

We can grow more good-looking apples today than our great-grandparents could a century ago. And our orchards can be as organically managed as theirs once were. Alternatives to a synthetic chemical agriculture are in the offing, and they will work for innovative farmers who inspire their communities to make local farms the mainstay of a vibrant, local economy.

APPLE GROWING A CENTURY AGO

Looking back a hundred years or so can provide direction for today's organic fruit grower, both in the orchard and in the market. Spray options were just beginning to be recommended—a Bordeaux mixture as a fungicide, the arsenicals for the bugs—and orcharding was for the first time becoming a major commercial industry. Much apple growing was still casual, though, with most orchards having only a dozen to sixty trees located out in the farm pasture or along stone walls. Many more people lived on small farms and endeavored to raise fruit in home market orchards—one map of New York State in 1875 is practically blackened throughout with dots representing every five thousand planted apple trees. Horticultural societies met to share fruit-growing discoveries and to compare notes on hundreds of varieties. Rewards of as much as fifty thousand dollars were contemplated in an attempt to focus human ingenuity on finding an effective means to control plum curculio damage. The crop was consumed by the farm family, mostly as cider, with a few barrels of prime-quality fruit going to the general store or being shipped to the cities. Insects and disease certainly got their share, yet people survived.

Local economies were better then at providing a sustainable living for the community at large. People lived within their means and by the sweat of their brow rather than juggling interest-bearing notes and credit accounts. Markets were accessible and equally bound to local prosperity. Hard work gave as much meaning to life as "time to go fishin'." Tractors reproduced themselves as horseflesh. Federal income taxes weren't collected, nor had insurance companies convinced folks they needed a policy just to breathe. Families were able to focus on the fundamentals of stewarding the land and providing for themselves, with a little extra to trade or sell for that which couldn't be grown on the farm. There's a context here we should remember, not only as we explore the possibilities of organic orcharding, but as we try to make sense of our own increasingly specialized, high-tech society.

Few fruit from these farmsteads of a century ago would have met current grading standards; people accepted nature's offerings beneath minor surface blemishes. Many orchards were essentially unmanaged except for some livestock grazing and winter pruning, but the agricultural experiment stations were looking to change all that. Commercial plantings were encouraged to supply expanding city markets, and with such investment came greater risk. Not only did costs have to be covered, but now there was Coca-Cola . . . cider was no longer "it," and Prohibition would soon bung up great-grandfather's barrel. In the face of such changes, fruit packout needed to improve, and fast, to ensure a higher percentage of fancy, table-quality fruit.

There's fascinating information to be gained in the pre-chemical bulletins and orcharding books written at the turn of the last century. Researchers were making detailed studies of insect life cycles to reveal their points of vulnerability through various cultural practices. Such a humanistic agriculture stresses a depth of understanding in working within the orchard ecosystem. It was observational science taken as far as the human eye could then see. Both the intensity of the research and its universal appeal led to volumes upon volumes of minutiae about all aspects of orcharding concern. Practical techniques were pulled from the improbable, and promising results began to show.

TODAY'S INTEGRATED PEST MANAGEMENT

That emphasis on cultural promise gradually got dropped with the advent of arsenical poisons, which eventually led to DDT, which launched the chemical mindset in earnest. Fortunately the circle is coming round again with today's emphasis on integrated pest management (IPM), an approach to orcharding that stresses only minimal, well-timed applications of chemicals along with other non-chemical management techniques. The gap in human understanding between these two eras is a fantastic opportunity for organic fruit growers. We can make links with a past that hungered to know the dynamics of biological orcharding and apply today's broader understanding of both specific problems and general ecological systems. Today we have better formulations of elemental fungicides and gentler sprays to apply. Beneficial organisms have been identified that can help balance out pest populations. Apple varieties and rootstocks have been developed with inherent resistance to disease. The scab pathogen itself is now understood in ways that allow greater reliance on cultural control.

By the 1970s, resistant and induced pest species had created a need to discover ways of reducing the spiraling use of pesticides in conventional fruit orchards. More and more sprays were needed to stay ahead of the bugs, which were no longer held in check by a natural balance now altered by chemical intervention. Costs were going up, but, as is too often the case in agriculture, net profits were not. Integrated pest management offered a scientific approach aimed at reducing costs by linking the need to spray to actual pest pressure in the orchard. Its evolving appeal also addressed liability concerns with neighbors and planted the idea of environmental safety as a marketing tool. Monitoring with traps, tracking fungal infection periods, and taking advantage of beneficial insect populations are now considered normal practice. Pesticide use has been reduced by a third to a half from what it was when spray applications never wavered from an unyielding ten-day schedule. IPM is a personal gain for growers as well, for, contrary to outrageous public perceptions, no one likes to spray all those poisons. It's one thing to wipe pesticide residues off an apple you're about to eat; it's another thing entirely to be standing in the midst of swirling chemicals.

Dr. Ron Prokopy, an entomologist at the University of Massachusetts, has identified four levels of IPM strategies. The first level is commonly referred to as *chemically based IPM*, in which sprays are held back until potential pest damage exceeds the cost of application. Some cultural techniques may be employed to lessen damage from particular pest groups. *Biologically based IPM* goes further by integrating orchard practices for common gain. Thus, in a second-level IPM orchard, sprays are withheld after June to allow beneficial populations to rebuild, summer maggot fly incursions are trapped at the border, drops are removed to limit in-orchard pest pupation, and fall sanitation is used to reduce disease inoculum the following spring. Third-level IPM comes into play on a diversified farm where surrounding crop practices and composted manures improve orchard dynamics yet again. Finally, fourth-level IPM steps off the farm and embraces all aspects of society to make possible a profitable life for all. Ron adds, "Integrated pest management is a philosophy not unlike that practiced earlier this century, before DDT. The difference is that we have gone through an evolutionary process and, armed with a somewhat better understanding of the basic biology of pests and with a somewhat greater variety of technologies available to control pests, we are in a position to deal with pests in a more illuminated and sophisticated manner than we used to be. . . . It remains to be seen just how far farmers will in fact be able to proceed toward a more ecological approach to managing pests and thus toward a world of less pesticide."

The point of this book is not to label some growers as better than others. The tremendous work and risk of farming is shared by any orchardist. We each face certain economic constraints that often play our hand for us. Pest pressures vary tremendously in different regions. Integrated pest management is an attempt to restore some semblance of beneficial balance by limiting pesticide applications and choosing more target-specific materials. It is a positive start that has stimulated both growers and researchers to broader ways of thinking. Yet somehow we as a society need to find a way to balance the human factors that keep us from going even further. Now, in the marketplace, appearance is paramount. The fruit harvest must be close to 100 percent unblemished to pay the farm bills. And then just

TRY ADDING A NOTE LIKE THIS TO THOSE PECK BAGS OF APPLES . . .

Customer Pledge

Each of us shares in the lasting success of local agriculture. No longer will I assume food just appears at the supermarket regardless of the season. The local growers that provide my sustenance are people I need to know. I understand their livelihood is intimately connected to the vibrancy of my community. It matters to me how my food is grown and that it comes from nearby. Paying full worth for a life-enhancing food supply is more than a matter of shopping for the lowest price. Making agriculture sustainable is as much my responsibility as the farmer's.

barely. We need to place greater value on safe food and on the small-farm way of life to go beyond first-level IPM.

BRINGING IT ALL TOGETHER IN LOST NATION

Pome and stone fruits represent the final organic frontier because the challenges found in the orchard are so complex. A long growing season allows up to several generations of insect injury and gives disease plenty of time to run rampant. Sixty species of insects can cause economic damage to apples east of the Continental Divide. Nor do trees lend themselves to crop rotation, a proven organic practice for renewing soil fertility and breaking pest cycles. Hand-thinning is but one example of the intensive labor involved: we can't go out in one day and cover acre upon acre of orchard with carbaryl (a synthetic thinning agent) but rather must go from tree to tree, picking off excess fruit. Lastly, marketing "aesthetically challenged" fruit can sometimes tip the scales on even a farmer's innate optimism.

The first scouts on any frontier are few in number until the trail stands further revealed. Fruit growers are a conservative lot looking for results that are known to work. IPM methods were not adopted overnight, despite the potential for immediate cost savings. It's an attitude reconcilable with tenured investment in a place where dreams are planted tree by tree. Organic fruit growing may be the ideal, but it is still far from fiscally practical for most orchardists. Yet tentative steps are being taken on many small farms to show what can be achieved in an integrated organic orchard.

Lost Nation is the name of one such orchard in northern New Hampshire. It's an actual place name from an era when winter snows proved too deep for horse travel out of the region. Here is where my partner, David Craxton, and I grow organic apples and squeeze cider on a hundred-year-old press. There's a ring to the Lost Nation name that is fitting to equate with an approach to orcharding that once was and wants to be again. So while I briefly describe our apple farm to give you, the reader, an understanding of our particular orchard reality, please understand that the story of Lost Nation orchard is only one of many. It's a mere footnote in a much larger book about sharing the bounty from that one tree in the center of the Garden.

David and I got together in the winter of 1992 to enact a plan to lease a run-down cider mill business with two plus acres of essentially unmanaged apples. Our wives both teach in nearby schools, giving their organic husbands some fiscal latitude to pursue farming in a depressed paper mill economy. The North Country is not an apple growing region (though in the southern part of New Hampshire orcharding is a proud Yankee tradition) because spring frosts and early autumn freezes offer no commercial certainties. Yet we've found one district advantage . . . plum curculio doesn't overwinter well here.

Ours is a rural area: Lost Nation is located between Groveton and Lancaster, each with three thousand people; there are no larger towns within a forty-five minute drive of our cider mill. Fall foliage brings tourists to the White Mountains in droves, giving us an intense marketing window of three weeks to claim the majority of our direct sales. The mill is water-powered in both the traditional and modern sense: a hydroelectric turbine now powers conveyor and grinder motors, but the press still relies on original water pumps to pressurize the piston beneath the cider tray. David welcomes customers back to watch the cidermaking process, beginning with the dumping of bushels of apples into the conveyor bin and ending with the emptying of the pomace cloths after the squeezing. People are fascinated to experience this age-old process and then be given a taste. Fresh cider is drawn from a

Lost Nation Orchard with Cabot Mountain in the distance.

refrigerated bulk tank in the front of the mill where apple varieties are displayed along with other farm products.

Our bearing apple trees—mostly Paulared, McIntosh, Cortland, and Spartan on M7 rootstock—are located right by the mill. Two new plantings are located on the rising slopes of the Pilot Range that frame our spectacular view. These five acres consist of seventy varieties that range from disease-resistant Liberties and cold-hardy Minnesota selections to classic cider apples like Pound Sweet and Ribston Pippin. Mountain ingenuity provided the opportunity to set up a gravity-feed drip irrigation system with these trees on MMiii, M7, and M26 stock. Additionally, the deer are working with me to establish a sixty-tree farmstead orchard on standard rootstock at our home farm just down the road. Much of this future production is accounted

for with Maine apples currently being trucked in to meet market demand. These apples from Abbott Orchards and others are not organic (we offer two ciders and clearly label all fruit appropriately). Our big thrust is to process a line of organic apple products we can sell direct by mail and wholesale through New England natural foods markets.

Every small farm eventually must face the labor issue. Finding the right apple partner is one of the best moves I ever made. David is a wonderful friend and a knowledgeable grower. Our farm skills and marketing talents dovetail nicely. I love the trees and spending entire days out under crisp blue skies picking apples; David takes charge of fence work and equipment maintenance. David is our "meticulous master of the squeeze" and sound businessperson rolled into one; I dabble at marketing and balance the checkbook. We bounce ideas off

JILL BROOKS

David Craxton and Michael Phillips, Lost Nation apple partners.

each other and entrust entire responsibilities to the other's care. David boils down cider jelly at a maple sugaring house and I jar the Yankee apple butter. A family can certainly do all the work of farming too. The point is we all need a good *someone*.

I would be wrong to give the impression that everything is hunky-dory in Lost Nation. There are times when it feels more discouraging than not. Out in the orchard, hopes pinned on a particular repellent strategy sometimes turn out totally reversed. A new planting on ground scouted as dry had two dozen drowning trees the first summer when it rained and rained. One stormy night the neighbor's Highland steers discovered the electric fence out, and those succulent apple shoots on the other side became cattle fodder. We have incredibly

loyal customers but far too few locally to have yet turned our efforts into a proper living. Our first mail-order catalog brought back just over twenty orders. One percent return may be considered an acceptable start by marketing standards, but it's pretty dismal in a farmer's heart. There are struggles in small-scale orcharding just as in any meaningful human endeavor.

CONVENTIONAL WISDOM

Each orchardist needs to define his or her constraints, both economic and environmental, and proceed from there. Doing the best you can do at this particular time is enough — ecological growers are doing just as much now to further marketing appreciation of orchard dynamics as organic fruit growers. Few people can afford to go totally organic on any kind of significant commercial level, yet it's vital that here and there we begin to figure out integrated organic systems. Small growers can lead the way for larger growers to take what are now perceived as incredible risks. Strongly held beliefs are not changed overnight. Clarity is needed to answer questions like these put by conventional grower friends: Why are you willing to risk using garlic (a rather broad-spectrum repellent) but not a target-specific petrochemical? How are you going to change consumer perceptions about what constitutes an acceptable apple? If I'm barely surviving now with a top-notch packout, how can you even begin to tolerate having a third of your crop be anything less than fancy grade?

Conventional wisdom is established by each generation in the context of its time. Our great-grandparents would have been entirely satisfied by the results achieved in today's organic orchards. That we're *not* satisfied tells us more about changed economic constraints and public perceptions than about a lack of ability to completely control what takes place in the orchard. The fascination with

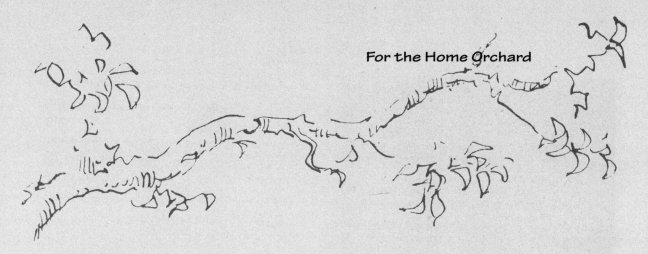

GROWING YOUR OWN

It begins in spring with the plum blossoms. Baby Grace and I delight in the pure ecstasy of a tree in flower. She teaches me how to taste plum blossoms. Together we witness the myriad of insects flying from blossom to blossom. Time stands still as a father and daughter are caught up in the perfect fragrance of spring. Apple buds at this point are pink and filled with the promise of an unblemished harvest.

Summertime brings lessons of acceptance and more moderate expectation. Some fruit have been lost to sawfly, others to curculio. But the apples remaining are swelling daily, taking on a rosy hue. I write my young friend Phil's name on a piece of transparent tape and he attaches it to an apple just beginning to color. Come fall we'll remove the tape and there will be "Phil" written in green on a deeply red background. The grass grows tall, but the swish of the scythe lays down a mulch carpet in preparation for gathering early windfalls. A glass of iced switchel — great-grandpa's restorative tonic of cider vinegar and honey — beneath the cool shade of the old Duchess tree is a grower's reward on this sweltering day. Read a leaf of Walt Whitman and reflect on the good life.

"Apples now. Hatfuls, bushel bags full, even a little heap under the stairs full!" The harvest is phenomenal. Juice drips off the oaken boards of the handscrew press in a steady stream. Family and neighbors lend willing hands to fill jug after jug. The best-looking apples are put into storage in the damp cellar, taste treats that will ripen varietally through the long winter ahead. The perfect smell of hot apple pie wafts from the kitchen. Later, when the orchard leaves have yellowed, bluebirds flock together to journey southward, calling a soft goodbye in the autumn air.

The first snowfall lays gently on the bare branches of the orchard. Timely, too, with the woodshed finally full, the fruity apple wood stacked right by the door. The snows soon deepen enough to bring out the cross-country skis . . . you slalom between trees to block migratory vole tunnels with packed snow. Deer tracks on the edge of the yard threaten next spring's buds but also assure you that you're not alone on this quiet day. Misshapen trees will soon stand to the attention of pruning shears. Orchard and orchardist rest now, reflecting on a year of past growth and the one ahead.

Growing your own is about so much more than just eating fruit.

Sticky trap for European apple sawfly.

"magic bullet" solutions for any pest dilemma just doesn't cut it. There are too many factors at play in the grand diversity of Nature for us to isolate each situation as unrelated to the others. Defining an acceptable answer to plum curculio as consisting of a single action—spraying such-and-such a chemical—overlooks our abilities to intelligently affect a reasonable balance through a series of integrated approaches. In the end, it may be that we have to work harder to get less of a "perfect crop" in order to have a healthy environment. A marginal gain of 30 percent control from knocking curcs out of trees isn't enough, but if commercial results are shown by introducing a repellent spray that funnels them to trap trees, aren't two or three offbeat ideas

combined worth something? Ultimately, all such thoughts depend on the people buying our fruit supporting us every step of the way.

We use a "trap lots of them" approach with European apple sawfly, putting the white sticky cards high in the tree canopy. Conventional wisdom says this pest cannot be fully trapped out; organic wisdom says get what you can if it improves your crop enough to justify the effort. Pollination advice includes mowing down competing bloom—some bees will work the dandelions instead of the apple blossoms—but such cutting of the understory drives tarnished plant bugs up into the tree canopy to wreak havoc on fruit buds and also frees scab ascospores from an entrapping cover. Herbicide use is recommended in the tree row these days to eliminate grasses, which use nutrients and water intended for the tree. Questioning that proposition leads to a range of crop-improving alternatives where only Monsanto (the maker of Roundup herbicide) is the loser.

Some discoveries are accidental. Bordeaux mixture was first used by a French farmer in 1878 in hopes of deterring travelers from picking his roadside grapes. The copper sulfate in Bordeaux tints the vines and fruit a bluish tinge. It's not known if passersby continued to gobble this fellow's grapes, but Bordeaux mixture's effectiveness as a fungicide was quickly noted. Researchers began to look at separate applications of copper and sulfur some sixty years later. And here we are after almost another sixty years learning that certain stickers can keep sulfur on the leaf surface through a rain and that early-season copper can be very effective against fire blight bacteria. And all because of blue grapes!

Patient trial and error will lead the way. Orchardists need to know fungal and insect life cycles to envision variations on potential approaches. No idea is too bizarre, but only results replicated over the course of several growing seasons will prove its ultimate merit. Techniques are always evolving. What you are about to read is an ongoing discussion. It too contains "conventional wisdom." Take to heart what sounds right for you in your orchard.

THE SMALL COMMERCIAL ORCHARD IN CONTEXT

Growing apples with chemicals in these times is considered a proven science; growing apples organically in a revived local economy is a long-lost art. The assumption that successful fruit growing hinges on chemical use is just entering its first centennial of belief, based on an economic context of recovering large-scale investment by selling fancy-grade fruit cheap. It's true in an *agribusiness* where only the big guys survive. The organic apple, however, is grown by an *agriculture* that stewards the land and involves the people drawing sustenance from it. We can bemoan local economy no longer: it would be just as well if the global economy found another planet. The revival of small farms is intimately linked to any sustainable food system.

There is a tremendous opportunity to inspire local marketing by bringing fresh-grown quality and taste back into the food people eat. Getting prices that will make local agriculture viable is key; this is the challenge that makes even getting a good grip on curculio seem attainable in comparison. Customers appear to be willing to pay as much as a 50 percent premium for organic fruit, be it on the wholesale or retail level. The ninety-plus organic growers in Washington state receive four to five dollars more per bushel box from the packing houses than is paid for conventional apples. Cynthia Anthony of Bear Well Orchard in Searsmont, Maine, gets $34 a bushel from the Boston co-ops for her 96-count Liberty apples. Lost Nation apples average eighty cents a pound for "selected orchard run" grade at our cider mill. Ned Whitlock of Dharma Farma apparently tops us all, getting as much as $60 a bushel (sold as fancy tray packs) at the Fayetteville Farmer's Market in Arkansas.

You can begin to make a living when bushel returns are decidedly better than the $8 to $12 conventional wholesale markets offer. Direct sales are a caveat of economic survival for a small farm. Another is adding value to fruit that would otherwise be worth less than what it cost to grow: be it dried apple rings, a line of organic jellies and fruit butters, or hard cider on tap at the local microbrewery. The organic fruit grower needs to find good value across the board for his or her crop. Appearance can no longer go unchallenged as the sole basis of fruit worth. Perhaps offering to teach Lessons on Eating the Minor Blemishes in area schools will help restore some sanity to the public palate.

Another twist on this story comes when you understand net bushel value in the light of rising costs. What good is a 90 percent conventional packout when wholesale returns, adjusted for inflation, pay less today than they did twenty years ago? The organic premium alone can make the difference for growers reaching urban markets directly. People will pay six to eight dollars a gallon for a good organic cider in the city. Costs per acre in an organic orchard vary with equipment investment, intensity of pest pressures, and fertility inputs, just as they do in any conventional system. Big orchards need to buy in everything, and chemicals don't come cheap. The more a small orchard can be integrated into the farm as a whole, the better. Raising animals can provide compostable manure as well as efficient digestive systems for drops. The tractor that pulls the sprayer can also harrow the pumpkin patch. I've daydreamed about growing tropical ryania shrubs in a solar greenhouse, but recognize that supplying garlic juice as a homegrown bug spray is far more likely in northern New Hampshire. Don't get me wrong. We need good suppliers (and boy, do suppliers need us!) to provide the inputs necessary in

LETTER TO AN ASPIRING ORCHARDIST

Dear Doug,

Growing apples organically calls for several qualities in you to start. You need to be dedicated to the organic approach. You will be tempted to take care of a recurring pest with a chemical spray or two, particularly when economics enters in. Persevering means remembering bigger goals: you are a vital part of a humanistic agriculture nourishing both the land and our people. Success will come over the years if you take this holistic view. Truth is, we humans know so little. You need to be an inquisitive and patient observer to sense the lessons of your particular orchard.

Farming demands an acceptance of living with less money than can be made elsewhere. Don't be deterred. The reward of a healthy life spent outdoors has great value. Still, the price of food is deliberately kept low in this country, though the hidden costs to our health and environment are more than an intelligent people would tolerate if they thought about such things. Which is another one of your jobs: inspiring folks to realize that small farms are worthy of their support. In other words, be a good marketer.

What size organic orchard a person can comfortably take on depends in part on equipment investment, where you'll be marketing your fruit and apple products, and to what extent you need other income to supplement your farm earnings. Up to an acre of orchard is a good place to start and, possibly, to stop. Most farms at the turn of the last century had anywhere from a dozen to sixty full-size trees. Pruning, hand-thinning, and harvesting would always be fun at that scale, not overwhelming. Using a scythe and a backpack sprayer would keep equipment costs very low. The fruit harvest will be just a part of your farm income, backed by other crops and ventures in those years when frost strikes the blossoms. Marketing could be as simple as a circle of friends and an old-fashioned general store in town. A hand-screw press could squeeze the cider apples. It all sounds perfectly idyllic.

A passion for growing apples will likely lead you to planting a couple more acres after a while. Hold off on planting more until consistent results show your methods are working, and have a marketing plan in mind before you plant that first tree. Investment in the requisite equipment and deer fencing needs to be incorporated into a long-range farm plan. More of your labor time will need to be directed to orchard management — know what you can afford both financially and spiritually. Too many people lose sight of the fact that what we do for a living should be fun. Too large of an orchard can be overwhelming, and when things get neglected, they aren't fun. The best equipment is often too expensive to be justified over minimal acreage. No family looking to do the work themselves should consider going much over ten acres of organic orchard, and that's pushing it.

Good luck!

Michael

achieving a profitable level of fruit quality. Determining the cost-effectiveness of such inputs is one basis of first-level IPM; any savvy producer needs to look at costs per acre and the results obtained in analyzing orchard management options.

Localized conditions at each orchard site certainly affect the bottom line. Jack Honercamp hand-traps gophers in Nebraska when clouds of grasshoppers aren't descending on his fruit trees, but then he hasn't seen any disease problems in twelve years. When orchardists from the West Coast fill out a grower's survey, one or two pests at most get listed as economic concerns. I mentioned earlier that we don't have any plum curculio to speak of in Lost Nation, but don't think the good Lord overlooked us unfairly: European apple sawfly, apple curculio, codling moth, lesser apple-worm, apple maggot fly, and red-banded leafroller more than take up the slack. Every orchard is different, just as every orchardist is different.

Can you make a living growing organic fruit? Assessing the feasibility of an organic fruit operation starts with a commitment to allotting several marginal years to get all the pieces in place. Your learning curve as a grower is part of this commitment, for each orchard site will present its own peculiarities and challenges. Small orchards work best, given the intensive labor required to manage fruit trees organically and the likelihood of needing other sources of income. Be clear to yourself about your goals and your limits. This is frontier territory and some of the natives are restless, particularly in the humid East. The answer to the $64,000 question remains a qualified yes.

SUSANNAH BECKER

Before investing in an apple orchard, both the locality and specific site should be carefully considered. Circumstances may often prevent the free choice of a locality, but the site of the orchard is usually within direct control of the grower, and may determine largely the success of the enterprise.

—J. C. FOLGER AND S. M. THOMSON,
The Commercial Apple Industry of North America (1921)

CHAPTER 2

The Orchard Site and Its Climate

Fruit growers in different regions face different challenges. No one simply plants a tree and then goes out come fall and reaps a harvest. Disease pressure varies greatly: scab predominates in the Great Lakes region and New England, fruit rots and sooty blotch in the humid South, cedar rust in the Midwest and across to Virginia, and powdery mildew throughout the Northwest. Fire blight rates universal concern across North America. Insect woes range from the extreme pest pressure of the Northeast and mid-Atlantic states to the multiple generations of orchard moths in areas that have long growing seasons. And, almost anywhere east of the "tree line," where woodlands are indigenous—sight in on Fort Worth, Texas, and veer north to Winnipeg—the presence of plum curculio complicates organic prospects immeasurably.

Yet disease and insects are merely challenges to making a dependable living at fruit growing. Ultimately, your ability to bring in a reliable crop in the first place, year in and year out, will determine whether the commercial investment of planting and maintaining an orchard is worth the risk in a particular region. For instance, damp, rainy weather during bloom often puts a damper on a fully pollinated crop in the Midwest. The grasslands of the Central Plains don't have many native trees for a reason: steady winds desiccate bud tissues all winter long when frozen root systems cannot supply moisture. Hail damage to trees gets old quickly where violent thunderstorms frequently clash, as in the Virginia hill country. Killing blossom frosts can strike anywhere from Idaho to New Mexico to the Carolinas. The danger of early frosts is even greater in milder winter climes, where orchards get set up by a warm spell and break dormancy too early. Northern varieties, on the other hand, harden-off with more certainty and can withstand greater cold. Yet total crop failure is unknown in the Wenatchee district of Washington state, from whence come far too many Delicious apples.

Proximity to bodies of water bodes well for protection from cold. Water holds heat and does not respond quickly to atmospheric fluctuations. The larger and deeper the water, the greater is its equalizing effect on temperature. In spring, low water temperatures hold back vegetation and thus thwart early frosts, while bloom may be delayed by as much as ten to twenty days within ten or twenty miles of a large body of water. In summer, water cools the air by day but keeps nocturnal temperatures fairly high. In fall, warm water lengthens the growing season by warding off early frosts. Growers in Michigan, Ontario, and western New York benefit from being on the leeward side of the Great Lakes (truly "big water"), but smaller lakes and deep rivers have moderating effects, too.

All locations have their plus and minus sides. The chief asset of a particular site is the soil, both its fertility and drainage. An orchard's isolation from wild fruit trees and from other plants that serve as alternate hosts for pests helps to ease insect pressures. Low rainfall can limit the severity of fungal disease, provided that the water needs of the fruit trees can be met through the use of moisture-conserving mulches or irrigation. Warm nights work against good red apple color in southern growing zones. Established fruit-growing regions offer the advantage of more suppliers and experienced growers to tap for advice. Then again, being

"the only show in town" is a market edge second to none. Lastly, the costs of production and yield vary widely by region, creating a competitive disadvantage for local growers up against the economy of scale of big agribiz. "Cheap fruit" will doubtless remain a problem until a time when energy and transportation costs are factored into the cost of food.

The search for favorable organic orcharding conditions might suggest that we all move west of the Line of Curculio Demarcation. Yet our farms are located in the perfect place for each one of us. The choice we really have is in siting our orchards to the given lay of our land. Apples can be grown in Alaska . . . you've no reason not to try on your home turf. In the end, local sustainability cannot and should not be limited by regional perspectives.

SACRED SLOPES

Cold air is denser and therefore heavier than warm air. It pours down into valleys from the surrounding hills on still nights, giving rise to river fog as it condenses. Frosts settle in the low spots of undulating terrain. Avoiding this cold air is a basic tenet of fruit-growing success. Orchards located on

DIVERSIFIED FARMS

One century ago the consolidation of fruit orchards on diversified farms into a specialized industry was begun. The economy of scale gained by large plantings allowed fruit to be grown at a lesser cost per acre, a savings theoretically intended for the grower. Yet fruit prices never kept up with inflation, and the tables have turned. Today, vast orchard investment needs to be protected from the vagaries of nature. Chemicals provide assurance of a crop and the need for much less hand labor. Regional vantage defines the boundaries of such capitalized ventures, not local markets.

Ecological orchardists seek a different context. The scale of investment cannot overwhelm the desire to work within the balance of Nature. Some years, in some places, there will be light crops or even outright failures, be it from frost or lack of pollination or unresolved curculio problems. Yet life, and the orchard, needs to go on. Returning to the diversified farms of our great-grandparents' era is part of the answer to putting pleasure back in the bottom line.

sloping land have a better chance of missing a devastating frost at blossom time.

Perfectly flat land is nearly always frosty when conditions warrant because it lacks drainage for cold air. On the other hand, very high land also tends to frost because air temperatures decrease by 1°F for every 300 feet of elevation independent of latitude. The warmer air below holds more moisture, which helps limit radiational cooling. Cold air draining downslope pushes this warmer air part way up, forming what's called an *inversion layer* that acts to protect an orchard positioned to full advantage. A difference of as much as 15°F in temperature can result from the natural drainage of the air. This only works in still air where winds don't stir up the temperature gradient between the elevations. The best elevations in northern zones for tender fruit lie 100 to 300 feet above local rivers and lakes, as the water adds to the humidity of the inversion layer. A wood dividing the slope can block the atmospheric drainage and leave a narrow belt of dead air downhill of the timber exposed to frost danger.

Which is not to say all fruit growers need to take to the far hills. Localized elevations experience air drainage, too, though not quite as dramatically. Farms somewhat lifted above the general contour of flat country may well suit fruit trees. Rolling sites offer benefits over mountainous terrain: choice

of more exposures, less gusty winds, and ground level enough to cultivate. The soils are the rich earth washed down from above. Orchards located on such hospitable ground likely are nearer at hand to the rounds of daily life than an elevated slope up a steeper hillside. Difficult access to a remote planting works against late afternoon strolls through the fruit trees to check if deer are getting through the fence. Thus, the thermal gradient of an ideal slope may be outweighed by other, practical considerations.

THE FOUR POINTS OF THE COMPASS

Some of us have no choice in the lay of our land, but, all things being equal, what's the ideal direction for an orchard to face?

Good ripening and fruit color result on a south-facing exposure if it can be had without the danger of losing blossoms to an early frost. Avoid planting early-blooming cultivars on south or southeast slopes where the spring sunshine accelerates bud development. Also be wary of a southwest orientation where sunscald is a problem. A wind-pummeled exposure should be avoided: gales coming predictably out of the northwest, for instance, may be worse than the prevailing breeze. Northern slopes retard bud development and so are often

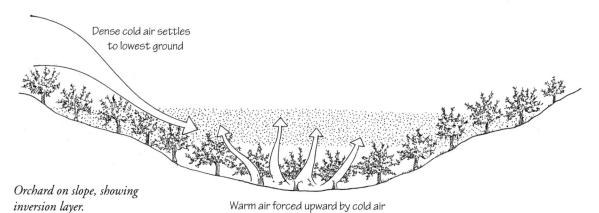

Dense cold air settles to lowest ground

Orchard on slope, showing inversion layer.

Warm air forced upward by cold air

used for tender, early-flowering stone fruit like cherries and plums. Finally, orchards planted near a lake or river should always face the water to benefit from its mellowing effects.

The great horticultural writer L. H. Bailey left this question of aspect unresolved: "There is the greatest diversity of opinion respecting the proper exposure for fruits, some growers contending that the northward slope is always the best, and others preferring a southward exposure. The truth is that no one exposure is best in all cases. Much depends on the location and the particular environment of the fruit plantation, and on the kind of fruit it is proposed to grow." Successful orchards can be found sloping toward every point of the compass.

DRY GROUND

Solving the problem of a fruit tree floundering in wet ground is easy . . . provided you act before the tree ever gets planted. Trees planted in saturated soils literally drown. Roots and trunk crowns deprived of good aeration fall victim to rot fungi. Marginal ground may not immediately cause a tree's demise, but vigor and thriftiness will lack until a wet summer comes along to settle up the account.

Apples are adapted to medium-textured soils six to eight feet deep that are neither too dry nor too wet. Pears tolerate more wetness as their roots will regenerate after sitting in waterlogged ground. Peaches require less moisture but better aeration than apples, so sandy soils are favored for them. Plums will tolerate heavier soils than any other stone fruit.

The groundwater table should not be higher than three feet during the growing season; if it is any closer to the surface, the tree's submerged feeder roots can no longer function properly to feed the tree. Tile drainage to this depth may improve drowning soils, if the excess water can be directed beyond undulating terrain. Soil drainage often follows the

The standing water around this young tree appears every spring but soon disappears when the land begins to dry out.

same principles as good air drainage: an orchard located above adjoining lands is upslope of the problem.

The subsoil also deserves consideration in evaluating a potential orchard site. Farmers who know the qualities of their soil only as deep as the bottom of a plow furrow don't know enough. Soils that drain satisfactorily to a depth of four feet are good, and six feet is even better. To examine your subsoil, get out a spade and dig. Keep in mind that a soft, mucky subsoil can be as much a barrier to root growth as solid bedrock. Roots have a boring power to force their way down in any ordinary subsoil, even fractured rock. But undrained ground lacks the air necessary for roots to penetrate further.

On heavy soils, where occasional standing water may be a problem, trees can be planted on berms or mounds to improve drainage around the crown of the trunk. Some rootstocks are more susceptible to crown rot than others, though all suffer under poor conditions. Berms are formed before planting out trees by taking topsoil from the aisles: each berm should be two to three feet wide and at least six inches higher than the adjacent ground after settling. Trees set on wide spacings can be planted on mounds. Ditch-draining low-lying pockets of surface wetness can be more appropriate than planting on berms or mounds. When siting your orchard remember that the fertility of thin soils can always be improved, but wet ground is hard to rectify once the trees have been planted.

ZONE HARDINESS

The zone hardiness of fruit varieties corresponds to the woody plant's ability to acclimate to winter conditions. Peach trees simply will not survive where winter temperatures dip much below minus 20°F. The severity of winter cold that cultivars are known to survive is often listed in the varietal description. Conversely, trees have specific chilling periods in which buds do not break dormancy until a certain number of hours between 32°F and 45°F have accumulated. Hardiness is lost rapidly once growth resumes. A late January thaw won't harm a Honeygold apple tree in Zone 3, but a Stayman Winesap awakening after a moderate 800 hours of chilling may find the next deep freeze deadly. That same Stayman would flower erratically—if at all—in the Deep South or California valleys. Apple plantings in Zone 9 are limited to low-chill varieties like Winter Banana and Reverend Morgan. Granny Smith, Pink Pearl, and Gravenstein are the next step up the chilling ladder with 600 hours required.

Shortening days put an end to summer's growth, but it's the first frosts that initiate hardening off in the fruit tree. Heavy crop loading, late irrigation or cultivation, and fall pruning can adversely affect this acclimatization of plant tissues. Too much nitrogen applied late in the season (after petal fall) will prolong growth and thus delay plant maturity, predisposing the tree to early winter freeze damage. In the clean tillage systems of our great-grandfathers, an August cover crop enhanced tissue maturity by reducing nitrogen levels and absorbing excess moisture in late summer. Grass sod works in much the same way. Yet cultural controls can never make up for a tree that is planted in a location outside the limits of its innate hardiness. Certain rootstocks like MM111 and M7 tend to shed their leaves earlier, thus allowing the grafted cultivar to harden-off earlier. MM106 and M26, on the other hand, defoliate late in the season and don't accentuate varietal hardiness. Interestingly, hardier scion cultivars often decrease the rootstock's hardiness, and more tender fruiting wood increases the root's ability to withstand winter cold.

The date of the last spring frost means slightly less to an orchardist than a gardener. Buds and opening bloom are hardier than a tomato plant on the ground. Deep freezes on the other end of the season affect the ability to properly mature late varieties of apples. Air temperatures below 28°F raise concerns for both bud survival and the keeping qualities of unharvested fruit. The length of the growing season—stretched beyond the usual gardening sense—between a heavy frost in spring and a substantial freeze in fall determines which varieties can be expected to set fruit and ripen in any given zone. Golden Russet is a classic cider apple that rarely gets to tree-ripen most years in Lost Nation, yet we have a few trees that are more than hardy enough to grow on the northern edge of Zone 4. An apple like Fuji requiring 170 to 190 days to ripen, does best in Zones 6 through 8.

All varieties chosen need to be winter-hardy in your climate. The moderating effect of the Atlantic

HARDINESS ZONE MAP

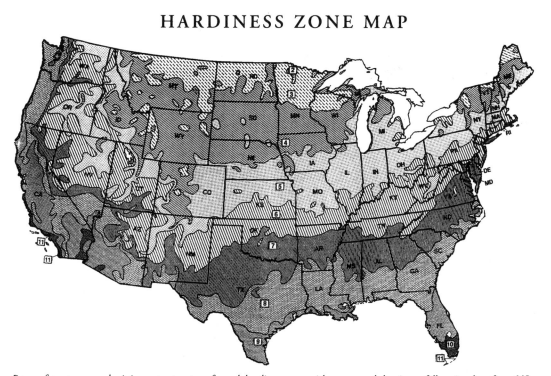

Range of average annual minimum temperatures for each hardiness zone, with recommended spring or fall sowing dates for wildflowers

ZONE 1	below -50°F	Sow seed in early spring when soil can be worked	ZONE 7	0° to 10°	Spring: February 15–April 15 Fall: September 15–November 15
ZONE 2	-50°F to -40°	Sow seed in early spring when soil can be worked	ZONE 8	10° to 20°	Spring: January 15–March 15 Fall: October 1–December 1
ZONE 3	-40° to -30°	Spring: April 15–June 15 Fall: September 1–October 1	ZONE 9	20° to 30°	Spring: January 1–March 1 Fall: October 1–December 1
ZONE 4	-30° to -20°	Spring: April 15–June 15 Fall: September 1–October 1	ZONE 10	30° to 40°	Spring: January 1–March 1 Fall: October 1–December 1
ZONE 5	-20° to -10°	Spring: April 15–June 15 Fall: September 1–October 1	ZONE 11	above 40°	Spring: January 1–March 15 Fall: October 1–December 1
ZONE 6	-10° to 0°	Spring: March 15–May 15 Fall: September 15–November 1			

Reprinted courtesy of Wildseed Farms, Eagle Lake, Texas

and Pacific oceans shows up on a map delineated by growing zones. Hardiness sweeps upward along both coastlines where winter lows aren't as extreme as they are at comparable latitudes further inland. Mountainous regions extend lower (less hardy) zones southward. Recommendations can be pushed to the next zone northward if your orchard's micro-climate is favorable, but the risk of "pushing the envelope" too far is yours as the grower. Pruning such borderline trees too early in winter can undo great hopes: the fresh cut stimulates cellular activity which dehardens the tissue at the wound. Subsequent sub-zero freezes within the next two weeks can put you back to square one.

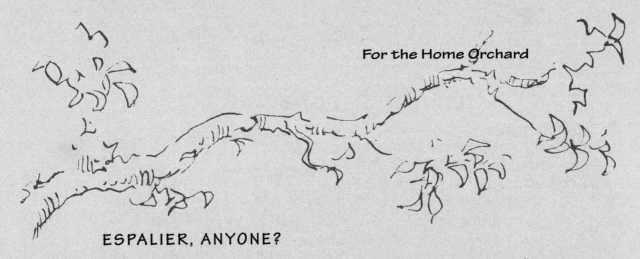

ESPALIER, ANYONE?

You can gain a zone of hardiness in a backyard setting by training dwarf fruit trees like vines against a sunny wall. Apples and pears lend themselves to espalier much more readily than stone fruits. The emphasis in this traditional pruning style is as much on artistic form in a small space as fruit production. Keeping the tree within the single plane of a supporting trellis does limit the overall harvest, but where else do you get to pluck a Tolman Sweet apple from a candelabra-shaped tree?

The support structure for the tree should be placed at least eight inches away from the wall to allow air movement behind the branches. Sturdy posts (set every eight feet) hold up the wire trellis: the first wire runs three feet above the ground, with four wires above that at a foot apart. End posts will need to be braced to prevent the wires from eventually sagging. Plant each tree just in front of the trellis plane, midway between the posts. Start with a one-year-old whip so you can train each chosen branch as it grows.

An espalier will need frequent pruning and pinching throughout the growing season, particularly in the formative years of setting a complicated pattern. Only branches growing in the right direction are kept, and these are tied to the trellis with twine. All other buds are pinched back. Be careful to leave the stubby spurs that will bear fruit once your tree matures. Root pruning — done by jabbing a sharp spade into the earth at the outer edge of lateral growth in early spring — might be useful to check vigorous top growth.

Northern growers will want to try an espalier against a south-facing, stone or masonry wall to maximize solar gain. In warm climates, choose a spot that doesn't get direct sun all day, ideally one with a white wall to reflect excess heat, which can wither the leaves. Espaliered fruit ripens earlier than its varietal counterparts grown in the windy open spaces of the orchard.

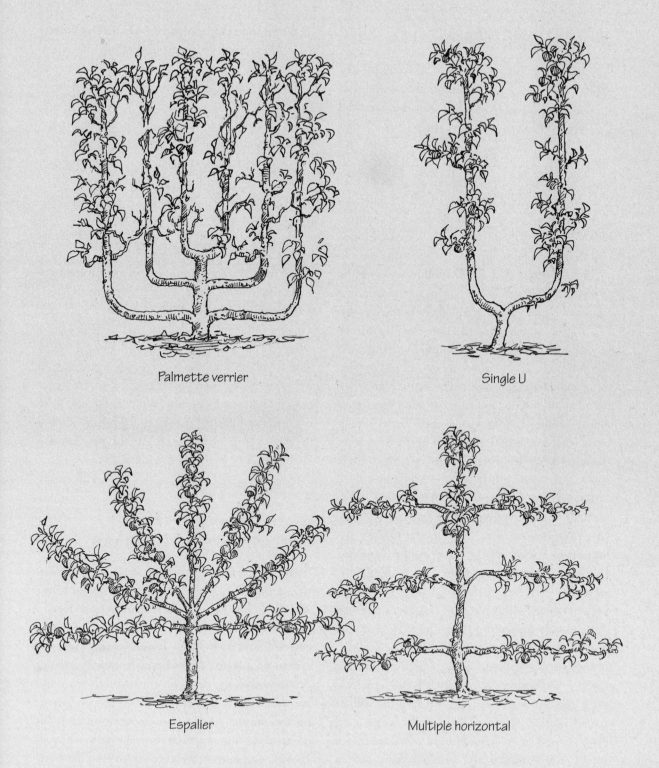

Palmette verrier

Single U

Espalier

Multiple horizontal

WINDBREAKS

Protection from high winds must be accomplished without interfering with the normal movement of air that provides frost drainage and quickly dries the trees after a rain. Choosing an orchard site that is naturally buffered can be difficult: the high and rolling lands best suited for tree fruit are often exposed to stouter winds. A storm just prior to harvest can put much of the mature fruit on the grass. Trees topple over in wet ground when leaf canopies billow like sails on the high seas. Wind-whipped transplants can be snapped off at the bud union.

The subtleties of a good windbreak should be appreciated as much as the sparing of the crop in a September gale. Snows retained along the leeward side of the woods prevent deep freezing of the ground and help delay early bloom. Dormant buds not desiccated by dry winds are less subject to winter injury. Pollinators find blossoms up high when the air is still but stay low on gusty days. Trees grow quicker and straighter; crops ripen earlier. Songbirds (that eat bugs!) are more likely to nest in sheltered branches. Prospects for getting a spray application where it belongs are vastly improved.

Forests and topography provide natural windbreaks. Orchard ground located just above a steep lake embankment benefits from the upward deflection of a wind off the water by the shoreline. Eastward slopes protected from the prevailing westerlies may, however, catch the fallout from a howling nor'easter. Winds lifted up and over a forested slope leave a sheltered pocket above the tree line. Too dense a wood, however, can block the drainage of cold air falling down the slope on a crisp spring night. Fruit blossoms immediately below a forested slope also are in greater risk of frost in the still air passed over by the inversion layer of dense cold from above. Tree rows bordering a windbreak often receive less sunshine and produce fruit with a higher degree of disease damage.

Windbreaks can be planted when an orchard site offers everything but protection from the wind. Choose trees that are thrifty in your growing zone and least affected by the fungi and insects that attack fruit trees. A tight hedge to block cold, drying winds as completely as possible is recommended for an inland location. Evergreens fit this bill during all seasons of the year. Allow some openings in a hedge on the downhill side of an orchard so frost-laden air can escape. Sites influenced by large bodies of water are best surrounded by a more open hedge that checks wind strength but still allows humid air off the water to pass through in winter. Either deciduous trees or scattered evergreens serve well on a leeward shore. Siberian pea shrub (*caragana arborescens*) planted four feet apart will reach a height of fifteen feet or more and survive Zone 2 winters. Pollinizer crab trees grown along a woven wire fence are sometimes used as a windbreak in conventional blocks despite being a source of insect pests and disease inoculum. Windbreaks should be planted one hundred feet away from fruit trees in dryland regions where moisture competition is a factor and fifty feet away anywhere else.

BIODIVERSITY IN A FRUIT ORCHARD

An orchard is much more than the sum of the fruit trees growing therein. A rich soil underfoot teems with microbial life on which healthy trees depend for both nutrient breakdown and absorption. Herbs and wildflowers provide home for hundreds of species of insects, some of which directly balance pest populations. Birds fill the air with song and also play a role in this pest/predator balance. Woodpeckers are the percussion section, drumming out borers and moth pupae beneath the bark. The soil, air, sun, and rain perfect the background harmony in which a tiny cell grows to become a bud to become a blossom to become a pollinated ovary to become the beautiful apple in your hand.

An orchard floor favoring broadleaf weeds is more suitable for fruit trees than a grassy turf. Fescues and other types of grasses have dense root systems that apples avoid, but goldenrod, buckwheat, plantain, and clovers are more congenial about "sharing the humus." Mixed cover like this also provides food sources for voles as an alternative to tender tree trunks. Raspberries in or near the orchard are another example of a tree friend. Unlike blackberry canes, which harbor summer disease inoculum, raspberries lack the waxy cuticle that sooty blotch calls home. Predatory mites, however, do favor this bramble fruit, and its blossoms furnish nectar for certain parasitoids. Raspberry canes compete very little with apple trees for nutrients and water, but hinder the growth of grasses that do. And though you might get scratched trying to pick fruit from a standard-size tree that is surrounded by raspberry canes, what's tastier than a ripe berry on a summer orchard stroll?

Our great-grandparents often planted berries down the rows of a developing orchard. That way, they could enjoy years of small fruit production from the cultivated ground before the orchard trees filled in their allotted space. Beans provide both a marketable crop and nitrogen fixation on their leguminous roots. Such interplanting is an appropriate form of biodiversity, so long as the soil is built up and protected. Vegetables like potatoes or winter squash can be followed with a cover crop rich in organic matter. The planting aisleway decreases in width as the tree roots seek out the enriched earth. Shallow cultivation here does not overly compromise young trees: roots encouraged downward access moisture and subsoil nutrients. The resulting good tilth from added organic matter more than compensates returning feeder roots with rich humus. Mature orchards continue to benefit from interplanted spaces deliberately left

between varietal rows or where a tree has succumbed to crown rot. Letting go the notion of an engineered orchard—"Monoculture or Bust"—makes room for the full circle of life needed to sustain, frankly, life on Earth. Small orchards can reap diversity benefits from nearby borders of native plants and garden ornamentals in addition to the creative expression provided by interplanted crops between the trees.

Biodiversity applies to overall farm management as well. An underlying principle of biodynamics is that of the farm as its own organism. You might say the biodynamic farm has the ability to be sufficient unto itself without relying on any outside inputs. Sir Albert Howard in his book *Soil and Health* shared this observation about fruit growing on the Indian subcontinent just prior to the First World War:

The tribesmen invariably combined their fruit growing with mixed farming and livestock. Nowhere, as in the West, did one find the whole farm devoted to fruit with no provision for an adequate supply of animal manure. This method of fruit growing was accompanied by an absence of insect and fungal diseases: spraying machines and poison sprays were unheard of: artificial manures were never used. . . . The quality of the produce was excellent: the varieties grown were those which had been in cultivation in Afghanistan for centuries. Here were results in disease resistance in striking contrast to those of western Europe.

PROXIMITY TO MARKETS

This book presumes local markets as vital to sustainable agriculture. There's no advantage of scale in a family-size orchard to embrace brokered returns. The location of your farm will determine the best venue for direct marketing of your fruit: either at a farm stand where people come out from town or at a farmers' market where you bring your produce in to town. Local markets can readily become hooked on the great taste of tree-ripened fruit, with

One day our cider-mill sign proved irresistible to an antique car club on tour.

peaches being particularly astounding compared to the rock-hard or mealy, disappointing specimens found in the supermarket.

Tourists can make up the difference where local traffic is lacking. Idealistic thinking might lead you to believe a town of several thousand folks will provide a viable market for a small farm—everyone has to eat, right?—but reality brings only a relative few who are willing to pay a premium for locally grown food. A drive greater than five to ten miles to the farm significantly discourages repeat sales. However, placing brochures at bed and breakfasts, inns, campgrounds, roadside information booths, and local attractions helps fall travelers find you.

Natural food stores are always thrilled to find a source of ecological apples. Direct wholesaling to such markets increases word-of-mouth exposure about your orchard. Help set up a display that says

where you are. Be on the lookout for music festivals and alternative gatherings that draw an organic crowd. One weekend away at the right event may bring in more sales than a month of Sundays down on the farm, especially if you offer an expanded product line and irresistible treats (hot apple crisp and ice cream) for eating out of hand.

The familiar realtor's maxim, "Location, location, location," echoes the sound advice about farmstand marketing. Small operations that can't justify staffing a fruit stand off the farm might be able to swap occasional sales coverage for space in a more prominent vegetable stand. Location plays the pivotal role in how many potential customers will find you. Poorly maintained roads and complicated directions may outweigh the charm and flavor of an outlying farm in some minds. Roadside signs are essential for attracting attention and

FRANK SITEMAN

Customers stocking up on apples at the Lost Nation Cider Mill.

pointing the way. A good sign should bespeak your quality, be limited to six to eight words laid out horizontally, and use color combinations (like dark green on white) visible to the fast-moving eye. Advance signs a quarter to a half mile from the entrance to your farm stand give drivers time enough to react. Once your customers have found you, encourage thorough shopping by alternating high-demand items like fresh apples and cider with related items like peeler/corers and cider doughnuts.

Impulse items—your value-added product line— should be placed to catch the browser's eye at every turn. Display and marketing techniques are as valuable as orchard layout and soil preparation in "growing" your farm.

Processing adds shelf life to fruit. Seriously consider doing some value-added products to make the most of an organic harvest. Such product diversification can free you from the drawbacks of an isolated location or bad weather. Livelihoods that depend on the fall season being bright and sunny to bring out the crowds may lack the flexibility to survive hurricane rains on Columbus Day weekend. A grassroots mail-order catalog and nonbrokered sales to natural food stores and gift shops within your state expands your farm's reach throughout the year. Tourists on holiday look for items they can pack away for gifts. No path is simple however: the specialty foods market is highly competitive and bureaucratically ponderous, and it oftentimes requires an appreciable investment.

Other draws to the farm can help the fruit business, both in season and throughout the year. A field of cut-your-own Christmas trees, for instance, gets out a different crowd that invariably asks about all those apple trees up on the hill. Offering a fruit growing workshop for backyard orchardists can lead to sales of extra nursery stock and orchard supplies. Hay rides and fiddle festivals provide entertainment for families who might just as well stock up on fruit while the getting is good.

Plowing under a cover crop in spring. (Source: The Principles of Fruit Growing, *L. H. Bailey, 1897, 1926)*

The supplying of artificial plant-food materials to fruit trees introduces a problem on which there is some difference of opinion among authorities. . . . The original conceptions of this problem were based largely on the findings of chemists, for it seemed logical to conclude that the elements found in the plant and its products in greatest amounts were the ones to return to the soil in like proportions. This doctrine led the horticulturists somewhat astray for a time, for valuable as it is, such a theory does not take into consideration the mechanical or physical condition of the soil or the important role of microorganisms to soil fertility.

—J. H. GOURLEY, *Textbook of Pomology* (1922)

CHAPTER 3

The Enriching of Fruit Lands

Life on earth is based on the fragile top inches of our soil. There, unbeknownst to our eye, lie teeming trillions of bacteria and other microscopic flora and fauna that are the very engine of our existence. A half cup full of fertile soil contains more microorganisms than there are humans on the planet. Organic agriculture begins with the recognition that these microbes are what feed the soil which feeds the plant (which feeds the animals) which feeds our bellies. There is no chemical shortcut to this existential truth.

MICRO-ORGANISMS AND YOU

The miracle of life that began with a single-celled bacterium coexists with and will end with single-celled bacteria. Our very bodies rely on the microbes lining our intestines to initiate the digestion of our food. Raw organic matter from plant and animal tissues can't become humus until metabolized by soil organisms. Even rocks, ground to fine dust by time and weather, yield their inorganic elements to these feeders in the soil. This degrading of mineral and organic molecules into an available form that can be readily assimilated by plants is the basis of our being.

Peter Tompkins and Christopher Bird, in their wonderful book *Secrets of the Soil,* relate the fertile gist of the matter: "Microbes first attack the substances that decompose most readily, such as sugars and cellulose. When these are used up, most of the microbes die, making up with their bodies half the total of the soil's organic matter; and a staggering number of dead microbes are decomposed and consumed by other microbes, in never-ending cycles. The oxidation of plant tissues being incomplete, lignins, tannins, fluvic acid, kerogen, and waxes—which resist the action of the microorganisms—are formed into a humus that undergoes a slower degradation, conferring to the soil its hydrophilic, water-loving capacity, its colloidal structure, and its resistance to erosion."

The foundation of organic orcharding lies in stewardship of the soil. Building humus is always the goal. Feeding a population of thriving microorganisms a diverse blend of organic matter results in a continuing humus. Nature's perfect fertility plan loops round and round on itself to the utter chagrin of the fertilizer companies: there are no profits to be made from a self-enriching soil. Plants and algae create organic matter through the process of photosynthesis. Animals eat plants and so on up the food chain, consuming what amounts to the stored energy of the sun. All plants and animals eventually die, and the nutrients from their bodies return to the soil through the action of microorganisms. Bacteria, fungi, and actinomycetes secrete different enzymes that begin the decomposition process. These microbes absorb the available nutrients first released—especially carbon and nitrogen compounds—and use them to reproduce.

Decomposition proceeds rapidly as each microbe multiplies by as much as 300 million a day. The resulting humus satisfies the nutrient needs of the fruit trees in more ways than one.

The residue left after the extensive decomposition of organic materials that we call humus contains 60 to 70 percent of the total organic carbon in soils. Here too are chains of sugar molecules that help cement soil aggregates together as well as the countless billions of bacterial bodies whose proteins will be further reduced into available plant nutrients. Stable humus is resistant to further microbial decomposition, thus holding the soil carbons somewhat in place. These form active chemical structures known as *humic acids,* which provide for long-term nutrient storage, expressed as the soil's "cation exchange capacity" on soil tests. Positive ions like calcium, magnesium, and potassium latch into place until such time as they are

EARTHWORMS FIRST!

Microorganisms that can't be seen by the naked eye are fine and dandy in theory. But every cultivated flock needs a shepherd: the humble earthworm fits that bill in our soils. The earthworm incubates enormous numbers of microorganisms within its digestive tract, which are then excreted, enriching the earth. Worm castings are five times as rich in nitrogen, seven times as rich in phosphates, and eleven times as rich in potash as anything else in the top six inches of soil. Furthermore, these humic nutrients are readily absorbed by the tree roots.

Each earthworm can produce its own weight in castings daily. One acre of fertile farmland will be renewed by over five tons of castings in a year. Earthworms burrow down as deep as fifteen feet, mixing and sifting soils as they go. Some carry down leaf debris and other organic matter; others return with mineral nutrients to the top. Earthworm-worked soils drain four to ten times faster than those without worm tunnels. Porosity gets reversed for the better in sandy soils, where worm castings retain a good rain. The night-crawling earthworm will remove 90 percent of the fallen leaves in an orchard when natural fertility is allowed.

A soil teeming with life by the quadrillions teems with earthworms by the tens of thousands. Cleopatra once decreed (remember, ancient Egypt thrived on the fertile soils along the Nile's flood plain) that the earthworm be revered and protected by all her subjects as sacred. Orchardists would do equally well to consider the earthworm when applying herbicides, pesticides, chemical fertilizers, and even organically approved copper and sulfur.

taken up by the root hair (in *exchange* for a hydrogen ion). Chemically speaking, the humic acid has become a humate. A dead soil requires applications of soluble fertilizers to make up for its lack of humates.

Yet chemical fertilizers cannot begin to rival nature. Hers is a twofold process by which plants draw their nurture from the soil. And, again, microorganisms are at the heart of the matter. Masses of living fungal threads, collectively called a *mycelium,* invade young roots and are gradually absorbed in turn, providing organic nitrogen *directly* to the root system. Underground chambers were built at the Malling Research Station in England in the 1920s to study this apple root interaction with soil life. The mycorrhizal association between the active root hairs and the penetrating fungi in fertile soil could be seen from beginning to end. The mycelium proteins digested by enzymes in the root soon enter the sap current of the tree as soluble nutrients. In soils where humus is lacking, this symbiotic feeding suffers. The tree is then limited to the absorption of soluble salts. It's never as healthy, as resistant to disease and insects, nor nutritionally as productive as a tree growing in fertile, living soil. Two philosophies of agriculture have just been described . . . which are you going to choose? Nature has quadrillions of aces up her sleeve awaiting the biological steward of the soil.

COMPOST AND SOIL AMENDMENTS

The health of the good dirt beneath our feet is where any organic farm system begins. There's more to this than providing chemical nutrients in specified proportions. Only a sound cycle of returning quality organic matter to the soil will make agriculture sustainable. Soils that have been mined of their nutrients and pushed to low levels of organic matter offer a reduced population of microorganisms little option but to compete with plants for nutrients, rather than each mutually benefitting the other. Soluble salt fertilizers do produce high yields at first, but as soil health declines, so does the crop unless more and more fertilizer is applied. Fruit grown in chemical soils—with lowered proteins, less vitamins, and poor mineral content—looks good in the market but never nourishes our bodies as completely as apples plucked from a tree flourishing in a living soil.

Compost makes that kind of soil happen. Good compost is akin to good wine: a full body of organic matter, the aroma of sweet earth, and the taste of all essential nutrients. By contributing the building blocks from which micro-organisms renew humus, compost is the quintessential fertilizer. The diversity we seek afield counts equally in the compost heap. The amount of nitrogenous material available determines the population of microbes that will flourish to make compost. The carbon to nitrogen ratio in organic matter expresses how nitrogen stands in relation to carbon content. Ideally, for rapid decomposition, this ratio is 20:1. Leaf mold, straw, cornstalks, and moderate amounts of sawdust (from stable bedding) are much higher in carbon than nitrogen. A rule of thumb in setting up a compost pile is to mix green and brown plant materials fifty-fifty to achieve a good C:N ratio, with interspersing layers of fertile soil to provide microbial inoculum. The volatile nitrogen in animal manures serves the same end as grass clippings and vegetable wastes. The nitrogen is stabilized into microbial bodies. The activity of these microbes reaches a crescendo in those first days after a well-aerated compost pile has been made, and in turn they yield up their nutrients to successive generations of decomposers until the pile arrives at an effective humus condition—the uniformly dark, rich, crumbly substance we know as "finished compost."

The spreading of fresh manure in the orchard is not allowed under most organic certification programs. Nor is it well-advised. Raw manure is similar to synthetic nitrogen fertilizers in its effect on soil. Harmful bacteria will survive sixty days (and even longer in cool weather) in manure. "Most probably, all pathogenic E. coli are destroyed between 150° and 160°F," says Jonathan Collinson of Woods End Agricultural Institute in Mt. Vernon, Maine. Although there is no definitive research on exactly what temperature destroys E. coli O157:H7 (the strain currently of most concern to fruit growers) in a compost pile, Collinson adds, "We haven't heard of any situation where compost application can be blamed."

A commercial orchard of an acre or more either needs to invest in equipment to make good compost or purchase their "black gold" elsewhere. Farm-scale composting requires a small tractor with a power take-off, a PTO manure spreader, and a second tractor with a front-end loader. Piles of organic materials are arranged parallel to the windrow-to-be. A homegrown source of manure is ideal but not absolutely essential. The loader delivers raw material to the manure spreader from alternate piles. As the windrow reaches four feet in height and six to eight feet in width, the spreader is inched ahead until all materials are mixed. Millcreek Manufacturing Company makes a line of compact spreaders that will fit between orchard rows as well. Eight to twelve tons of compost per acre are typically applied on a market garden. We spread just two to four tons to the acre beneath our M7 trees, as the ol' shovel-throw method allows accurate placement under the dripline. Our compost comes from a nearby dairy farm that windrows the cow manure with shredded newspaper bedding and crop residues. Given my druthers, I'd opt to spread more composted manure—and all from organically raised animals—but there are times when you just do the best you can.

The squeezings left from cidermaking can be incorporated into the compost pile. Left unmixed,

David Craxton spreads compost beneath Lost Nation trees in early spring to hasten the decay of potentially scab-infected leaves from the year before.

however, pomace remains slimy for years. Apple pomace contains trace amounts of nitrogen, phosphorus, and potassium. Great-grandfather used pomace as a natural herbicide: spread three inches thick over thistles and wild elder, the apple pulp destroyed every root of the targeted plant. The old literature also says that a thin dressing of pomace on an old tree will return it to bearing. However, you'll never find a more surefire deer attractant.

A well-balanced orchard soil may need no other fertilizing beyond an annual application of compost, either in late fall or first thing in spring. Mulching and cover cropping are essentially supplemental composting in the field. Trees that make good terminal growth—twelve to twenty inches in the nonbearing years, eight to sixteen inches once established—and have foliage of a rich green hue that holds well into fall are doing well. When the fruit harvest seems to falter, be it in annual yield or in quality, and soil tests point to a mineral deficiency, it might be wise to introduce additional fertility with soil amendments.

Soluble mineral fertilizers are used to replace depleted nutrient reserves caused by leaching or an agriculture that does not replenish organic matter. Most ecologically acceptable soil amendments are slow-acting rock powders. These often are cheaper than the chemical alternatives if you consider the total nutrient availability over several years. Rock powders cannot "burn" plant roots or cause a salt buildup in the soil. Ground rock is less effective in soils low in organic matter, as the microbes that need to first consume the mineral are lacking. Protein sources of nitrogen also need to be made organically soluble before becoming available to the tree.

Unconventional NPK

The big three of conventional agriculture are nitrogen, phosphorus, and potassium. Soluble chemicals are applied directly to the root system for immediate uptake by the fruit tree. Much ado is made about nitrogen, although a healthy tree favors a lean diet in this respect. Each one percent of organic matter content contains about a thousand pounds of captured nitrogen, of which twenty to forty pounds per acre are released yearly. Bearing orchards in a fertile soil probably have the one hundred pounds of actual nitrogen per acre needed for a fruit crop. Unabated sod, of course, complicates matters by commandeering about the same amount of nitrogen as the trees. Blood meal, cottonseed meal, and various animal tankages are organic sources of nitrogen to consider if you are "feeding the grass" (figuratively speaking), but traditional sod mulching makes more sense. Grass cut at haytime (after bloom) and allowed to lay as a mulch beneath the tree somewhat smothers the sod while providing nutrients to the tree. Weak trees are one exception to the no-add rule, where an application of four to six pounds of nitrogen fertilizer per mature standard tree can provide a marked boost. Smaller trees should receive proportionally less fertilizer. Rapid growth in young trees is encouraged with extra nitrogen to develop the fruiting structure. We use a general organic blend like Pro-Gro (5–3–4) in the first several years after trees get planted, at an increasing rate of one to four pounds per tree per year.

Apple trees primarily need phosphorus for root development. Mycorrhizal fungi are adept at making phosphorus reserves in organic matter available to the root hairs. Bringing soil levels up to par with rock phosphates prior to planting is likely the last time you'll need to consider this element. Black rock phosphate contains 30 percent total phosphorus and a whopping 48 percent calcium; colloidal rock phosphate contains 18 percent total phosphorus in a colloidal clay base that helps bind sandy soils. Both release their mineral reserves over the course of many years, thereby reducing the nutrient losses and pollution caused by chemical phosphate runoff. Bone meal is a costlier form of soluble organic phosphorus. Dried whey contains 10 percent available phosphorus, with a nitrogen boost on the order of 5 to 6 percent.

Potassium dances with an entirely different crowd than the conventionally assigned NPK entourage.

The Cation Waltz

Cation balance needs to be achieved between calcium, magnesium, potassium, and sodium in proper proportion. In the 1940s Dr. William Albrecht of the University of Missouri developed a base saturation range for these three positively

BONES FOR APPLE TREES

"There is no more valuable fertilizer for apple trees on most soils than bones. . . . It has been recorded by a reliable authority that near the graves of Roger Williams, the founder of Rhode Island, and his wife, there stood a venerable apple tree which had sent two of its roots into the graves of Mr. and Mrs. Williams. The larger root had pushed its way through the earth till it reached the precise spot occupied by the skull of Roger Williams. There, making a turn, as if going round the skull, it followed the direction of the backbone to the hips. Here it divided into two branches, sending one of them along each leg to the heel, where both turned towards the toes. One of these roots formed a slight crook at the knee, which made the whole bear close resemblance to a human form. There were the graves emptied of every particle of human dust. Not a trace of anything was left. There stood the guilty apple tree . . . caught in the very act of robbing the grave. The fact proved conclusively that bones, even of human beings, are an excellent fertilizer for fruit trees; and the fact must be admitted that the organic matter of Roger Williams . . . had bloomed in the apple blossoms, and had become pleasant to the eye; and more, it had gone into the fruit from year to year, so that the question might be asked, Who ate Roger Williams?"

Sereno Edwards Todd, THE APPLE CULTURIST (1871)

charged elements. Such cations are attracted to the negatively charged molecular sites on a colloidal clay or humus particle. Overabundance of one can interfere with the availability of another, thus the recommended base ratios with which to compare your soil test results. A high cation exchange capacity indicates that more nutrients can be kept available in the soil for root uptake, yet relatively safe from leaching. Acid soils are low in fertility because too much of the cation exchange capacity is occupied by either hydrogen (which is not a plant nutrient) or aluminum (which is toxic to plants). Liming soils affects cation balance by the substitution of calcium and magnesium for excess hydrogen. Some acidity in the form of hydrogen ions is necessary to make other nutrients available, which is why the most fertile soils have a range of pH somewhere between 6.3 and 6.8.

Calcium is essential for cell wall structure and membrane integrity. Higher fruit calcium results in more rigid cell walls, leading to firmer fruit after storage. Potassium regulates the absorption of calcium in the tree, and to a lesser degree so does magnesium. An excess of either can cause bitter pit calcium deficiency. Hay mulch can reduce calcium uptake by making potassium overly available. Even phosphorus gets into the game by precipitating out calcium at a high alkaline pH. A look at soil amendment options — in the context of cation balance — becomes important since fruit calcium levels determine fruit quality.

We lime orchard soils to neutralize acidity, often without realizing that the choice of lime is not a neutral matter. Dolomitic lime is high in magnesium; calcitic lime favors the exchange of calcium. The carbonate component of both is what converts hydrogen ions into water and carbon dioxide, thus reducing acidity. Aragonite is a calcium carbonate mineral that comes from oyster shells. It is used in soils already high in magnesium when calcitic lime is not available. Limit surface applications (without incorporation into the soil by tillage) of lime to 2.5 tons per acre in any one year so as not to upset topsoil ecology. Lime overdone significantly accelerates the decomposition of humus.

Sulfate of potash-magnesia (sold as Sul-Po-Mag or K-Mag) adds both potassium and magnesium where calcium levels are adequate. Potassium is needed to renew what has gone into the fruit and to increase tolerance to winter cold and spring frosts. Sulfate of potash contains 51 percent soluble potash and 18 percent sulfur. Hay mulch contributes potassium as well. Gypsum is a naturally occurring calcium sulfate that is said to lighten compacted heavy soils without raising pH and to displace excess magnesium and potassium. Calcium stewards will appreciate Bio-Cal from Midwestern Bio-Ag—this lime kiln dust contributes a whopping 150 pounds of soluble calcium per ton (compared to 2 pounds for calcitic lime and 20 to 25 pounds for gypsum). Greensand is a slow-release source of potassium with exceptional moisture-retaining ability. Wood ashes, which contain large amounts of potassium and 32 percent calcium oxide, have a definite alkaline influence. Cation amendments aren't meant to be juggled, so make wise choices based on soil test results *after* adjusting pH.

And Now a Good Word for Sulfur

Organic orchardists who use sulfur as a fungicide should rightfully be concerned about high sulfur levels in the soil. Excess sulfur can lock up available calcium to form calcium sulfate. Yet sulfur is an essential element for photosynthesis. Sulfur balance permits fruit trees to better withstand cold weather. Soils high in organic matter generally have sufficient levels of sulfur. A quite modest use of sulfur-based fungicides has not upset our soil balance. Any effect on pH apparently is countered by our dusting the fallen leaves with lime after harvest.

Soil Remineralization

Excavation damage to a fruit tree often results in renewed vigor as subsoil minerals are brought to the surface of the orchard. Similarly, trees planted above "rotten ledge" (subsurface rock that is crumbling in place) seem to take off. Both examples bespeak the philosophy behind soil remineralization. Phenomenal results have been reported in Austrian forests where ground volcanic rock has been deliberately spread. Recently broken stone of a fine particle size releases various minerals that trees respond to with gusto. Granite meal is available commercially, but a scrounger will do better by taking a trip to the local rock quarry. Rock dust that accumulates beneath the crusher is usually available for the asking. Glacial till, mixed and churned by moving mountains of ice, contains many of the required elements necessary for plant growth. Azomite, an ancient aluminum silicate clay mixed with many marine minerals, has similar attributes to rock dusts. Fruit trees respond with increased vigor and pest resistance to its naturally chelated trace minerals.

I'm particularly intrigued by the concept of paramagnetism in rock. Given that our earth is subject to various energy forces—from gravitational pull to electromagnetic attraction—it's not surprising that some people consider plants equally beholden to influences beyond our current agricultural ken. Eco-farming advocates like Dr. Phil Callahan deem paramagnetism an essential attribute of a living soil. Good virgin soil is highly paramagnetic; all plants are diamagnetic. Healthy crops result when the bio-polarity of the soil (if you will) resonates with the cosmic growth initiative. Dr. Callahan estimates 60 to 70 percent of our soils are depleted of paramagnetic energy. Volcanic basalt from the Canadian Shield has a high paramagnetic reading.

Doug Murray, an IPM orchard consultant in Paw Paw, Michigan, recommends incorporating rock chips into the soil before planting to prolong the basalt's effect, as powdered rock disintegrates that much more rapidly. I'll be broadcasting this rock for the first time in 1998 under selected apple trees in side-by-side comparison trials. You'll be sure to hear this orchardist's opinion on the merit of paramagnetic theory if indeed Yankee skepticism can be allayed by Nuthin' But Rock (one Canadian source of basalt).

FOLIAR FEEDING

Foliar application of nutrients provides a way of supplying essential elements directly to the leaves and fruit when they are most needed for good growth. Plants absorb foliar sprays twenty times faster than soil-applied nutrients. The resulting increase in photosynthesis stimulates the root system in turn to increase the uptake of soil nutrients. Cold soils in spring often limit the uptake of nutrients by the root system. Likewise, the intensive pace of growth following bloom can surpass the rate at which nutrients can be transported to the foliage and developing fruit. Nutrient-deficient soils can miss the boat entirely until sufficiently amended. Yet more harm than good—or just wasted money—can result when foliar application rates are wrong or poorly timed. Differences in tree size and planting density affect the appropriate amount of material to be applied per acre. Nutritional sprays need to be put on the leaf with enough water to ensure wetting time is sufficient for uptake by the foliage. Slow drying conditions favor maximum absorption. Early morning finds the leaf stomata (pores) open and receptive to taking in foliar nutrients.

Two schools of thought exist in the organic camp on the subject of foliar feeding. Some growers opt for a high-energy program, intending to stimulate the tree into the fullest production possible. Liquid fish emulsion or hydrolyzed fish powder applied at pink stage adds nitrogen to the flower buds to prolong ovule fertility and thereby encourage improved fruit set. Nitrogen can be particularly beneficial following a heavy crop year when leaf analysis levels are low. Foliar humic acids promote the goodness of humus up high in the tree by increasing the uptake of other nutrients. Biocatalysts like Spray'n'Gro, said to increase fruit size and color, leave me wondering what production process justifies charging one hundred dollars a gallon for any product. Peaceful Valley Farm Supply's Brix Mix gangs up many of the high-energy options for the express purpose of raising sugar levels in the tree. On the other hand, the low-key approach goes more with the daily flow, content to enhance leaf sheen with seaweed extracts and plug any specific nutrient holes revealed in the leaf analysis until the soil processes can catch up. Your reliance on foliar options will be defined in part by the depth of your wallet and by the perceived results you wish to obtain. The only dynamic fully understood here is this: foliar nutrients supplement soil-building but never serve as a substitute for true soil health.

Seaweed extracts are bottled as a concentrated liquid or dried into a soluble powder for foliar application. The plant growth hormones contained in seaweed stimulate cell division and promote larger, healthier root systems. Its chelated trace elements include boron, molybdenum, copper, iron, zinc, cobalt, manganese, and selenium in naturally balanced amounts (being derived from a living plant). Increased fruit set and Brix (fruit sugar) levels have been demonstrated in treated orchards. Foliar applications begin at pink and can continue weekly through midsummer, since any nitrogen contribution is negligible. My inclination is to include seaweed powder in the spray tank most times out at a low "tonic" rate of a quarter pound per acre. The trees receive what amounts to two to three gallons of liquid concentrate per acre each season . . . we grow a great crop of organic leaves in

Lost Nation. North Country Organics offers the best bulk deal in a soluble seaweed extract. In truth, we don't know which nutrient is the least common denominator at any point in the growing season. Seaweed eliminates any guesswork by making available a wide range of trace nutrients in infinitesimal amounts. Avoid the nitrogen boost of liquid fish after petal fall so as not to delay winter hardening in the trees.

Chelated minerals are readily absorbed by plants to provide a short-term fix for known deficiencies. Such chelation occurs naturally in the soil when a metallic ion combines with an amino acid or other organic molecule chain. Organic chelates are preferred to synthetic EDTA chelates because the organic bonding agent assimilates in the plant's cellular system, whereas the other can continue to react with exchangeable elements. Foliar calcium use is explained as one remedy for bitter pit in chapter 6. Magnesium can be applied to the leaves by spraying Epsom salts (hydrated magnesium sulfate), as chelated forms have a low magnesium content. Chelated micronutrients get mentioned at the end of this chapter.

BIODYNAMIC SOIL TREATMENTS

The astral science of Rudolf Steiner is obscure on first reading. Yet the sense of the whole expressed in Biodynamics is one and the same for the enlightened organic fruit grower. The apple tree lives and breathes in an orchard system that is a being unto itself. The trees are rooted in the earth—Steiner's mineral sphere—and reach their branches upward towards the cosmos. Spirit enters through the light streaming down from the sun by day and the stars by night. Beautiful fruit is produced in a balanced system where all the existential elements of creation are expressed. Low productivity, unchecked insects, and disease are merely symptoms of depleted soils and our own estrangement from the

land. Biodynamic preparations
out" to growers lacking a spiritua
sults gained by its practitioners d

The Biodynamic preparations
hance soil life and plant metabolism. The nourishment of a healthy tree depends upon the interplay of soil decomposition and the photosynthesis of light energies. Horn manure spray (BD preparation 500) is applied on the orchard floor after spreading compost in late fall and again in early spring on a warm overcast afternoon. It's considered central to the method that horn manure be stirred in rhythmic spirals for an hour before applying to fully invoke the vortex of cosmic energies. A small whisk broom dipped into the stirred pail is traditionally used to fling the liquid in a wide arc onto the ground. Biodynamic compost should be high in animal manures and treated with the special herbal preparations indicated by Steiner in his 1924 agricultural lectures. Horn silica spray (BD preparation 501) is applied to both the foliage and the ground cover on a sunny summer morning. This quartz-crystal substance increases light assimilation in green plants. Silica also helps to ripen the leaves after harvest (sprayed while leaves are still on the trees) in anticipation of quick decomposition to reduce overwintering scab inoculum.

The preparations are rooted in enhancing the digestive processes that in turn feed the soil. All are available from the Josephine Porter Institute for Applied Biodynamics in Virginia. Whether we choose to embrace this cosmic outlook in our fruit growing or not, it's good to consider wider spheres of thought.

COVER CROPPING

Orchard ground should be cover-cropped prior to planting. Ideally, two or even three growing seasons are invested in building up the soil with the understanding that tillage access will never be as good once the trees get planted. Sod is turned the first spring and planted to the first of two buckwheat smother crops. Lime and rock phosphate are best incorporated at the start (if needed) to sweeten the microbial decomposition process. Interplant winter rye with hairy vetch in September to combine the nitrogen fixation of a legume and the organic bulk of the rye root mass. Red clover interplanted with oats offers a similar two-bit gain. Green manure options can include bulky Sudan grass, deep-rooted alfalfa, and Hardin soybeans. Choose what works best in your region to most benefit your particular soil type. Most clovers and alfalfa require a full year's growth to get the maximum benefit of added nitrogen. A basic turf of orchard grass and Dutch white clover can be established during the year of tree planting if no further row cropping is envisioned.

The cultivated orchards of our great-grandparents were put into a cover crop late in the summer to protect the soil over the winter and renew organic matter. The spring harrowing was essentially a "composting in place" that allowed for aerobic decomposition in the top several inches of disced earth. The fruit trees had no immediate competition during the peak of the growing season for soil nutrients or moisture. Additional cultivations after petal fall kept weeds from taking hold. The planting of a summer cover would be delayed in a dry year to reserve soil moisture for the sizing fruit. But not for too long. The growth of the cover crop helped check tree growth and thus hasten winter hardening.

I like the ideal of maximum soil preparation as much as anyone. But the reality of planting an orchard often comes with one year of lead time. Nor does a rocky incline lend itself to tilling up the entire field. Here at Lost Nation, we embrace humus-building with a tad of Yankee practicality in our new plantings. The sod in each marked tree-row-to-be gets tilled in a four-foot swath to either side,

The rye cover crop around these young trees will soon be scythed and left to lie as a summertime mulch.

creating an eight-foot-wide planting strip. The pasture left between tilled strips becomes the grass aisles. The buckwheat smother crops have been followed by winter rye in the year preceding tree planting. Oats are a better choice in a northern zone: a wet spring delays the tilling under of the vigorous rye, whereas an oat cover would have winter-killed. Turning in oat straw rich in carbon ties up soil nitrogen in the decomposition process, so let it lie as mulch. Our planting holes were dug within the center of the rye and the edges harrowed in later. These immediate edges can be worked for a year or two while the trees are small. Annual nitrogen-fixers like field peas or soybeans lead into a later sowing of oats. Some tree feeder roots may initially get harrowed in the cover crop zone, but the gain in organic matter may justify the effort. The in-row strip between trees grows to winter rye and self-seeded buckwheat, but wildflowers and other grasses eventually gain the stronger foothold. Any quackgrass that survives year one can be a nuisance around the gravel mulch base that surrounds the young trees, mandating hand-hoeing and/or flame weeding. Gravity-fed irrigation lines ensure our young trees get enough moisture despite the surrounding growth.

Green manure crops should be incorporated into the soil while still green and succulent. Clovers can fix up to 150 to 200 pounds of nitrogen per acre when properly managed. Grasses are better at increasing soil organic matter, primarily due to their high lignin content and fibrous root systems. Pathogenic fungi can be suppressed by disking in a green manure: the high nitrogen content results in rapid decomposition, which in turn stimulates germination of dormant spores of the pathogen. Since the trees are not yet planted, the germinated spores, having no food source, get attacked by other microbes. Annual legumes grown alongside the tree row should not be directly disked in green in late summer, as the release of nitrogen may delay hardening off. Mow the legume crop to lie in place, wait a few days, then sow a grass-type cover into the dried green mulch. A biennial legume interspersed with a scattering of oats could be mowed but then left to grow through the fall for shallow incorporation the following spring. The nitrogen boost would come when needed, the winter-killed oats would improve tilth, and the now open ground could be left rough until the summer planting of the next protective cover.

PONDERABLE MULCH

Sod does compete with tree roots for nutrients, but the problem involves more than having enough nitrogen, et al., in the organic matter to go around.

Early illustrators of fruit books were apparently prone to seeing curious businessmen in cover-cropped orchards. (Source: The Principles of Fruit Growing, *L. H. Bailey, 1897, 1926)*

The symbiotic fungi providing nutrients to the feeder roots are a *shallow* reinforcement: the active humus which supports mycorrhizal gain is uppermost in a fertile soil. A thick carpet of grasses drives fruit tree roots down beneath this organic advantage. Subsoil nutrients may well be adequate, but feeder roots are now limited to soluble uptake only.

Aeration enters in here as well. Roots metabolize carbohydrates photosynthesized in the leaves by taking up oxygen and releasing carbon dioxide as they grow. The surface roots of most fruit trees dive downward to avoid the carbon dioxide given off in a topsoil thick with sod. Inadequate subsoil aeration, caused by poor drainage in certain soils or cultivated hardpan, lessens this vital metabolism in roots down low. Where it's feasible, breaking up the subsoil with a deep chisel-type plow before planting can do wonders.

Mulch gives fruit trees a fighting chance to feed in the trebly rich humus layer. The surface-oriented main roots that spread two to three times the breadth of the tree up above extend in all directions beneath the topsoil. These send feeder roots into the organic residue towards the surface and even into the decomposing bottom layer of a moisture-holding mulch—but not into a dense sod. Roots grow as much as two inches each week from April through October, but nutrient demand above lessens with cessation of terminal bud growth in mid-summer. Mulch can be less of a success later in the season in suppressing the grass in the orchard.

A fruit tree that is not yet bearing needs to establish a strong root system and develop its branch structure. Sod competition is too much to ask in this case. A thicker mulch is desirable at first to prevent any perennial weeds like quackgrass from taking hold later in the season. Established trees have greater nutrient reserves in the "wood" that enable them to survive—though not actually thrive—in grass. Mulching the rows of dwarf trees (with close tree spacing) like a raised garden bed works well. A five-foot-wide bed is minimal, with a few inches of soil left revealed around each trunk. Purchased hay mulch can run as much as several hundred dollars an acre. Cover-cropped strips along the tree row are more cost-effective in these early years when tree spacing gets to be more than ten feet. Larger orchards may opt for mechanical cultivation or a steam machine to maintain an open planting strip indefinitely. Standard trees are probably best ring-mulched as described in the sidebar on page 38 (Mulch Donuts), unless dwarf trees planted temporarily between (to boost the first harvests) justify cover cropping or cultivation.

Orchardists tending much more than an acre of fruit will want to opt for a sod mulch system once the trees come into full production. No mulch will hinder other plants from growing forever, even if we want to continue bearing the expense. Fortunately, the orchard liberates us from the gardening sentiment of absolutely controlling "weeds" from taking root. *Haphazard mulching* in the orchard does great good, and nowhere is this better demonstrated than by traditional sod mulch. The grass is left to grow for one cutting, which takes place a couple weeks after petal fall. The resulting hay gets spread beneath the trees, knocking back most of the sod found there. Apple feeder roots are quick to respond, for as you'll see in the great grass debate of chapter 5, better yields are obtained by a sod mulch approach. The soil beneath the tree is kept friable with a sod not quite as dense.

Basic mulching gear consists of a pitchfork and gloved hands on a small farm. Baled hay or straw can be spread much more easily than a huge round bale. Loose hay is another option if you have a spare field to cut. Seeds in the hay aren't an issue as they would be in the garden. And a mulch layer four to eight inches thick doesn't compromise soil aeration. Two mechanized mulching systems are available if your acreage and management style justifies the cost. The Pro Chopper from King Machine Company chops and distributes bales of straw from a truck or wagon. The Millcreek Row Mulcher conveys wood chips, compost, and chopped hay or straw out the side of a five-foot-wide hopper powered by a tractor.

Mulch offers other benefits beyond suppressing sod and conserving moisture. "We mulch like crazy and never feed compost to our trees, as the older mulch on the bottom becomes compost," say Laurie and Shannon McGowan of Annapolis Royal in Nova Scotia. "Mulch is great for peaches too . . . laid on thickly in late winter, it blankets the frozen soil so the cold stays around the roots longer, delaying bloom time beyond those late killing frosts." Lower soil temperatures under a mulch in summer favor the root uptake of potassium needed for next year's return bloom. A sod mulch in place before "June drop" suspends curculio-infested fruitlets atop the hay to shrivel in the sun. And if renewed before harvest, a thick mulch makes the gathering of fallen apples a cinch.

Herbicides have taken the place of mulch in today's conventional orchards to limit the competition for nutrients. Yet the bottom line resulting from the dearth of soil life where herbicides are used is crop reduction, which can only be reversed by massive inputs of chemical fertilizers. In contrast, a sod that breaks down annually renews soil

GROWER MANAGED TRIALS

WANTED: *Fruit growers to ascertain the validity of organic orchard techniques. Must be willing to replicate results. Observations are as important as hard data. Sharing interpretations of paired-comparison trials is vital to our mutual learning curve.*

Let's face it. Each one of us often has figured out an approach to a pest problem or fertility issue that we fully implement one season but then never know for certain if it made a difference. Perhaps alternate spurs are stripped of fruit on a heirloom variety to encourage annual bearing. Or parasitic nematodes are applied to the ground beneath the trees to target sawfly larvae. Maybe we initiate a trial — garlic is sprayed as a repellent on one block of trees three times, neem on a different lot of trees just once — but then have no control by which to ascertain results. Some ideas appear to help. But what if it was just the year? Was the additional labor justified for a slight improvement in the crop? What if a promising idea like homebrewed garlic beer (rather than purchased extract at eighty dollars a gallon) is one nuance away from working as envisioned?

This orchard floor trial affirmed that tarnished plant bugs are quite content to stay in a ground cover left unmowed.

Organic fruit growers need to take more responsibility for understanding orchard dynamics and pointing the way towards effective solutions. Experiment station research is mostly funded by people with products to sell and rarely done in an integrated organic context. The growing season gets to be overwhelming, but if we don't undertake this research, who will? Each of us needs to understand what makes a comparison trial valid and pledge to do one a year. Replications are crucial, because each set of treatments provides a "second opinion" on the question at hand. Randomizing treatments avoids the biasing effects that the wetter ground, for instance, one row over might cause. Locate sets of varietal trees throughout the orchard to compare. Block treatments are necessary for a strategy based on influencing the environs as a whole. A small section of the orchard left untreated can serve as an indication of success when other plantings aren't available to set up replications. Data can be as simple as fruit damage assessments taken at harvest or comparison photographs or an accurate accounting of costs.

Cynthia Anthony of Bear Well Orchard in Maine never lacks for ideas worthy of a proper trial. Her row-mulching research involved four replications of four treatments — hay, hay over newspaper, wool mats, and cardboard — to see which method best controlled quackgrass. The root rhizomes in each plot were weighed and labor cost per acre figured into the analysis. Here's Cynthia on the final score: "In the future I will manage quackgrass by applying cardboard (any type that is available) on heavy infestations and the newspaper/hay mulch on the remaining rows."

MULCH DONUTS

Apple trees do better without immediate sod competition when first planted. Row mulching works on dwarfing rootstock where the tree spacing is close. Clean cultivation of the entire orchard was recommended at the turn of the last century, with a soil-building cover crop planted in late summer to provide winter cover. Some larger orchards have invested in a Weed-Badger, a rotary cultivator rigged behind a tree guard that mounts off the side of the tractor, to maintain in-row cultivation. Herbicides eliminate plant life and soil micro-organisms in IPM orchards at the cost of good tilth.

Hay mulch is perhaps the best option for the home orchardist if pine voles are not a problem in your area. A peastone mulch fills the inner ring of the mulch donut, extending two to three feet in diameter. Hay that is placed right up against the trunk of the tree retains too much moisture and provides cover for meadow mice who find apple bark a tempting lunch. A gravel mulch does neither, yet proves equally effective at suppressing weeds. A ³/₈-inch-diameter stone is best, spread several inches deep. Stone makes searching borer cavities that much easier too, as the clean peastone can be readily scooped aside if the borer has descended towards the roots. The gravel can be replenished in the early years of growth if spring cultivation of quackgrass proves necessary.

A bale of rotted hay forms the donut ring around this gravel "hole." Obtaining mulch hay a year ahead of time allows it to be out in the weather to rot. You'll find that wet hay lays much nicer and stays in place on windy days. The hay ring should be a bale-leaf wide, just enough to keep the sod from creeping up into the inner gravel mulch.

The sixty standard trees on our farm were planted in what had been an overgrown pasture. Tree spacing is thirty feet by thirty feet, as measured by the eclectic eye. That leaves a lot of grassland between trees. I use the mulching bar attachment for my BCS walking tractor to cut the lushest sections, and a scythe where the terrain gets rugged. The swathes of cut grass amount to a second round of mulch hay that is practically in place, readily forked around the spring mulch to knock back the quackgrass till fall.

The hay mulch is all thrown aside in late fall when you prepare the orchard for winter. Inevitably, voles will have nested under all this protection, and, once snow covers the ground, access to the vulnerable bark won't be denied them. Pulled back in fall, though, the rotting hay adds nutrients and organic matter to an ever-widening circle around your tree. Next spring, the open ground beneath the former mulch ring can be lightly forked to remove any remaining quackgrass runners.

Meadow voles can prove a nuisance with their tunneling beneath the mulch. Whenever their subterranean subway system extends into the gravel mulch (and thus surely along tree roots), I stamp the ground down hard all around and renew the peastone. My trees are thriving, despite this potential concern. Pine voles are another story, being root herbivores, and if that's your situation, forego the hay and practice the fine art of shallow hoeing around the gravel.

Mulch rings work well in the home orchard.

organic matter. The favorable ground resulting from mulching or a cultivated cover crop has the diversity of life needed by the tree to thrive. Herbicides offer no such benefits. Ponder that the next time you heft a bale of hay.

SOIL TESTS AND LEAF ANALYSIS

The cost of a soil test and plant tissue analysis is a small price to pay for knowledge—particularly when test results show that soil amendments are not necessary. Home orchardists can get by with checking in every several years, but any commercial orchardist looking at spending hard-earned apple profits needs sound justification for adding to per acre costs. Testing to see if topsoil conditions are

being maintained in an established block can be undertaken every three years, but plant tissue analysis should become an annual habit. Leaf analysis will point to those great big blank spaces where nutrients aren't available in the tree despite good soil results. Testing for every micronutrient gets expensive, but certain ones are worthy of appraisal.

Soil tests done before planting reveal the mineral deficiencies of your chosen site and indicate whether substantial differences exist between the topsoil and subsoil. A soil probe beats the dickens out of a spade if you want an accurate profile, so spend twenty bucks (check either the Forestry Suppliers or Ben Meadows catalog) for the economy model or "farm pool" with the neighbors and buy a longer core sampler. Ten to twenty cores taken to a depth of eight inches from randomly scattered sites throughout an orchard block—mixed together in a clean pail from which two cups worth can be forwarded to the soil lab—will provide a good assessment of the feeder root zone. Labs utilize numerous salt and acidic solutions to extract each nutrient being tested, with the proper extractant procedure determined by soil type and region. An orchard established in variable soils can have an area with low test values and another with high test values. Creating distinct management blocks of an acre or more to accommodate radically different soil types makes sense. Subsoil samples from a depth of eight to sixteen inches give a better indication of inherent soil fertility not yet influenced by previous surface liming and cultivation. Heed recommendations to incorporate the right type of lime (based on pH results and cation saturation levels) prior to planting the trees. The topsoil should ideally be raised to pH 6.3 to 6.8 and the subsoil in the sampling range to at least pH 6.0. Lime works its way very slowly down through the soil otherwise. Always keep cation balance in mind when liming. Soil phosphorus level is next in line for receiving attention during soil preparation.

Leaf analysis recommendations are based on standards established by research in actual orchards. There is no point in submitting a leaf sample for analysis unless it can be compared to those standards. Leaf nutrient levels change throughout the season. Early in the season, levels are increasing rapidly, but many mineral elements decline by harvest time. The most stable time for sampling is after shoot growth ends in midsummer, about sixty to seventy days after petal fall. A hundred leaves from one main-crop cultivar, taken halfway up current-season shoots on several same-age trees, are submitted. Recent spray or foliar residues should be removed (a quick triple rinse in distilled water does the trick) to avoid showing enhanced levels of iron, manganese, zinc, and copper. The sampling form from the lab will ask for other pertinent details that might influence leaf analysis results.

Brix levels in the tree can be monitored with a refractometer. High sugar content correlates to increased disease resistance, ability to withstand climatic stress, and better fruit quality. Refractometers first came into vogue to determine sugar levels in fruit to gauge optimum maturity at picking. Nowadays growers use Brix throughout the season to monitor that overall nutrition is on course. Plants with a Brix reading of 12 or more are said to have good "immune systems." The sap from either the leaf or fruit—sap extractors make this impossible-sounding prospect possible—is squeezed onto the glass plate of the refractometer, which, turned towards the sun, provides the sugar percentage from the calibration scale in the viewer. Be prepared to spend one hundred dollars or more to set yourself up in Brixville. Pike Agri-Lab offers the best deals in refractometers.

Soil test values for each nutrient are normally divided into five categories: very high, high, medium, low, and very low. Only very low values are a specific call for attention. Certain ratios of nutrients are also suggestive. Imbalances involving calcium, magnesium, and potassium show up as base saturation levels of the cation exchange capacity. Recommended values vary by soil type, but generally conform to a 58:12:2 ratio for Ca:Mg:K in a conventional orchard. Advocates of the Acres U.S.A. philosophy of eco-farming like to see calcium levels seven times higher than magnesium and at least fourteen times higher than potassium. A base saturation ratio of 70:10:3 achieves this. Pay attention to the relative levels of zinc and phosphorus, as high levels of the latter can lock up the zinc needed for shoot growth and fruit set. Boron is one micronutrient to check repeatedly, as it's toxic when overapplied, but associated with calcium deficiency and poor pollen germination if lacking. Keeping tabs on copper and sulfur levels helps monitor the danger of an elemental fungicide program on earthworms. Last but certainly not least, organic matter content is your "badge of honor" . . . get it up to 5 percent if you can.

Leaf analysis tells what the actual nutrient levels are in your tree, regardless of how good things might appear down below. Nitrogen levels in apple leaves should fall on either side of 2.2 percent according to tree age and the firmness of the cultivar. Fresh market apples like Gala and McIntosh should have leaf nitrogen of 1.8 to 2.2 percent; the harder keeping varieties should have leaf nitrogen of 2.2 to 2.4 percent. A living soil supplemented with compost usually provides adequate amounts of nitrogen. Trees with biennial-bearing tendencies that have a low nitrogen reading may well benefit from a light application of Chilean nitrate or blood meal in early spring to complement the fall spreading of compost. Low leaf calcium *can* be a problem of uptake rather than lack of adequate calcium in the soil. Correcting a boron or zinc deficiency *may* be what's needed to get leaf calcium up to the 1.6 to 2.0 percent range. Leaf values for these two trace minerals *might* confirm if this is the approach to take. A fruit calcium deficiency (as evidenced by bitter pit) *may* well be more a function of drought, as this nutrient translocates to the leaves from the fruit under moisture stress. Whew! The "sum of the parts" can get downright confounding.

Too much can be made of the visual symptoms of nutrient deficiencies. Going straight to extension literature to see that yellow paling of leaf tissue, for instance, is a magnesium deficiency does not account for the many factors at play in the orchard. Magnesium may indeed be the problem, but so might overly wet ground or an excess of potassium. Deficiency symptoms tend to appear when the mineral in question is in highest demand by the tree. Iron, boron, and zinc deficiencies, for instance, tend to appear at bloom. Eroded land with shallow soils is more likely to exhibit symptoms than the bottom of slopes. Trees in decline that are scattered throughout a block suggest the problem is due to voles or borers, though a varietal pattern in an eclectic planting may be nutrient-related.

Cornell's *Orchard Nutrition Management* brims with information on acceptable nutrient levels and the dependent relationships thereof. The current rub of soil and tissue test results, from an organic perspective, are the chemical recommendations. These are rarely "translated" back to acceptable organic materials except by astute independent labs. Paul Sachs lists close to fifty testing facilities in his excellent soil primer, *Edaphos: Dynamics of a Natural Soil System.* You need to be familiar with soil amendments and foliar sprays—and their approximate cost per acre—to make the best choice for your soil. All test results are merely indicators of soil health. Keep emphasizing humus-building regardless of how complicated the numbers seem to get.

TRACE MINERALS FOR EVERY TREE

Micronutrients are minerals that are important in very small amounts for the proper functioning of the tree system. These play a major role in the creation of over five thousand different enzymes necessary for life functions. A well-balanced compost generally suffices to provide most essential trace minerals. Seaweed extract also supplies many chelated trace elements as a regular addition in the spray tank. Leaf analysis may reveal a particular shortcoming that can be remedied by either a granular application to the soil or a specific foliar spray. Good things can be overdone, however, and the line separating nutrient from poison can be easily crossed when isolated trace minerals are applied.

The availability of copper, manganese, and zinc is reduced at higher pH levels (above 6.3) and thus is more of a concern when orchard soils are properly limed. Integrated Fertility Management offers a line of amino acid chelated nutrients called "metalosates" that can be foliar-applied to meet specific trace deficiencies. Amino acid chelates are compatible with the cell chemistry of the leaves and thus are readily metabolized. Calcium and magnesium metalosates are available in addition to iron, zinc, manganese, and copper; rates vary from twelve to forty-eight ounces per acre depending on leaf tissue analysis.

A moderate level of boron is important for good fruit quality. Boron deficiency can cause cork spotting and internal browning in apples. Excessive levels, on the other hand, lead to increased levels of water core at harvest. Boron's influence on the movement of calcium into the fruit helps prevent bitter pit. Surface applications of borax (11.4 percent boron) are readily mobile in the soil and needed for good root growth. One rule of thumb is to band twenty-four pounds per acre every three years beneath mature tree rows to account for leaching. Half this amount would be used on non-bearing trees. Subsoil toxicity can become a concern in certain soils however. Solubor (20.5 percent boron) can be applied twice each season, once at pink and again ten to thirty days after petal fall, at a foliar rate of one pound per hundred gallons per acre if leaf analysis indicates the need to supplement fruit boron.

TAPROOT DYNAMICS

Trees with roots reaching deep into the substrata are able to call upon mineral reserves as yet untouched by the organic cycling at the surface of the planet. The dissolving power of soil water makes the rock minerals available to be absorbed by roots. These minerals are then passed into all parts of the tree, including the foliage. Autumn leaves bring the minerals, now in an organic form, back to the ground to be incorporated into humus. The land stands renewed to a degree by the trees themselves.

Outside the orchard, this vast natural circulatory system is suffering. The destruction of forests around the globe is coming back to haunt us in many ways. The greenhouse effect, the encroachment of deserts, and mineral-impoverished soils relate directly to our disrespect for trees. Some propose the cycling of glaciers — every ten thousand years (or so) ice has ground rock to dust and scattered it over broad areas — as the earth's way of renewing fertile possibility. We could conceivably invest our technological prowess into grinding glacial till to remineralize all soils. First and foremost, we need to realize that our existence on this humble planet hinges directly on holistic stewardship of all we have been given. Hugging trees starts to make sense when we wake up from consuming everything in sight.

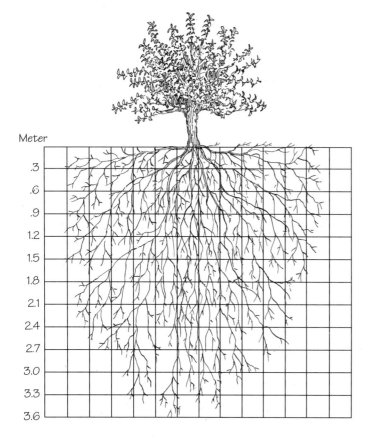

Meter
.3
.6
.9
1.2
1.5
1.8
2.1
2.4
2.7
3.0
3.3
3.6

Roots of an apple tree in good soil will normally spread two to three times as far as the upper branches. A permanent water table or impervious layer of rock checks the downward growth. (After Emanuel Epstein, "Roots." Copyright 1973 by Scientific American, Inc.)

Why do we need so many kinds of apples? Because there are so many folks. A person has a right to gratify his legitimate taste. If he wants twenty or forty kinds of apples for his personal use, running from Early Harvest to Roxbury Russet, he should be accorded the privilege. . . . There is merit in variety itself. It provides more contact with life, and leads away from uniformity and monotony.

—LIBERTY HYDE BAILEY, *The Apple Tree* (1922)

CHAPTER 4

The Trees and the Planting

Creating an apple farm begins by planting one tree at a time. Rows fill out inside a field that, if you're on the ball, is already fenced in from deer. Those just-planted fruit trees now become a harmonious whole: *your orchard*. There is a sanctity to this ground that the vegetable garden or rolling wheat field never quite attains. The trees stand permanently in position through all the days of the year. The plantings never rotate, but rather, the spring air mixes into the summer sunshine that takes on the robust scents of autumn to finally greet the gently falling snows on the awaiting limbs. The trees frame this seasonal portrait, providing a fixed perspective to the many changes in our own lives. The stoic Duchess, her trunk long split in three yet held together by a chain now embedded in the bark, was here eighty years before we bought our farm. Grace picked her first apple at age two from the Green Sweet tree. Over yonder grows a Falla-water, long ago dedicated to the memory of my Dad, where I still go for father-and-son chats. We

pinned our commercial prospects on those Sweet Sixteens and Honeycrisps, and by golly, we were right. A grower's passion for this entity we call an orchard runs deep.

CULTIVAR SELECTION

Choice of cultivar is akin to religion, choice of rootstock is a political stance: no grower tells another grower what to plant. What we can do here is allude to some of the better varieties and establish the parameters any orchardist dealing with a fickle public needs to consider. Ed Fackler of Rocky Meadow Nursery has a savvy sense of what works commercially for direct sales: "I think one should consider no more than thirty varieties. Offering your customers two or three different high-flavored varieties at the beginning of the season will greatly enhance later season demand for more and different kinds. Ideally, one would offer at least a sweet type and a tart type at any given time during

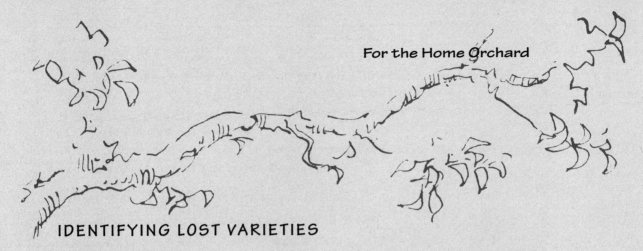

IDENTIFYING LOST VARIETIES

Have you ever wondered what kind of apple that big tree in the backyard might be? It's been there as long as anyone can remember, yet the folks who planted it have passed from living memory. There are ways you might be able to figure out if your tree is a Duchess or a Snow apple or just a wild unknown. So come along, Watson, and let's see what the old folks and nearby fruit growers have to tell us about regional favorites.

Many antique apple varieties are in truth just chance seedlings resulting from the cross-pollination of unknown parents. The genetics of modern apples is known: the pollination being done by hand at agricultural experiment stations or in home orchards by devoted amateurs. Creating additional trees of the same type of apple can only be done by grafting budwood of that favored cross onto another rootstock. The Rhode Island Greening is one cider apple that literally gave its all to colonial approval: travelers took so many budwood cuttings for grafting that the original seedling tree, in the dooryard of a Mr. Green's tavern in Newport, Rhode Island, died.

Word-of-mouth of such favored seedling apples led to the propagation of several thousand named varieties by the close of the nineteenth century. Apples were selected for taste, preferred use in cider or cooking, and keeping ability. Books like S. A. Beach's *Apples of New York*, published in 1905, provide detailed descriptions of each fruit's characteristics as well as color plates for confirming the varietal identity. Any notions as to what kinds of apples were grown in your area a hundred years ago will help narrow your search. Your state library system might be able to provide such reference works. Members of the North American Fruit Explorers (see the NAFEX listing in the appendix) can borrow such classic volumes through the group's mail-order library. My friend, Vicki Caron, is currently working on a series of field guides for identifying apples in a given region like the Northeast, much like the ones birdwatchers use for figuring out a new bird sighting.

Large trees set at a consistent spacing indicate grafted origins. Seedling trees sprouting under the dripline are likely the windfall progeny of the mother tree, and any bearing fruit should be tasted with that genetic potential in mind. A single tree near an old farmhouse or stone wall has good potential of being a named variety as well. Still, if your family detective never gets a handle on that name, don't despair. Tell your friends it's the old Homestead apple and enjoy!

the sales season. Also, colors (including russets) should be mixed at any given time during the sales season."

That old adage about variety being the spice of life is the major advantage a small orchard has over the limited offerings in the supermarket. A well-planned market orchard features an eclectic mix of old and new favorites. Don't overlook local preferences—some of our customers won't even consider apples other than McIntosh—but don't feel confined by a Red Delicious mindset either. Enjoy your niche market by inspiring people to loftier tastes. Your enthusiasm for favorite varieties will create loyal fans out of naysayers. Offer someone an explosive Honeycrisp apple . . . who could possibly resist? Trendy apples like Gala, Fuji, and Jonagold have gained followings for good reason. Enticing the non-sweet crowd with the classic fullness of an Esopus Spitzenberg or a Stayman Winesap makes sense. Apple connoisseurs will respond to the complex flavors of Sweet Sixteen and Margil. Let people know Bramley's Seedling and Calville Blanc are especially high in vitamin C. Expound on the virtues of a Roxbury Russet cider.

Climate and soil types make or break certain varieties. The delicate flavor of Cox's Orange Pippin—Britain's classic dessert apple—seems to be brought out only in a lake- or ocean-moderated climate. New Englanders love their Macs precisely because our rocky soils and early autumn frosts bring about that perfect blend of sweet tartness. Jonathan has an affinity for the Midwest, sizing better there than anywhere else. Mollie's Delicious is a Southern belle in more ways than one. A good nursery catalog will list the "better flavor zones" of its cultivars. And Warren Manhart's book, *Apples for the 21st Century*, is a fun and valuable reference.

Talk to other growers in your region about yield and cropping habit. The ability to bear annually rates high, though planting a few Baldwin or Newtown Pippin trees should remain any apple-lover's

prerogative. Organic growers need to recognize their thinning limits: varieties that set heavy crops are often maintained as annual bearers with the use of chemicals. We could never grow enough Macoun apples to satisfy local demand, but on the thinning hand, limiting such detail work to sixty Macoun trees keeps us sane. The venerable Northern Spy is notoriously late in coming into bearing, while precocious varieties like Braeburn and William's Pride soon begin providing a return on investment. A wonderful apple like Spigold sometimes needs encouragement to bear: Ed Fackler recommends double-girdling the trunk with a razor knife one to two inches apart beneath the lowest scaffold in year four (ten days after petal fall) to shock it into production.

The inherent resistance of some varieties to pest pressures should not be overlooked. Plant breeders have done their best work with disease resistance. A block of scab-resistant varieties like Pristine, Redfree, Liberty, and Goldrush won't require any fungicide sprays in early spring. Similar plantings could be based on resistance to cedar apple rust, fire blight, powdery mildew, or fruit rots—whichever represents the greatest concern in your orchard. Yet in Nature such solutions are never complete: these varieties remain susceptible to sooty blotch and fly speck, and European strains of the scab fungus are showing *resistance to the resistance*. The hope of insect aversion to particular fruit unfortunately contradicts our own harvest desires. The flesh of fruit contains few allelochemicals (particularly after ripening) that might ward off insect feeding and oviposition. Otherwise it would be bitter and thus undesirable to us as well as the pests. Still, varietal inclinations show up in mixed blocks. Apple maggot flies go for early apples over harder winter keepers. Both Arkansas Black and Idared are reported to be less bothered by curculio. Grower networking on insect preferences—likes and dislikes—may point the way to some interesting realizations. Ultimately, a healthy tree produces better fruit than a stressed tree with whatever amount of resistance.

All varieties chosen need to be winter-hardy in your growing zone. Nursery catalogs often state the proven range of possibility, yet a cultivar may bear well in a transitional zone if the microclimate is favorable (see chapter 2). Trial plantings are the best way to discover what makes sense on a commercial scale. Choice of rootstock can impart tenderness or hardiness to the scion in some cases. Late varieties may survive as trees in northern zones but rarely have a long enough season to dependably ripen fruit. Chilling requirements equally come into play on the northern and southern edges of appledom.

A planting strategy must also take into account the time for harvest of each cultivar. Summer apples initiate an early marketing season, but have nowhere near the sales volume of fall varieties. Frosts and the turning colors of forest leaves serve to remind people that apple season has arrived. Once the roadside trees are bare of leaves, your market can slacken dramatically. Some orchards close after October, others keep a holiday vigil, and still others—with satisfactory storage—never close their doors. How you utilize your crop fits into such planning. Most of our processing is done with late fall varieties, after the intense part of the marketing season has passed. Cidermakers should grow apples that enhance a good cider blend, particularly early in the season when dessert fruit tends to be puckery. Sweet Bough, Wickson, Milton, and St. Edmund's Russet may get little acclaim on the table, but in cider, cultivar value takes on a whole new meaning.

ROOTSTOCKS AND TREE SPACING

Rootstock choice need not be limited to full-size standards, though there's a lot to be said for the longevity and poetic presence of big trees. While it's true that dwarfing rootstocks were selected to have less vigor than seedling trees, it's something of an organic myth to imply that the smaller trees necessarily are less healthy than standard-size trees. Tree health comes from the soil, not from genetic traits that determine shortness or tallness. Dwarfing trees root proportionately as deep as more vigorous stock, but are less well-anchored since their brittle roots can snap under wind pressure. Super-high-density plantings probably are chemically dependent for the simple reason that the trees are

An overlooked virtue of dwarfing rootstock is the improved light distribution to the fruit in a smaller tree.

planted too damn close. Trees need space for air movement and root development. Dwarf trees come with more horticultural constraints, but they offer the commercial grower a quicker return on investment. By planting dwarf trees, home orchardists get to enjoy more varieties without being overwhelmed by harvesting five or more bushels per year from each one.

Rootstocks are the foundation of your orchard. They are selected for their influence on tree size, precocity, hardiness, adaptability to soil conditions, nutrient uptake, and resistance to certain pests and diseases. Each rootstock has its own set of characteristics. The eight most common in commercial use (in order from most dwarfing to full-size standard) are M27, Mark, M9, M26, M7, MM106, MM111, and seedling. The work on classifying Eu-

ropean dwarfing rootstock was begun at the East Malling Research Station in England in 1912. The Malling Merton (MM) clonal rootstock series originated in the 1920s by breeding rootstock with a specific purpose in mind: namely, resistance to woolly aphid and improved anchorage. Fifteen crosses were made between Northern Spy and the original Malling stock, of which the two "semi-standards" (MM106 and MM111) maintain commercial appeal. Virus-free clones (induced by heat treatment) receive an EMLA designation: the traits of an EMLA7 from an M7, for example, remain unchanged except for a slight increase in vigor.

More recent breeding work has focused on hardiness and disease resistance. The Budagovski series was developed at the College of Horticulture in Michurinsk, Russia, where temperatures plummet

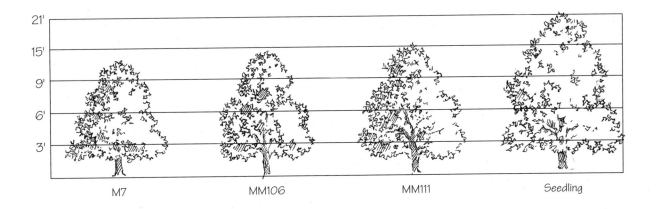

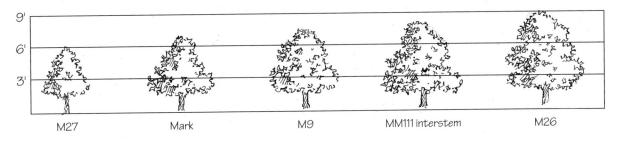

Relative size of apple trees on different rootstocks.

to −40°F almost every winter. Bud 9 produces a 30 percent size tree resistant to collar rot that crops in two to three years. Accordingly, despite susceptibility to fire blight, grower interest is high. Antonovka seedlings were crossed with Malling clonal stock to create the Polish series, with precocious P2 showing particular value as an interstem. The Ottawa series from Canada highlights Ottawa 3 as hardy into Zone 2 with no burr knot problems. Herb Aldwinckle and Jim Cummins at Cornell's Geneva Research Station created the Geneva series by inoculating hundreds of thousands of hybrid seedlings with collar rot fungus and fire blight bacteria. The survivors are few but precocious, well-anchored, and, of course, highly-resistant. Cummins Nursery is hard at work propagating commercial quantities of the Geneva rootstocks.

Rootstocks (other than seedlings) need to be produced by clonal means, much as buds are grafted to retain the varietal characteristics of the fruit. Propagation techniques range from inducing misted cuttings to root, and mounding over existing stock with sawdust, to high-tech tissue culture. The traditional argument against clonal rootstocks is valid —all trees in the orchard could be grounded on a single genetic system—but, on the other hand, we equally manipulate long-term diversity when we choose to graft favored cultivars again and again. A balanced approach finds room for a mix of both cultivars and rootstocks. I enjoy the beauty of a full-sized apple tree, and though the smallest dwarfs like M27 and P22 are too much like raising tomato plants for my tastes, the challenges and rewards of the many intermediate rootstocks are as fun as any seedling orchard. Nor is every open-pollinated seedling tree equal. The vast taproot on Antonovka stock helps it resist drought and its Russian heritage assures hardiness. Another Russian seedling, Beautiful Arcade, offers a natural dwarfing ability—75 percent the size of a standard with a tendency towards early bearing—without the clonal risk of virus infection. Deliberately crossing two such varieties to produce seedling stock ensures all desirable qualities. "Run-of-the-mill" seedlings sprouting from the pomace pile can have wide variability in growth traits. Commercial arguments aside, standard trees endure beyond our lifetime: plant a few for your great-grandchildren.

INTERSTEMS

Trees that have been twice grafted have three distinct cambium genetics at work. The wood between the rootstock and the fruiting cultivar is called the *interstem*. Such trees appear to offer the best of all worlds: the root can be vigorous and have good anchorage, the interstem provides the desired dwarfing effect, and the fruit above sells like hotcakes. The degree of dwarfing varies with interstem length, with a six- to eight-inch piece of stem wood generally considered sufficient. M9 interstemmed on M111, for instance, produces a tree about 35 percent of full size which crops early. The cost of producing a three-component tree — whether double-grafted in the dormant season or budded in successive years — can offset the advantage of growing small, yet self-supported trees. Most nurserymen recommend that interstem trees be planted with the lower graft union three inches below the ground surface to minimize any tendency towards suckering. Some growers have expressed a concern about "interstemmed" fruit being undersized or the trees themselves being unthrifty in shallow soils.

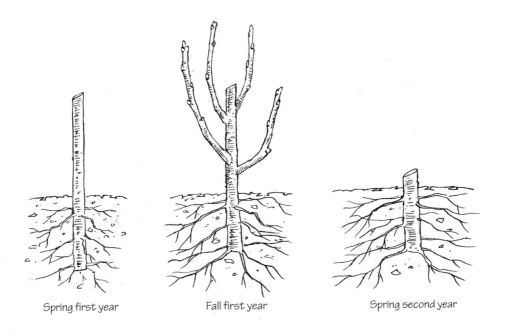

Spring first year   Fall first year   Spring second year

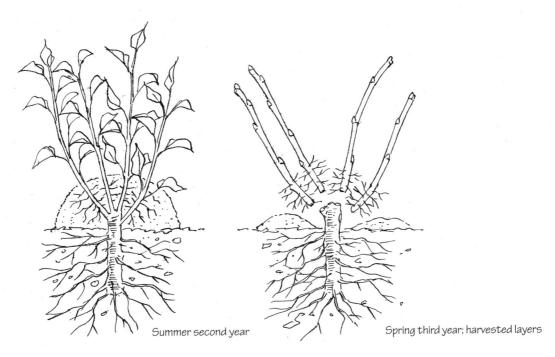

Summer second year   Spring third year; harvested layers

Mounding rootstock regrowth in moist sawdust produces "shoots with roots" that offer the original root genetics to the subsequent grafted cultivar.

You owe it to yourself to learn the characteristics of the rootstocks on which you're planning your farming future. Obviously, dwarfing stock is much easier to prune, spray, and harvest. Yet M27, M26, and M9 are quite susceptible to fire blight. MM106 suffers severely from collar rot in wet soils. The thick bark of M9 appears more palatable to voles. All small rootstocks like Mark are susceptible to apple measles (a manganese toxicity problem). M7 has not proved as winter-hardy as first thought, though here in Lost Nation that seems to be overcome by planting the graft union just above the ground. Vigorous growing stock can recover better from borer damage. MM111 tends to lose its leaves earlier, thus initiating winter hardiness sooner. Fruit size and yield are affected by rootstock, with soil type and climate being big regional variables in that interchange. Steve Johnson in Port Angeles, Washington, prefers trees on more vigorous roots like M7, M106, and MM111: "These trees are freestanding, need less weed control, have a more widespread root system for nutrient absorption, and can tolerate drought conditions longer. So what if I have to prune more to control their growth?"

Spacing recommendations for various rootstocks are made to get the greatest number of trees per acre. Often these are based more on chemical reliance than good air flow for disease control. Row spacing provides access for the equipment used on your farm. It isn't uncommon at all to want more room once the trees mature. Management efficiency can be a tradeoff on overall yield, but better fruit quality can make up the difference. Trees planted too close together will compete with each other and require excessive pruning. A rule of thumb is to restrict tree height to 75 percent of the row spacing so that treetops will not shade the lower branches in adjacent rows. Good light distribution in and

This Duchess apple tree on our farm was planted over ninety years ago. Only a seedling rootstock could provide such beauty for posterity.

around the tree makes for increased packout. The training system to be used on the trees influences planting distance. The slender spindle system used in some high-density blocks keeps trees contained within the narrow space allotted (typically four to five feet for M9) by tying lateral limbs to a horizontal position and even downward. Trees on dwarfing rootstock do not grow to a certain size and then simply stop. Branch-spreading to encourage early fruiting redirects vigor, which can vary considerably among cultivars: Idared on MM106, for instance, can be spaced closer than Mutsu on MM106 in the same soil type. Spur-type strains of certain varieties grow more compactly—more sunlight energy is put into fruiting spurs than lateral shoot growth. Northern or high-altitude growers find standard trees are often smaller at maturity than a southern tree would be, and modify tree spacing accordingly.

NURSERY SOURCES AND VARIETAL COLLECTORS

Trees are a big investment, whether propagated by the orchardist or bought from a reputable nursery. Purchasing top-grade stock is a given once you recognize the cost of waiting an additional year for a less vigorous tree to catch up. Any dollars initially saved per tree are not a bargain in the long term. Root development has proportionately more value than overfertilized top growth. Nurseries with shorter growing seasons may not be able to push growth as far along as in southern zones, but northern orchardists will appreciate buying stock that is acclimated to their conditions. A one- or two-year-old whip transplants more readily than older stock: root growth is less disturbed, allowing the whip to overtake those fully branched prodigals after a year or two. A trunk caliper of ½ to ⅝ inch gives more bang for the buck. Feathered trees—with at least

three wide-angled laterals ini[...] 34 inches off the ground— [...] than a #1 whip. Accordingly, [...] a dollar more per tree for this [...]

The fruit varieties offered v[...] perception of what is comme[...] Market favorites and disease-resistant cultivars are touted in most nursery catalogs, with a few specializing in reviving the heirloom fruits of our great-grandparents' era. It's generally assumed that apples are planted for dessert eating, but if a quality cider blend or home keeping ability interests you, chat with the folks at the nursery. They'll be glad to talk about rootstock selection, tree growth habits, fire blight resistance, and whatever else might concern you as a potential customer. Nurserymen like Guy Ames and Ed Fackler are fruit growers as well, which adds immeasurably to a commercial discussion. Ultimately, tree quality and friendly advice mean more than who has the lowest price. The nursery business is as challenging as any kind of farming: ordering trends can be capricious, and with so many variety and rootstock options available, costs are going to be higher for smaller operations with less margin for an eccentric market. A custom budding order placed two years before the trees get planted can save you an average of ten percent: a one or two dollar deposit per tree gives the nursery assurance you really intend to buy these trees. The custom trees grown for us by Amberg's Nursery have always been top notch.

There are relatively few nurseries propagating fruit trees by organic methods. Fedco Trees and St. Lawrence Nurseries both emphasize northern hardiness on Antonovka seedling rootstock. Frank Foltz of Northwind Nursery specializes in the Minnesota selections like Honeycrisp, Keepsake, and Sweet Sixteen. Bear Creek Nursery prefers to get around the problem of unordered trees by selling custom benchgrafts: specify which of their four hundred apple varieties you want on a choice of elve rootstocks and come spring you'll be planting your own nursery beds.

We grafted most of the trees for our new plantings in Lost Nation ourselves. Buy rootstock by the hundred lot direct from either Lawyer's or TRECO. Varietal wood can be obtained from other local growers, members of the North American Fruit Explorers (NAFEX), living history farms, several of the smaller nurseries, and at statewide scion exchanges. The challenging part can be matching up rootstock diameter—each nursery seems to determine caliper differently—to the diameter of your scions. Ideally, whip grafts are made within several inches of the soil line to reduce aerial burr knots (unsightly bumps of tissue growth that attract dogwood borers) and the tendency of dwarfing stock to "dwarf too much" when overexposed. Mentally prepare yourself for clonal rootstock: "sticks without roots" isn't far from the truth in some cases, but given rich earth and plenty of water, miracles do happen. An experienced grafter can expect a 90 percent take, but factor in an additional 15 percent loss for spindly growth and other inevitable misadventures. Nursery beds should be laid out as single rows three feet or more apart with the trees eight inches apart in the row. Northern growers will want to increase the in-row spacing and go heavier on the compost to offset a shorter growing season. All this planning can only be fully rewarded a year later if the orchard soil is properly prepped. Some of our nursery trees weren't planted till three years after grafting, and boy, did we sing the blues about extensive root systems and the need to prune aggressively. Only drip irrigation saved the day from transplant shock.

GRAFTING AND PROPAGATION

Chances are good if you're an orchardist that you already know how to graft. If not, learning opportunities abound: spring pruning workshops spon-

Bench grafts planted in a nursery bed at Lost Nation Orchard.

sored by Cooperative Extension often delve into grafting basics; members of the North American Fruit Explorers receive a detailed handbook; town libraries have how-to manuals waiting on the shelf; nearby growers just need to be asked. Give it a try. Once you see a scion bud take and start to grow, your orcharding life will never be limited again.

Tree stock is either benchgrafted in early spring for planting out in nursery beds, or budded in August when the rootstock is already established in the ground. The resultant scion growth of a whip and tongue union can provide a suitable whip for transplanting out in the orchard the next spring, though less vigorous whips likely require another year's growth. Buds cut from one-year-old shoots are either inserted under the bark of the rootstock

The most common budding method is the "T" bud, in which a shield containing the desired bud is inserted into a T cut on the rootstock in late summer. The stock will be cut back just above this bud the following spring. Any lateral growth on the resulting shoot is pinched off up to a heading height of 20 inches.

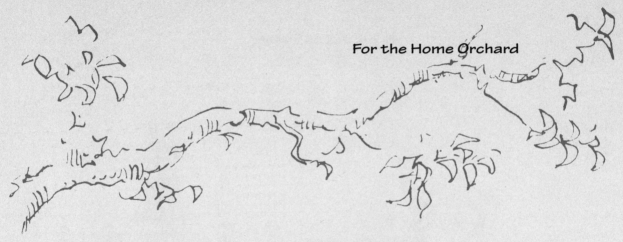

PLUMS, PEARS, AND PROMISES

Every orchard should have some tree fruits besides apples. The cultural approach to growing peaches, plums, cherries, and pears is much the same. Climate still points the varietal way. The few intriguing twists on the disease and insect front are often more manageable than the pest complex facing apples. But, ah, the flavors, the juiciness, the delightful aromas . . . even Johnny Appleseed wasn't beyond the pure pleasure of a tree-ripened peach.

Pears are a notable exception on the organic frontier. Other than fire blight — plant varieties with demonstrated resistance like Summercrisp, Magness, and Shinko — the "other pome fruit" often comes through the season relatively unscathed, despite being attacked by as many insects and mites as apples. The difference is one of degree. Dense pear sets don't succumb to a curculio sting or a tunneling "lep" near as often. Pear psylla and pear blister mites can be held in check with dormant oil. A dusting of wood ash on skeletonized leaves will control pear slugs. European varieties differ from Asian pears in that they don't properly ripen on the tree. All pears can benefit from the use of a bee attractant (either Bee-Scent or Bee-Here) sprayed on the low-in-nectar blossoms. Planting two or more different varieties of pears improves pollination dramatically. Magness is not a good pollinizer and definitely needs a partner. The popular varieties Bartlett and Seckel will not cross-pollinate with each other.

Plum varieties that offer a cross-pollination challenge can be obliged by planting trees in pairs just four feet apart. Bees working the blooms of these intertwined trees then become as effective as a pollen-carrying breeze. Japanese hybrids are hardier than the often self-fertile European varieties, which can handle heavier soils and are less prone to brown rot. Plum curculio — it earned this name

for a reason — can be a major contender for these sweet fruits of late
summer.

Cherries come sweet and sour, with the latter being preferred for pies.
Spring frosts occasionally kill the blossoms on this early-blooming fruit. Most
sweet cherries require two varieties for proper pollination — Stella is a black-
red exception — and sour cherries are always self-fertile. Sweet and sour varieties will not pollinate each other. Growers in Zone 5 and south can enjoy both
types, but northern growers can only have a cherry pie if the microclimate is
ideal. Naturally dwarfing Meteor and Northstar are among the hardiest
choices.

Peaches are reward enough for toughing out the mild winters of the middle
growing zones. The fun begins in early July with yellow Candor, carries into
August with the white-fleshed Belle of Georgia, and ends in September with
Redskin and freestone Veteran. Thinning early varieties to six inches and late-
bearers to eight inches achieves good fruit size and reduces the likelihood of
brown rot spreading from fruit to fruit. Cultivar resistance to peach leaf curl
and bacterial leaf spot never hurts with these short-lived (ten to fifteen years
on average) trees. The one dwarfing rootstock to bud to peach is Citation,
though standards like Bailey and Lovell are more cold-hardy. Peaches needing
adequate supplies of potassium and calcium appreciate a hay mulch and an
occasional liming.

Lastly, don't forget the plumcots and the apriums and the nectar peach-
cots. These stone fruit crosses combine all the glories of their parents. If, that
is, you thought apricots, nectarines, and the like needed improving upon.

("T" budding) or placed on the rootstock where a portion of the bark has been removed (chip budding). Height of budding on the rootstock varies, but it is usually three to nine inches above the soil line. The scion bud heels into dormancy, but the rootstock continues to develop roots through the fall. The rootstock portion above the bud union is pruned away before growth begins the next spring. Lateral growth on the ensuing shoot (up to a height of twenty inches above the bud union) is pinched two or three times throughout early summer. The budded tree usually develops four or more wide-angled feathers above this heading height and attains a total height of four to five feet with good irrigation. Next spring it's time to plant this up-and-coming whiz kid out in the orchard. A two-year budded tree has a jump start on production when compared to a one-year benchgrafted tree. There would be less of a difference if the benchgraft was also given a second season in the nursery, but a profit-wise nurseryman has little reason to provide it. The callus on bud unions tends to be more delicate. Benchgrafts make a dependable union that grows upright and straight. Wood growth out in the orchard eventually strengthens compatible unions equally after a few years.

The level of maturity in grafted wood steps beyond that of the developing rootstock. A seedling tree goes through a juvenile phase, during which it cannot be induced to flower. This is followed by a transition phase in which flowering can occur, but not as readily as when wood reaches fruiting adulthood. The wood tissues in the trunk of a seedling tree are perpetually juvenile: cut off a sixty-year-old tree at its base, and the resulting shoots from latent buds will be unfruitful until tissue growth again enters the adult phase. In contrast, scion buds taken from a fruiting cultivar and then grafted to seedling stock are entirely adult above the union. The "vegetative adult" phase of young grafted trees is very short in precocious varieties like Golden Delicious but seemingly interminable in Northern Spy. Adult wood on precocious rootstock accomplishes what our great-grandparents would have called impossible: Northern Spy initiating fruit set in its second year on G65 rootstock.

You can put your grafting talents to work in numerous ways in an existing orchard. If a row of self-sterile cultivars aren't getting sufficiently pollinated, try grafting a suitable pollinizer on replacement branches down low in each tree's framework. Bridge-grafting can save the day when rodents girdle unprotected trees. Watersprout scions are tacked every two inches around the trunk to span the missing cambium and then are coated with grafting wax or an asphalt emulsion sealer (this technique is more fully described in the vole section of chapter 6). Topworking comes into play when you realize your original varietal selection is nobody's favorite or prone to disease pressure beyond your ken. An established root system and tree framework in its prime can be worked over to a new variety by cleft- or bark-grafting scions into mid-diameter branch stubs, or by budding the sprout growth emanating from the edge of these stubs later in the summer.

THE SETTING OF THE TREES

The planting of a tree is a sacred act. It matters little that a hundred or more saplings will go into the row ahead. Each time we break open the earth, layer out the developing roots, and tamp the soil back in place we embrace our mutual destiny with trees. I like to recall the story of Elzéard Bouffier and the thousands upon thousands of oaks he planted in the Basse-Alpes region of southeastern France. Jean Giono, who wrote *The Man Who Planted Trees*, concluded, "When you remembered that all this had sprung from the hands and the soul of this one man . . . you understood that men could be as effectual as God in realms other than

NURSERY LINGO

Benchgraft — a propagation technique matching sized rootstock (out of the ground) to scionwood that has two dormant buds.

Budding — a propagation technique utilizing a single scion bud inserted into the bark of planted rootstock.

Callus — healing growth that develops over the graft union and binds the scion tissue in place.

Compatibility — the performance of scion and rootstock depends on a graft union that makes a strong physical connection and displays a physiological harmony of the two genetic systems. A number of incompatibilities in trees are induced by viruses. However, graft unions where the scion outgrows the rootstock (or vice versa) can be perfectly compatible.

Feathered tree — nursery stock that has already developed three or more wide-angled laterals.

Heading height — the height at which lower scaffold branches are trained out from a developing whip. A scaffold branch started thirty inches from the ground stays put on the trunk at that height. As the branch enlarges in diameter, it will actually appear to get slightly closer to the soil line.

Scionwood — a dormant shoot, ideally first-year growth, taken from a fruiting variety to provide grafting stock.

Whip and tongue union — the grafting splice used in making a bench graft.

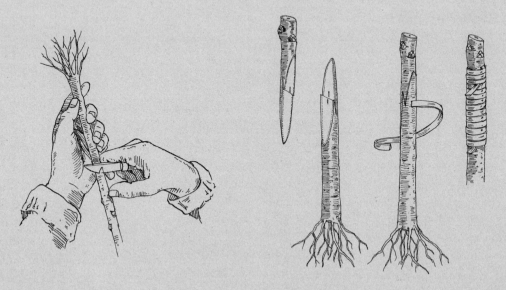

The common whip and tongue graft depends on the cambium zones of both the scion and the rootstock making intimate contact at one point. Wrap this union with surgical rubber and seal with grafting wax or an asphalt-based tree dressing to prevent any drying of the cambial zones. Be sure to seal the exposed end of the scion as well.

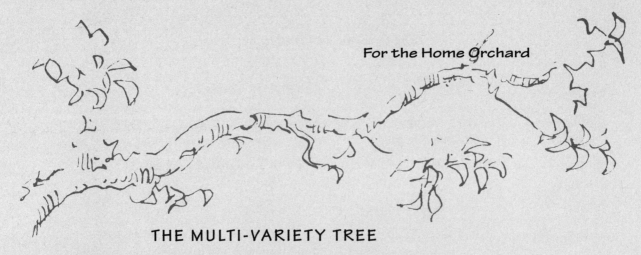

THE MULTI-VARIETY TREE

Henry Lang up in Milan, New Hampshire, has an apple tree with two hundred-odd varieties grafted onto it. Tags flutter throughout the tree in an attempt to keep track of which branch bears which fruit. It's a complicated undertaking — imagine pruning under the constraint of mistakenly clipping off all the budwood of Magog Red Streak with a single snip — yet a home orchardist can have a lot of fun putting just a few select varieties on a single tree.

Graft scionwood of the new varieties onto an existing tree in early spring. A young tree in training could readily have the chosen varieties spliced onto each pencil-sized scaffold branch. A vigorous wild tree has the advantage of established maturity, particularly where borers are numerous and browsing deer devastate young plantings. Such a tree may be beautifully shaped and healthy, and, given a few well-positioned grafts, may also bear palatable fruit.

Look for small wood near the trunk on which to place your whip-and-tongue grafts, be it a watersprout in need of spreading or lateral growth with existing scaffold potential. Grafting in the tree's interior allows a whole branch to eventually become a new variety, which is much easier to keep track of than twig wood in the outer canopy. Graft calluses can be painted over as a means of marking the point of varietal change.

A successful graft might grow three feet or more that first summer if tree vigor is good and competing shoots have been pruned away. Your chosen shoots can be bent under the wild scaffold branches or tied into place over the winters ahead. Prune away the

wild section of the tree slowly as each grafted branch fills in its envisioned space. Ten years down the road the wild branch structure will be gone, leaving you a tree with Arkansas Black, Fireside, Dudley, and Ashmead's Kernel forming the lower scaffold; Oriole, Rambo, and Melrose midway; and an entire new top of St. Edmund's Russet.

Graft the desired cultivars on shoots near the trunk to create the multi-variety tree.

that of destruction." An apple orchard may not be an oak forest, but it is a wonderful gift to posterity.

The size of the tree hole needs to be large enough to accommodate the roots without bending them. A three-foot diameter hole generally fits the bill. It's better to prune back an excessively long root than curl it back on itself (sometimes I trench out a channel for such a hearty root). Loosening the subsoil in the bottom of an eighteen-inch-deep hole provides leeway in setting the height of the graft union above ground. A buried graft union will eventually establish its own roots, which override the desired dwarfing effect of clonal rootstock. I aim to keep the graft union two inches above the soil line, planting only slightly deeper than the tree may have grown in the nursery. The settling of looser soils may bring the graft union down another inch or two, and if that has been your experience, compensate by keeping the graft union higher at planting. Trees on seedling roots are the one exception: the graft union can be buried one to three inches deep to encourage "self-rooting" of the scion cultivar. Forget any advice that tells you to mix compost or rich earth with the soil in the planting hole; the roots will soon extend much further into the surrounding earth for their long-term sustenance. We backfill the tree only with the soil that came out of the hole (plus a dusting of one pound of black rock phosphate for early root development). Tree nutrition in the years ahead will come from above to feed the top six inches of soil, where 90 percent of the feeder roots are found.

Backhoes are incompatible with fluffy soil and an intimacy with the land. Tractor-mounted augers and even shovels can burnish the sides of a planting hole, especially in clay soil. Roughly squaring up the sides helps fracture a too-smooth bowl. Growing roots need to readily penetrate into the surrounding soil, otherwise they may circle around the "glazed pot" inadvertently provided by a poorly dug hole. In heavy or clay soils, it is possible to

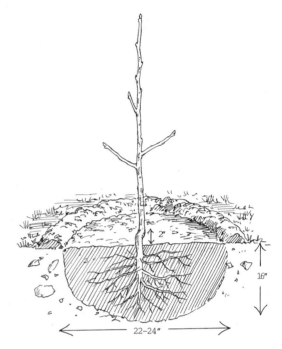

The value of a proper planting hole for a tree cannot be overestimated.

plant on raised mounds to lift the crown of the tree above any standing water that accompanies spring thaw or heavy rains—just be sure to break up the soil layers below prior to planting. Piling the soil on the uphill and downhill sides of the hole as you dig allows you to systematically plant from the row side without compacting the turned earth.

Prior to planting, you should never allow the roots of the tree to dry out. Soaking the roots in a bucket of seaweed solution can help reduce transplant stress, and wrapping in plenty of wet burlap ensures that the transported trees will stay moist out in the field. Choosing a relatively calm, cloudy day for planting is preferable to a sunny, windy day. Each tree either needs to be individually labeled or tied in bundles of ten to identify who's who in the planting plan. Digging holes ahead of time for a planting session is more efficient than a "dig then plant, dig then plant" routine. Broken roots should

HOLEDIGGERS IN THE SKY

Planting a new block of fruit trees calls for a heap of hole digging. David and I have put in the lonely effort, each spading out forty sizable holes in a morning's work, then planting the trees in the afternoon. But nothing beats an inspired group of friends helping out on the farm. Our Holediggers in the Sky club was born one spring weekend when we invited a dozen or so farm members to help. Amazingly, most of them showed up, shovels in hand and kids in tow. Two hours later, we had close to two hundred holes dug and the inkling of an idea.

That fall we issued certificates for a "thank you gallon" of cider. Andrea added the charming touch of the right to "visit your holes whenever you wish." Next spring's newsletter announced two hole-digging dates as we began to plan the planting of our Thayer block. The first Saturday the ground was too waterlogged for digging, so we put our volunteers to work in our bearing blocks: all the prunings got picked up, tree guards were removed from replacement trees, and the last of the compost spread. A group of willing souls hiked up the mountainside with us the next Saturday and dug all the holes for three long rows.

Placing trunk guards on young trees and the fall sanitation regime gets prioritized after the harvest is in. Explaining the why behind liming fallen leaves — to hinder the reproductive cycle of the apple scab fungus — added a fervent pitch to Pete and Erik's efforts to "stamp out scab sex." Moral crusades aside, these fun work sessions always end back at the cider mill for homemade cookies and apple juice.

Currently no new holes are planned, but, come spring, we still call on our trusty holediggers for the first of several days afield.

---

be trimmed off. A slight mound of soil in the bottom of the planting hole helps in spreading out the roots. Tamp soil firmly around each layer of roots as you backfill. Roots should radiate in all directions around the tree just as they grew in the nursery bed. With a little forethought, a rootless pocket can be left for a stake six inches from the trunk on the leeward side of dwarfing stock. Puddle water in the root zone to collapse any remaining air pockets before replacing the topsoil. Dancing a happy jig can equally serve for a final tamping of moist soil and to straighten out any errant lean to the tree. Deliberately slanting trees into the prevailing wind can somewhat counter its effect on exposed sites.

Whips are headed back at planting time more severely than a feathered tree. A one-year whip is snipped off thirty to thirty-six inches (based on its caliper) above the ground. This helps compensate for lost roots as well as invigorating lateral buds. When newly planted trees are not headed severely enough, they often develop laterals well above the desired heading height. Summertime training in this first year will establish a central leader from the set of vertical shoots responding to this heading cut. A single vigorous branch should be removed to bring lateral prospects back to an even keel. Feathers with narrow crotch angles are removed with a "bench cut." The small piece of branch remaining from this horizontal cut made alongside the leader will produce a more horizontal shoot. The central leader on a feathered tree is headed six inches above the highest feather.

(top left) Be sure to dig planting holes that will satisfy your dog supervisor. (top right) Grasping the upper roots in your hand helps in spreading laterals at the appropriate depths. (bottom left) Root laterals are meant to radiate out from the tree. (bottom right) Tamp the soil as you backfill with a hoe to avoid air pockets. (center) Now is that a straight row, or what?

The young orchard should be planted as early in the spring as possible after the soil has dried out sufficiently. Field preparation the year before is usually the key to getting the trees planted early. Cold soil temperatures promote the development of healing calluses at the tips of cut roots. Normal spring rains will then settle the soil around the roots before much leaf growth occurs. Planting delays do happen, however, and in that case nursery stock must be heeled into moist sawdust or sand in a cool place. However, never place your trees in the cooler with stored apples, as the ethylene gas from the fruit will induce bud break. Home orchardists often heel trees in the garden until proper planting holes can be dug. Trees planted after bud break may experience transplant shock, which can stunt both the upper tree and root development. Heavy pruning can help, but reliable irrigation is better.

Growers in Zone 6 and south can take advantage of fall planting. The root growth that takes place in mild winters gets the young tree established and raring to go by spring. Fully dormant trees can be transplanted from mid-November through December. Larger two-year nursery trees suffer less transplant shock when fall-planted and thus retain their head start on one-year whips. Roots continue to grow even though tops are dormant in regions where soil temperatures remain above 40°F. Damage to the roots is more likely in northern zones from the frost-heaving of recently disturbed soil.

Some of your newly planted trees may have to be "replanted" in later years. A furious wind that comes on the heels of saturating autumn rains may well blow over a tree that's still in leaf. Such trees will come out of the ground at a forty-five degree

(left) Heading and summer pruning a one-year whip.   (right) Temporarily "heeled-in" young trees.

angle, stopped only by the scaffold branches. Windward roots will likely have snapped and be poking upward. Use a tractor or team of horses to stand the tree upright again, digging the roots back in as best you can. Four strong guy wires will be needed to hold the tree in place until new roots reestablish the tree's permanency in the ground in three years time. However, this technique will not work in soils that tend towards being overly wet.

ORCHARD SIZE AND LAYOUT

Orchards evolve in time. An experienced grower with a grasp of marketing prospects can make plans to plant the "back forty." Most of us, however, need to grow with our trees, develop local markets and fiscal understanding of value-added ventures, gradually acquire the right equipment, and see if family income needs can be met by the fruit harvest. Keeping life fun is a big part of any decision to expand. The size of a monoculture—be it fruit trees or soybeans or golf course fairways—keys directly to ecosystem balance. The conventional wisdom that *bigger is better* has more to do with investment efficiency and marketing share than with insect populations and tree health. A few orchardists have interior organic blocks somewhat protected by outlying conventional plantings, yet plum curculio still finds the crop. Small plantings scattered about the farm integrate better into a diverse ecosystem, but deer fencing and the labor of clearing hedgerows of alternate hosts can make this an expensive trade-off. The availability of mulch and compost sets an acreage constraint on maintaining tree fertility. Good help can be hard to come by, and your own body can only do so much in a day. Large IPM orchards are made possible by the best equipment and chemicals supplanting the vast amounts of hand labor involved in an organic approach to growing fruit.

Not that large organic apple orchards don't exist. Both Turkey Ridge and Germantown Orchards in Wisconsin harvest over 100 acres of organic tree fruit. Reed Miller in Putney, Vermont, has transitioned his family's five-generation orchard into a full-fledged organic operation of 180 acres. Jim Bittner in western New York continues to convert blocks of conventional fruit to organic with an eye on the dried-apple-ring market. Larger orchards have the advantage of realizing economies of scale with equipment and storage operations. The challenge of curculio is met with an array of approaches: botanical sprays, garlic synergists, even limb jarring by high school students motivated by a "per bug" bonus. Precise timing of elemental fungicide applications and hand-thinning many acres of tree fruit to abet next year's bud set are equal challenges to being big.

Still, market connections are paramount. The direct sales caveat of sustainability shifts somewhat when orchard output tops 10,000 or more bushels: some of these apples are going to need to be wholesaled. Large orchards have the production to support an extensive value-added product line; however, recouping the higher labor costs of organic orcharding from a baby food or juice processor might be a legitimate alternative for the less-than-select half of the crop. If the weighted average price per bushel from all sales avenues turns a profit for the farm—where direct sales buoy up less profitable routes—a large organic orchard operation may indeed prove viable in your locale. I'd love to be growing more apples, but recognize that the orchard can only be a part of our farm's market mix in sparsely populated northern New Hampshire. The human factor once again sets the limits. Sustainable promise will ultimately be found in orchards and farms that hold us in balance as well.

But let's get to the *sine qua non* of orcharding: how does one plant a straight row of trees? Even one tree twelve inches out of line becomes a mowing or harrowing obstacle. Sighting back down a plowed furrow works better on flatter terrain; the wavy effect of a few inches of variance will seem less as the trees grow. Edging all four sides of a field with stakes to indicate every row and tree spacing allows two people to sight in each tree somewhat accurately. Ultimately, even cocky carpenters must use string lines in rolling terrain to get the trees close to true. A measuring wheel or spacing pole allows one person to mark out the tree spacing in such rows—mark each hole with a surveyor's flag or a handful of lime—whereas a tape measure requires two workers to get the job done right.

Orchard patterns vary from the simple four-point square to the multiple-row bed schemes of a super-high-density block. A hexagonal layout sets every tree equidistant from the others in any direction. Such a planting results from staggering tree alignment in every other row halfway between trees in the adjoining row. Slightly more trees can be planted per acre this way. The one advantage of the square—being able to run equipment horizontally between the rows—is offset by a 15 percent increase in yield from the additional trees of the hexagon.

Marking out a field begins with establishing a base line (the outside tree row) parallel to the surrounding woods or roadway. Leave twenty-five feet minimum between the first row of trees and the fence to maneuver equipment. Stakes are set at each end and more sighted in between. Parallel rows of stakes are then established at right angles to the base line by setting up a 3:4:5 triangle (using ropes in lengths of thirty, forty, and fifty feet helps lay this out). Row spacings are then marked along these triangulated lines. Curved rows laid out to match the contour of the land are necessary where crop interplanting is envisioned. Improved sunlight distribution in rows running in a north-south direction produces more quality fruit than east-west rows.

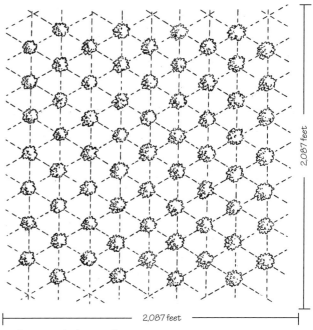

A hexagonal planting layout.

A typical standard tree orchard on a 30-by-30-foot spacing has about 50 trees to the acre; MM111 rootstock on a 16-by-24-foot spacing works out to just over 110 trees per acre. A valid concern in establishing such a *low-density* orchard—beyond the longer wait till first harvest—is the nonproductive ground that exists between trees until branch tips meet years down the road. The aisles can be hayed in a homestead operation, though fertility is being taken from the orchard. Vegetable plantings can be rotated with soil-building cover crops to more fully utilize the land in those early years. But perhaps best, from a fruit point of view, is to plant dwarfing trees in between the permanent trees. Eight to twelve cropping years could be gotten from these intermediaries before they would need to be removed. Fruit production would steadily climb the third year after planting. The initial investment in supplemental M9, Bud 9, or M26 trees would be recouped many times over. Great-grandfather often planted compact-growing Wealthy trees in his standard rows for an early crop gain. Temporary

TREE SPACING CHART
(Number of trees per acre)

SPACE BETWEEN ROWS OF TREES IN FEET	SPACE BETWEEN TREES IN THE ROW IN FEET										
	6	8	10	12	14	16	18	20	22	24	26
4	1,815	1,361	1,089	907	777	680	605	544	495	453	418
6	1,218	907	726	605	518	453	403	363	330	302	279
8	907	680	544	453	388	339	302	272	247	226	209
10	726	544	435	362	311	272	242	218	207	181	167
12	605	453	362	302	259	226	201	181	165	151	139
14	518	388	311	259	222	194	172	155	141	129	119
16	453	339	272	226	194	169	151	136	123	113	104
18	403	302	242	201	172	151	134	121	110	100	93
20	363	272	218	181	155	136	121	108	99	90	83
22	330	247	207	165	141	123	110	99	90	82	76
24	302	226	181	151	129	113	100	90	82	75	69
26	279	209	167	139	119	104	93	83	76	69	64

SOURCE: Hilltop Nurseries, Hartford, Michigan.

trees should remain unpruned until they are in heavy production.

Ned Whitlock tends eleven acres of organic orchard in Green Forest, Arkansas. He's got good equipment to do the work but admittedly has a hard time staying ahead of borers with that many trees. Ned is retrospective about orchard size: "I wish I could squeeze my best trees all together on six acres and cull the rest. Life would be a lot simpler and net earnings the same." Let's just call that a word to the wise.

HIGH-DENSITY PLANTINGS

The buzz word in planting systems these days is *super-high density*. Harvest can begin in the second year from a two thousand tree per acre planting. M27 or P22 rootstock are spaced three feet apart in double-row beds separated by five-foot-wide aisleways. The financial pressure to recoup investment costs goes up in such an orchard: the planting bill alone approaches ten thousand dollars an acre; a double trellis consisting of three wires is required in each bed; and irrigation isn't optional. Bill Jordan is an organic high-density orchard consultant in Granite Falls, Washington: "Less pest pressure in the West allows our direct-market growers to risk the high-density investment. Organic growers need to strip off the first crops, however, to give the trees another year or two to grow . . . these tiny trees will be growing in a low-maintenance turf (no herbicides, please) and so need to develop more branch structure before fruit production begins." The payback comes with crops of a thousand bushels an acre after six years. Polyvinyl row covers are often placed over the trellis to protect buds from spring frosts, limit the spread of fungal infection from rain splash, and warm up the pollinating scene on overcast days.

High density, of course, is relative. An East Coast orchard with five hundred trees per acre—typical of an M9 planting set at 6 by 14 feet—requires as much work with the same horticultural constraints. Mulching the tree rows is probably the best organic answer to keeping sod out, renewing long term fertility, and conserving moisture. Your continuing investment hinges more on labor than outside inputs. Steve Page and Cynthia Anthony model high density prospects on their one-acre orchard in Maine. Scab-resistant varieties are maintained under a vertical axis pruning system, crop production began to kick in with three hundred bushels in the fourth year, and the mulch (along with some hand weeding) is keeping quackgrass at bay. Cynthia adds, "We have borers like everyone else, but with the trees only six feet apart, we just roll to the next trunk on a soft bed of hay." How do you like them *high-density apples*?

DOWN TO THE NITTY-GRITTY

Varietal and rootstock choices have been made, orchard layout decided, and the trees themselves planted. Time now for the detail work of establishing an orchard: staking the dwarf trees, running irrigation lines (if possible), mulching each trunk zone with peastone, and giving some thought to equipment realities.

Staking

Dwarf trees with brittle root systems aren't anchored well enough to support a full crop. But this is not the only reason for staking a developing whip. A tree allowed to sway in the wind develops more thickness at its base. Trunk girth expands at the expense of leader development. The goal of earlier fruiting in a dwarf planting is partially achieved by not tipping back the central leader (other than to stimulate lateral branching) solely to stiffen leggy growth. A leader supported by a stake develops fruiting spurs in the terminal area sooner, which suppresses further vigorous top growth. This

in turn promotes better light penetration and fruit quality, all within reach of the ground.

Staking is absolutely essential for dwarfing rootstock like M9, Bud 9, and M26. Many cultivars budded to these roots develop fragile graft unions, which are more likely to snap in the wind until the wood matures. A single guy wire (supported by row-end trellis posts) just above head height aligns each tree's stake in tighter plantings. Some growers allow these stakes to dangle from the guy wire, others anchor them into the ground. The effect is the same once the tree is tied to the stake. M26 rootstock spaced ten feet or more apart, particularly in hilly terrain, can be independently staked. Some growers do this for precocious varieties on semi-

Lanky trees on self-standing rootstock such as this M7 benefit from the support of a temporary stake.

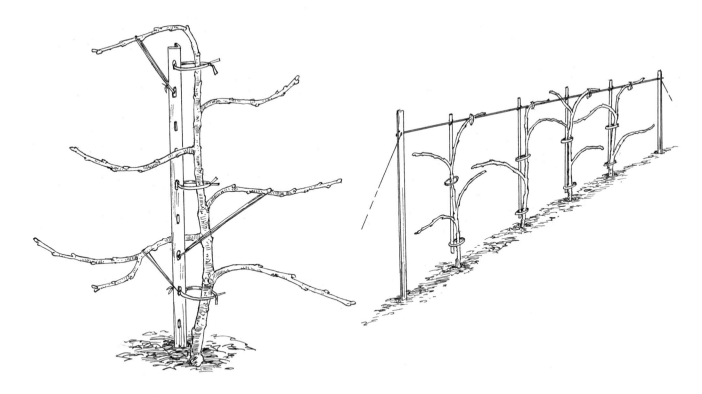

Individually staked trees grow faster because wind sway is reduced. Trees supported using a single guy wire (from which uprights dangle) can be encouraged into earlier production by training the leader to the wire.

dwarf M7 as well. Staking a three- to six-year-old tree on larger rootstock that has "runted out"— slowed down in vigor—helps considerably. Permanent stakes can be anything from electrical conduit or steel rebar to fiberglass or angle iron fence posts. Bamboo or hardwood will eventually rot but do serve to support early leader growth. Pressure-treated wood (other than for guy wire posts) is not recommended in living soils.

Irrigation

There are essentially three approaches to watering young trees: a water wagon (be it your sprayer or a tank on the bed of a pickup), overhead sprinklers, and trickle irrigation. Watering each tree individually often doesn't get done until the situation is dire. Sprinklers waste a lot of water in adequately

soaking the tree's root zone, but may be justified as a means of spring frost protection and manipulating scab ascospore release on a sunny day. Trickle irrigation is applied right where it's needed, and, given sloping terrain, may not require a pressurized source of water. Dripline tubing with built-in emitters spaced every forty to forty-eight inches provides a band of moistened soil up to five feet wide. The best tubing is both pressure-compensating— so water distribution is equal everywhere on the slope—and self-flushing. Watered trees get a big jump on root growth and fruit production regardless of rain. A second dripline can eventually be buried on the other side of semi-dwarf rows to irrigate expanding root zones in sod. Water deeply to get the moisture beneath the grass sod.

Trees should receive an inch of available water

each week. That's subject to many influences: soil type, tree size, drying conditions, temperatures, and competition from other plants. Newly planted blocks typically are trickle-irrigated twice a week for five to eight hours at a time, with adjustments made for natural rainfall. A home orchardist can feel good about slowly pouring four gallons of water around one- and two-year-old trees each week. Organic mulch goes a long way towards keeping moisture in the soil of orchards that have no readily tapped water supply.

Gravel Mulch

Herbicides are the conventional solution to keeping the immediate area around the trunk weed-free. This zone wants to be open to limit borer habitat and grass growth, which is conducive to vole damage and collar rot. Shallow hoeing works for a year or two, but, like many good intentions, eventually gets neglected. Hay mulch up against the trunk is not the solution . . . but peastone addresses all three concerns. Laid several inches thick, a gravel mulch suppresses germinating seeds. Invasive roots are another story, which is where circumferential hoeing and/or flame weeding is practical when quackgrass threatens. Harrowing a winter-killed cover crop alongside each row in the first years after planting also protects from perennial weed incursion, leaving just the in-row strip for such "bone of contention" treatment. Laying a three-foot-diameter piece of Agri-tex landscape fabric between gravel layers may inhibit sod even longer, until the tree is well established. A gravel-covered graft union is unlikely to scion-root. This mulch also helps stabilize young trees blowing back and forth in the wind, as the peastone trickles down the sway hole around the trunk.

Equipment Access

Aisleways between the tree rows are planned with six to eight feet of space allowed for equipment ac-

Gravel mulch around the base of young apple trees reduces immediate sod competition. Gravity-fed irrigation lines run down the length of every row on this mountainside orchard in Lost Nation.

cess, thus a minimal 16-by-24-foot spacing recommendation for MMIII recognizes the tree eventually will be contained within an eight-foot radius, leaving an eight-foot aisle for the tractor or team of horses. Tractor profile—with the proviso that PTO horsepower is sufficient to operate sprayers and mowers on a given terrain—defines what constitutes workable row spacing.

All of which assumes you understand your orchard equipment ideals long before you actually get to realize them. The ultimate options often prove cost-prohibitive on a small commercial scale. Money-poor idealists do the best they can. Back in your heyday you start with a scythe and a backpack sprayer. The market garden shows promise, thus a BCS tiller with a cutter bar attachment seems an astute compromise for mowing the orchard. But the vibrations prove too much, particularly now that the orchard has grown to two acres in size. A good deal in a vintage tractor comes along just when you've finally paid off those college loans, so armed with a home-built wand sprayer and a belly-mounted sickle bar, your row spacing finally makes sense. Thank goodness the trees weren't planted closer together when you were *certain* of being able to finance a narrow profile tractor and a sleek air-blast sprayer. It's all a process that, in a word, is called reality.

A neglected young apple tree. The tree pruned and branches spread.
(*Source:* The Principles of Fruit Growing, *L. H. Bailey, 1897, 1926*)

Persons complain that the thinning of fruit is expensive and laborious,
and this is true; but it is a fair question whether there is anything
worth the having of which the same may not be said.

—LIBERTY HYDE BAILEY, *The Principles of Fruit Growing* (1897)

CHAPTER 5

Care of the Orchard

The year-round tasks of orcharding lead to a perennial friendship with our trees. Caring for the orchard is about what we can give these good friends, so that they in turn can offer us the bounty of their many fruitful years.

INTUITIVE PRUNING

I expect to fully master the art of pruning by the time I'm eighty years old. You get only one shot at improving each year, the effects of which might not be fully understood till three more growing seasons have passed. An intuitive pruner works in several years at once: seeing the fruiting prospects of the current year; training a new scaffold branch to eventually replace old wood, making a stubbing cut to encourage side shoots further back on a pole-like branch; visualizing how the sunlight will reach within the tree when the leaves are full; and providing good access when it comes time to pick the fruit. These things aren't deliberately thought

through as much as felt. This oneness with the tree can only come with years of experience and confidence.

Approach each tree with an introductory intake of the breath. This meditative pause is when you take in the tree's framework and overall shape. How does it fit within the row? Are some branches too low? Is the leader beyond reach? Are the scaffolds balanced and properly spaced? Where does a new branch need to be trained to fill an empty hole? These questions answer themselves quickly in a well-worked orchard. Restoring years of neglect or tackling a past training system that was too dense is another matter.

There's a directing order to my pruning mantra: "Framework first, then the thinning, lastly see the fruit and how it grows." Nothing too mystical, but it's a beat that keeps me to task and includes all the important details. Thinning from the top down is a good idea, as this way you follow the path of the sun's rays to the fruit. It's easier to thin the lower

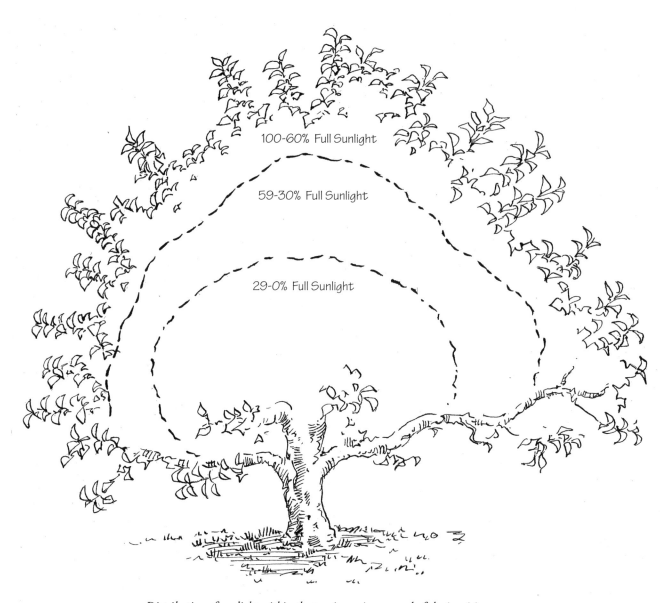

100-60% Full Sunlight

59-30% Full Sunlight

29-0% Full Sunlight

Distribution of sunlight within the tree is a primary goal of the intuitive pruner.

scaffolds—they're within reach—but more critical to achieve the topwork. Weak, drooping wood results from bearing branches that bend under load until they become too shaded to fruit well. Fruit buds are larger than those that leaf, whether placed on spur wood or the terminal bud of a longer shoot (St. Edmund's Russet is such a tip-bearing variety).

Be attuned to fruit bud distribution as you decide which branch to thin. You don't need every fruit bud to assure a full apple crop in a mature tree—5 to 8 percent will bring that about—but you also don't want to get so involved with pruning basics that nothing is left to flower. Be generous about leaving the pencil-thin laterals radiating off struc-

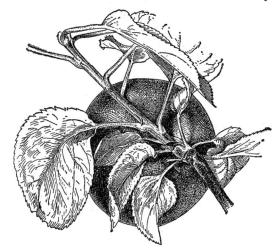

Next year's fruiting spur forms aside this year's fruit. (Source: The Principles of Fruit Growing, *L. H. Bailey, 1897, 1926)*

tural wood that will bear in future years. The growing points of the tree are those terminal buds left to leaf and photosynthesize the sunshine into root reserves and bud development for the year beyond. The delicate balance of pruning allows enough growing shoots while at the same time opening the tree up as much as possible to encourage fruit development and attain good disease control. It's a balance that can actually be quantified mathematically: twenty to forty leaves are required per fruit for best fruit size and yield. Shoot leaves, likely to be in direct sun, are more efficient at feeding the developing fruit than spur leaves.

Different varieties of apples have different growth habits. Cortland and Jonathan tend to be twiggy and want lots of thinning out at the branch tips. Sweet Sixteen, Winesap, Gala, and Northern Spy grow more upright, requiring attentive pruning to prevent weak crotch angles. The tops on such apical-dominant trees can be slowed down by a delayed dormant pruning (three weeks post budbreak). Strong, spreading trees like McIntosh, Jonagold, and Mollie's Delicious seem to grow just like you'd hope, though long branches might need to be braced under a full crop. Varieties that bear heavily need attention at fruit thinning time—Liberty and

Macoun, for example—a need an intuitive pruner should abet. Pruning one variety at a time helps me focus on that tree's particular growth habit.

The bearing wood on mature trees eventually peters out. By replacing this wood, you can keep a tree in full production longer. Overlarge limbs are often the result of too many branches left in a scaffold: the "poles" resulting when crossing side limbs get trimmed off puts the fruit buds further and further out from the trunk. Rejuvenation pruning in the top portion of the tree is an ongoing process of removing a larger lateral or two each year, while at the same time growing out replacement limbs a season or two before to take their place. Watersprouts emanating from the trunk can be spread to become such replacements. Renewing the bearing surface of the tree in this way avoids the stress of having to remove a trunk-size limb. The main and secondary branches of the lower scaffolds are considered an extension of the trunk—only fruiting laterals off these are renewed. Two-year-old spurs set a higher percentage of fruit than older wood. Fruiting laterals past their prime are never totally removed but are cut back to a pencil or upward-pointing spur to generate new spurs. The goal of a vertical-axis pruning system is to keep younger, more fruitful wood in close to the trunk. "Scoring" a barren limb can result in the initiation of fruit spurs: a knife cut made on the underside of such a limb about ten days after bloom activates latent buds.

Similar work takes place up top with the central leader. Either it eventually gets too tall, or, under a heavy fruit load, it droops down and totally shades the interior of the tree. Once the tree reaches its desired height, cut back the dominant leader to a weak, upward-pointing lateral. This is all the more de-vigorating if done around the longest day of the year. Letting the new leader grow a few years can help in the development of laterals to renew an upper scaffold.

PRUNING LINGO

Central leader — a style of pruning that develops one strong trunk in the center of the tree from which branches radiate at strong, wide angles that can safely bear heavy loads of fruit.

Dormant pruning — all large branch cuts and some thinning are done when the buds are at rest for the winter, generally after risk of a deep freeze is past in order to avoid winter injury.

Fruiting spurs — short shoots on wood two years or older that bear the fruit; best developed by a light pruning touch rather than invigorated into long, unfruitful shoots by heavy pruning.

Heading cut — the removal of the terminal bud on current or one-year-old wood encourages development of lateral buds, stiffens a lanky leader, and restricts vigor (if summer pruning).

Latent bud — a bud, usually concealed, more than a year old, which lies dormant in the bark tissue, until such time as severe pruning or bark injury causes that bud to grow.

Modified central leader — a style of pruning that eventually allows the central leader to branch off to form several tops; often easier to maintain than other forms of pruning, as trees naturally grow this way.

Open vase — a style of pruning that allows more light into the shady interior of the tree by creating an open center formed by branches radiating out from a topped main trunk.

Root suckers — shoots that grow from the roots of the tree, which, being below the graft union, will grow into a wild tree within your tree if not cut away.

Scaffold — the framework layers of the bearing tree, each composed of three to five main branches, which allow better sunlight penetration and air flow than could be had in an unlayered tree.

Stubbing cut — a pruning cut made into two-year-old or older wood to either stiffen or reduce the length of a limb; side shoot development can be encouraged on polelike branches by such cuts.

Summer pruning — the removal of watersprouts after terminal bud set helps light reach the interior fruit, while at the same time checking vegetative regrowth; heading and thinning cuts on trees-in-training are often made in summer to lessen their vigorous response.

Temporary scaffold branches — extra limbs left on the trunk for bearing purposes until such time as the chosen scaffold branches grow to fill in these areas.

Terminal bud — the growing point of the tree at the very tip of every shoot, which is deliberately removed in a heading cut to alter the tree's hormonal balance in favor of lateral buds.

Thinning cut — the removal of an entire branch at its junction with another branch or the trunk; these non-invigorating cuts are used to open up airflow.

Training — pruning and limb spreading as applied to the not-yet-bearing tree.

Vertical axis — a staked tree undergoing yearly rejuvenation pruning has a lower tier of semi-permanent scaffold limbs and an upper region of renewable fruiting arms. The majority of limbs on such a central-leader tree are kept "perpetually youthful" and thus easier to contain within the row.

Watersprout — a vigorous, vertical shoot arising from the trunk or main branch of a tree.

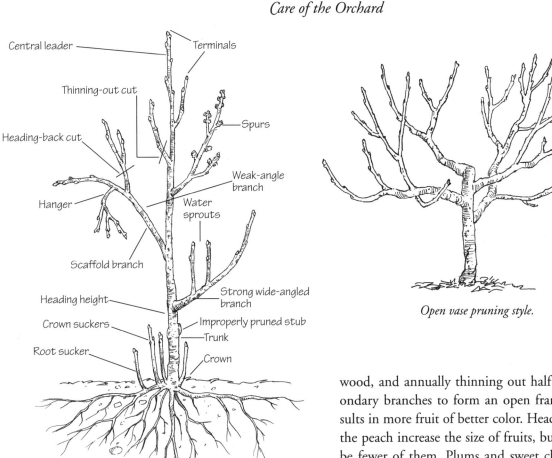

Central leader

Terminals

Thinning-out cut

Spurs

Heading-back cut

Weak-angle branch

Hanger

Water sprouts

Scaffold branch

Strong wide-angled branch

Heading height

Improperly pruned stub

Crown suckers

Trunk

Root sucker

Crown

A fruit tree subjected to pruning lingo.

Open vase pruning style.

Pears are worked in much the same way as apples: trained to a central leader followed by years of annual yet moderate thinning. Anjou is one exception, in that heavy pruning induces higher set in this variety. The degree of pruning for the pome fruits depends upon the vigor in a particular orchard. Annual shoot growth of eight to sixteen inches is a good indicator of balance—much more than this and you're either pruning excessively or overfertilizing.

The stone fruits lend themselves better to a modified central leader or open vase tree structure. Peaches initiate their flowers on one-year-old wood, and annually thinning out half of the secondary branches to form an open framework results in more fruit of better color. Heading cuts in the peach increase the size of fruits, but there will be fewer of them. Plums and sweet cherries bear their fruit on short spurs and require much less thinning after training, though the more vigorous Japanese hybrids need some heading back to prevent breakage of brittle branches under heavy crop loading.

Trees on dwarf rootstock can be pruned more severely than standard trees as the danger of invigorating excess vegetative growth is less (such being the genetically-weakened nature of the root). Ninety percent of the pruning and training on dwarf trees should take place between May and August, with only 10 percent corrective surgery left for the dormant season. A major concern with dwarfing stock in snow country is the breakage of limbs necessarily kept low—an icy crust will often pull such shoots off the trunk. M26 rootstock held by a rigid supporting pole is trained much the same as larger trees, just more compactly. Use of a trellis-

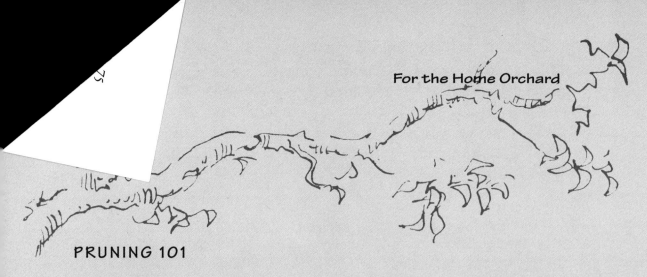

PRUNING 101

Pruning begins with knowing why you do what you do. Limiting a tree's reach is just one reason to thin out branches and make heading cuts. Pruning encourages fruit set and allows good air flow and sunlight penetration around the developing fruit. Old wood eventually needs to be replaced if the tree is to remain fruitful. The tree responds to different cuts in different ways, and an understanding of these variables is what will make you a good pruner.

Start with a vision of shape and lateral spacing. An orchardist will speak of maintaining a central leader within a framework of three scaffolds. Like a conifer, the base is kept broad and the top more upright to allow sunlight to reach the fruit buds on the lower branches. A scaffold consists of three to five branches radiating out from the trunk within a one- to two-foot span of the trunk. Having approximately three feet between scaffolds is a goal, with the first scaffold starting three feet or so above the ground on a semidwarf tree kept to twelve feet high. Lower branches are too much in the "fungal zone" to produce high-quality fruit, and they often interfere with mowing. Training a tree during its first several years in the ground will get you much closer to the envisioned ideal than coming in years later to reshape the tree's framework to your liking.

Overly tall leaders, crossing limbs, and those branches growing back towards the center or with narrow crotch angles are the obvious ones to remove. A heading cut on a lanky leader will stiffen the remaining wood and encourage the lower buds on the clipped shoot to set a satisfactory top scaffold. Crotch angles are best dealt with

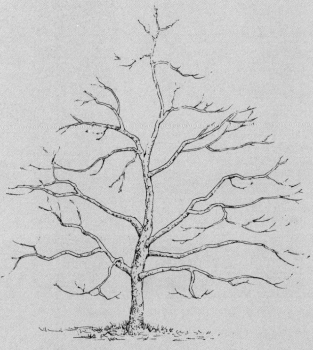

Scaffold framework

at a young age — you want branches to radiate out from the trunk in the horizontal plane up to a 45-degree angle. Branches that develop with narrower crotches form a weak union with the trunk because of included bark, and years later, be it under a heavy fruit load or in an ice storm, severe injury to the trunk is likely when the branches split. Broken or infected branches should always be removed.

Focus on thinning out branches on each scaffold once the basic framework is in place. Excess branches up high block sunlight to lower limbs and to those precious fruit buds in the interior of the tree. Remove branches that don't hold to the horizontal plane and that compete with other shoots at the end of the scaffold branch. It's a delicate balance to leave enough fruiting spurs and yet not over-crowd those remaining and prevent them from receiving the sunshine and nutrients needed to grow large, beautiful fruit.

A proper pruning cut is made flush with the branch collar on the trunk so it can completely heal over. Leaving a branch stub is an invitation to disease and rot, as the uncovered dead wood will serve as a point of entry. Shearing off the branch collar removes the protective tissue that will form the healing callus. Generally, all cuts are made at the union of a branch to its parent limb. A heading cut made along the branch (out from the attachment point) stimulates lateral bud growth. Buds nearest this cut will be invigorated more and bend towards the vertical plane, but further back, the hormonal balance brought about by a heading cut will favor wider branch angle development. Large branch removal can result in rampant sucker growth in the healing tissue around the wound, which is best reversed by back-to-back years of summer pruning.

Dormant pruning should be done in late winter when the risk of sub-zero temperatures has passed. A branch cut stimulates cell activity at the wound, causing the tissues to lose hardiness for ten to fourteen days after the cuts are made. Prune the hardiest varieties on the more vigorous rootstocks first to lessen the possibility of such winter injury. Summer pruning in early August, particularly of watersprouts and when training young trees, encourages fruit bud development over vegetative regrowth. It also allows better sunlight penetration to the ripening fruit, result-ing in better color and size. Summer cuts are best limited to branches with a diameter of one inch or less, which can fully harden-off before the winter months.

A well-healed pruning cut.

Long-reach shears help greatly with thinning out tops.

Branch trimmings left in the orchard aisle can readily be dragged out with large tarps to later be burned.

ing system for dwarf trees at a high density spacing introduces new considerations, but the basics of why you prune what you prune remain the same.

Every orchardist has his or her preferred pruning tools. A bypass hand shears is a must for training work and useful for thinning cuts. Felco shears fit the requisites for me: easy on the wrist, replaceable parts, and a handy holster for the belt. The Wheeler pruning saw is well-known in New England for making branch cuts one inch in diameter or more. The standard blade is okay, but Arthur Harvey (Greenleaf Sawblades, Canton, ME 04221) offers some refined options made from bandsaw stock that make the Wheeler my absolute favorite. Short-handled loppers might be a wise choice for pruners with too heavy a cutting hand—just right

for making the prime thinning cuts of whole branches but too big for getting involved with overly fine detail work. A long-reach shears is a useful extension of the arm to make a few thinning cuts up high but can be awkward to maneuver into a flush-cutting position. The pneumatic pruning systems used in larger orchards are expensive to justify in a small planting. Whatever the tool, sanitation is a must for preventing the spread of fire blight bacteria and the like throughout an orchard. Pruning tools should be wiped down with rubbing alcohol or 5 percent Lysol, or dipped into a pail containing a 1:10 bleach solution between trees. Removing an obviously infected limb means a wipe-down right after such a cut. Amberg's Nursery sells Felco's bypass shears and seventeen-inch loppers rigged with a hand-pressured spray device that sanitizes the blade after each cut.

Prunings either need to be removed and burned or chopped up in the pathways of the orchard with a flail chopper. Pruned twigs can become heavily colonized by the fungi that cause the various rot decays of fruit if left piled. Rot spores may continue to be produced for six years on branches trimmed from the tree. However, if the brush is chopped, the pieces are quickly decomposed by other fungi before rots can affect the fruit.

TRAINING THE YOUNG TREE

Sereno Edwards Todd in his 1871 *The Apple Culturist* had a knack of speaking to the truth of the matter: "The man who purposes to produce a profitable orchard of beautiful trees, which will yield bountiful crops of fruit for an age after he has passed away, must begin right, plant right, train right, and cultivate right. Then his reward will be as certain as the vicissitudes of the seasons."

Training starts in year one. The developing whip should have all growth rubbed off its bottom twenty inches once three to four inches of new growth shows up top. The height from the ground to the eventual lowest branch can be more with MMiii and standard rootstock, but the whip needs to grow this first year before removing laterals too far up. Midsummer is the time to snip back the four or so invigorated top shoots (caused by heading the whip at planting time) to the chosen leader. Laterals just below these sharp-angled upper shoots are left to develop as scaffold candidates for the following year.

Next spring, before growth resumes, select the first scaffold branches at the desired heading height and remove all others in the lower span of the trunk. The three to five laterals left should be as evenly spaced around the trunk as the growth whorl allows. Clip on a clothespin above a shoot if a crotch angle isn't close to the horizontal. Head back the leader to stiffen the central shoot and encourage lateral bud development for higher scaffolds in vigorous rootstock. Dwarf leaders are left to grow to encourage earlier fruiting. Don't head any scaffold branches unless one is way ahead of the others and needs reining back. Shorter laterals up high can be left to provide that good green foliage necessary for photosynthesis. Later in summer some higher scaffold choices can be encouraged by pinching off sharp-angled shoots that compete with desirable laterals.

It helps to understand the role of hormones in training a young tree. Auxin is produced in the vigorous upper shoot tips and young leaves. Its flow down the trunk helps to widen crotch angles by causing greater cell growth on the upper side of a branch. Heading a growing tip stimulates the three or four buds immediately below the cut to make a vigorous turn towards the sky. These become growing tips themselves, producing even more hormones. Buds beneath these dominant upper shoots are encouraged horizontally as auxin also inhibits the upward curvature of a tip shoot towards the light.

The permanent framework of the tree begins to show itself in the third growing season. Each scaffold branch should be of equal vigor and have a strong crotch angle of no less than sixty-five degrees. Branch angles will narrow with age as the limbs grow, so paying heed now saves split trunks years down the road. Keep an ample supply of limb spreaders on hand. Scaffolds are separated by one to three feet of trunk growth depending on rootstock. Interim laterals can be left in trees trained to a wider spacing until the permanent scaffold fills its envisioned space. Scoring into the bark with a sharp knife above a bud in April will promote branching should an open spot on the trunk be in want of a limb.

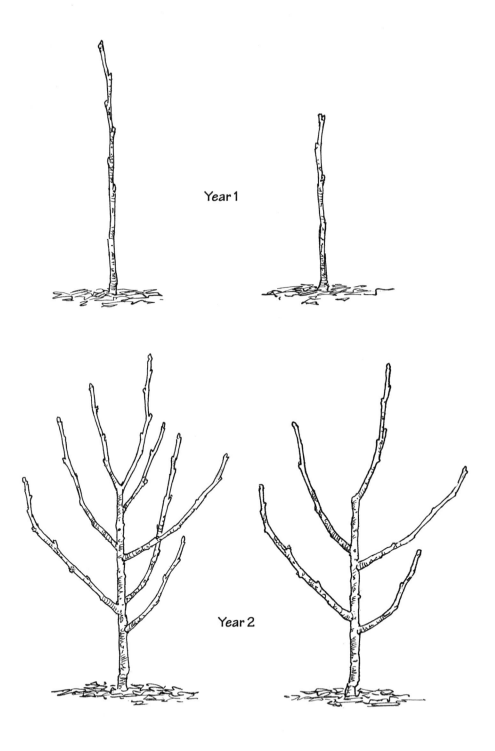

Year 1

Year 2

Training trees in the early years of an orchard makes for strong scaffold branches capable of bearing a full crop. Head back a lanky leader on vigorous stock, but leave dwarf trees alone to abet precocious bearing.

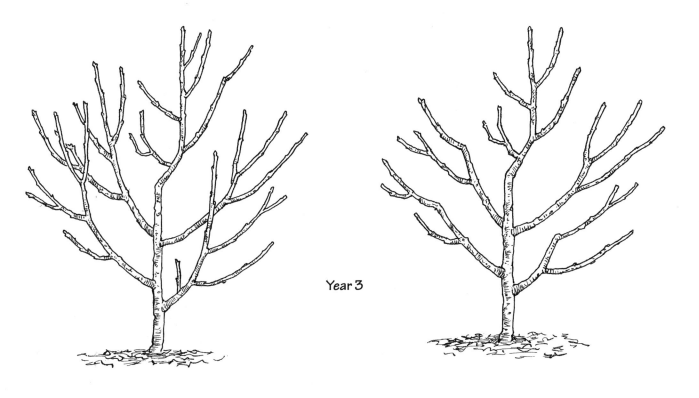

Year 3

Year 4

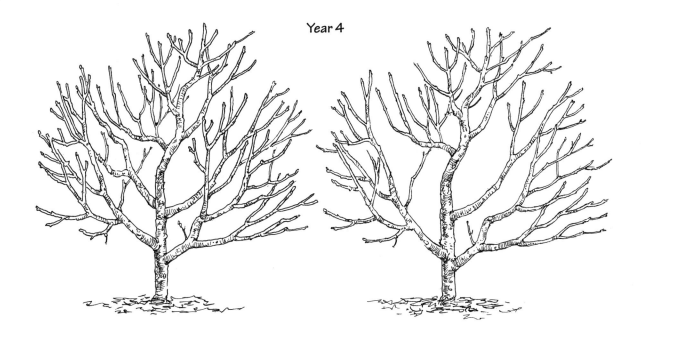

LIMB SPREADERS

Limb shoots are best spread in spring, when the flowing sap makes wood tissue more pliable. A wise orchardist will spread branches in a young tree before pruning to help make the scaffold framework more readily seen. Jutting a clothespin off the leader just above a short shoot sets a wide crotch angle. Red plastic wyes in incremental lengths from three to twelve inches (available from Occupational Services) work well to spread slightly longer shoots. The pointed metal spears do the same job, but, if lost on the ground, present a mowing hazard. One-inch-square hardwood spreaders up to three feet long are made with double-ended nails to prevent scaffold branches from turning back to the vertical despite a good crotch angle; a gradual incline of thirty degrees holds well under future crop-loading. Lathe boards notched on each end achieve this without leaving puncture marks in the bark. Wilson Orchard Supply offers the wire *branch benders* typically used in high-density blocks. Lightly twisting a branch beforehand helps reduce crotch-splitting caused by too great a pressure on the spread angle.

Branch spreaders come in incremental lengths.

Rig up a tool tray with compartments to carry your spreading array out into the orchard. Keep mixed lengths of lathe and hardwood spreaders in a five-gallon bucket. I like to include a few "rockpins" in my kit — attach a clothespin to clean rocks about the size of a small fruit with Liquid Nails. Once dry, these can be clipped onto lanky shoots to simulate crop-loading. Larger limbs can be weighted down with "cement Dixie cups," prepoured with a short length of electrical wire projecting from the cement as a hanging hook. Or try bending down such limbs to stretch the bark tissue along its upper surface. Though the shoot likely will spring back to its original position, the bending influence is established into future growth.

The "rockpin" simulates fruit loading.

Replacement limbs in the upper scaffolds of a mature tree can be tied into position off of a lower branch. The A.M. Leonard catalog offers a poly twine that can be used for two or three seasons. Amberg's Nursery sells a paper-based cord that will disintegrate after locking the branch in place, a useful attribute if you're not inclined to remove your tiedowns later on. Leave a loop around all branches so bark growth is never constricted. Hefty bottom branches (never trained at the proper time) can be tied down to concrete blocks on the ground. Notching the underside of a badly angled scaffold allows such a branch to heal into a better position. Chainsaw cuts are quick, but a series of three narrow saw kerfs made one-half to two-thirds of the way through leaves less of an air pocket behind the callus tissue.

Tie downs in bearing trees establish replacement limbs.

The fourth and/or fifth and sixth growing seasons are the teen years of the tree. The first crops are light compared to the harvests that will come at full maturity. Permitting the scaffolds and leader to grow with as little pruning as possible will hasten fruit bud development. Dwarf and semidwarf trees will have started to bear, and the weight of the fruit will add greatly to the spread of the tree. Spreading laterals up high in standard trees helps the scaffold branches below reach outward in search of sunlight until annual crop-loading begins.

A properly trained tree will need only minimal corrective pruning over the years to maintain this "naturally spreading" shape that you've diligently trained from year one. The fruiting wood of a productive tree is continuously pulled downward by annual crops. A limb never regains its full height once bent by the weight of fruit, even after it's picked. Eventually scaffold laterals droop and fall below the horizontal plane. Such lower fruiting branches are thinned and removed as a matter of course. New upright growth appearing on the upper portions of the scaffold limb rotates in to take the place of the spent wood below. Thus, a vigorous tree planted twenty-odd years ago is mostly producing fruit on wood only three to nine years old.

egg cells apiece. Cultivars may be self-fertile, partially self-fertile, or self-sterile. Triploid apples like Jonagold, Mutsu, and Gravenstein have defective pollen. Placement of pollinizers (the "guy trees," so to speak) within the orchard to provide viable pollen becomes more critical when you are growing such cultivars. See the table on page 99.

Large orchards must have bees brought in to get the crop pollinated. An orchard monoculture often lacks the diversity needed to support a wild pollinator population throughout the year, particularly when pathways are frequently mowed and the tree row itself is kept barren with herbicide. Great-grandfather had the same problem under a clean tillage system. Smaller blocks of fruit trees of four acres or less literally have a pollinator edge because of the wildflowers and nesting sites to be found in the surrounding hedgerows. Add to that a ground-cover plan that supports diversity within the orchard and importing honeybees can be entirely unnecessary.

But sometimes it's nice just to be sure. You can keep bees, rent hives from other beekeepers, or barter apples and cider for use of a hive. Hive

POLLINATION AND FRUIT SET

Fruit trees grow to produce seed. The fruit is merely part of the package from the tree's perspective. Seed development hinges on pollination. That transfer of pollen from the male anther to the female stigma can either be done by wind or insects. The cross-pollination required by most fruit trees is performed by bees, wasps, and syrphid flies, which are attracted to the showy flowers. Upon reaching the stigma, the pollen grain germinates and grows a tube down the style to the ovule. Each seed that grows in most apples and pears is the result of the separate pollination of five stigmas leading to two

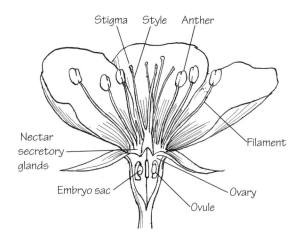

The anatomy of an apple blossom.

Larry Gates brings his beehives to Lost Nation Orchard in trade for apples and cider later in the fall.

rentals run $35 or more, which, at a recommended density of one strong hive per acre, makes domestic pollination costly. Stronger hives containing six or more combs of brood are likely to work the bloom at lower temperatures. Weaker colonies must keep all its members clustered together in weather below 50°F to maintain a core hive temperature. Hive strength can be critical, particularly when blossom time turns out to be cool, cloudy, and windy, as it often does. Really strong hives containing ten combs of brood provide enough worker bees to cover upwards of two acres of fruit trees.

Hives should be placed in the orchard the evening after 10 percent of the blossoms have opened. Any earlier and the bees may lock in on other sources of nectar and pollen. Dandelions stretching through high grasses can be selectively scythed if a yellow orchard floor rivals the fruit blossoms for the bees' attention. Getting the pollen deposited on the fruit blossom as soon as it opens is important, because the female ovule begins to decline after the flower opens. The ovule has a maximum life of between two and three days. The honeybee is at work for seventeen hours of that time if the weather is good, with a potential three bee visits per hour per blossom. Researchers have determined that it takes sixty-eight bee visits by the somewhat ineffective honeybee to produce a fruit with a high number of seeds. More seeds—apples have a potential of ten—means a better chance of fruit reaching maturity, a larger and well-rounded pome, and a significant increase in fruit calcium. Seed development draws calcium into the fruit; bitter pit is related to calcium deficiency and can be worse in those lopsided years when overall pollination is incomplete.

Hive placement is a question of facing the rising sun. The longer the hive is in shadow, the later the bees will start work in the morning. Distributing the hives throughout the orchard is useful for those inevitable windy days when the bees prefer sheltered bloom close to home. The colonies should be placed on a platform about six inches above the ground to keep tall grass from obstructing the hive entrance. Pollen inserts placed in the entranceway work when the bees walk through a compatible pollen that is then carried on the insects' legs to the blossoms. Purchased pollen can be necessary in single-variety blocks, or where early bloom comes too soon for that one late variety. Hand-pollinating one blossom out of every four flower clusters is another option: make two gentle thrusts per flower with a blunt brush or a finger dipped in the collected pollen. Some growers place bouquets of the target variety sprayed with a sugar solution near the hive to garner bee interest. Foliar boron applied

APPLE BLOSSOM CHARTS

The timing of bloom with cross-pollinating varieties is somewhat ensured in a we
chard. Bear Creek Nursery in Washington has put together this chart to help orchardis
riety placement in the orchard with bloom-time overlap in mind. Crab apple pollini
within each row (bees tend to fly down the aisles) are effective in solid varietal blocks. The flower
color of the pollinizers should be similar to the blossoms of the cultivar to be fertilized, because
bees tend to visit flowers of like color.

Early Bloom

Beacon
Chestnut Crab
Coles Quince
Cornish Gilliflower
Dolgo Crab
Duchess of Oldenburg
Dudley
Early Cortland
Early Harvest
Early Joe
Egremont Russet
Fameuse (Snow)
Golden Russet
Hazen
Hibernal
Idared
Irish Peach
Jerseymac
Jonamac
Jonared
Lakeland
Liberty
Lodi
Lowland Raspberry
   (Livland Raspberry)
Maiden's Blush
Manchurian Crab
Mantet
Margil
McIntosh
Norland
Nova Easygro
Oriole
Parkland
Primate
Quinte
Red Astrachan
Red Gravenstein
Red Melba

Sinta
Smokehouse
Summer Red
Swaar
Tetofsky
Twenty-Ounce Pippin
Vista Bella
Washington Strawberry
Westland
White Winter Pearmain
Wickson Crab
Yates
Yellow Transparent

Mid Bloom

Akane
Arkansas Black
Black Gilliflower
   (Sheepnose)
Blue Pearmain
Braeburn
Calville Blanc d'Hiver
Canada Reinette
Champlain
Chenango Strawberry
Claygate Pearmain
Connell Red
Cortland
Cox's Orange Pippin
Empire
Esopus Spitzenburg
Fireside
Freedom
Gala
Golden Pearmain
Grimes Golden
Haralson
Honey Gold
Hudson's Golden Gem
Idamac

James Grieve
Jefferis
Jonagold
Jonathan
Kidd's Orange Red
King David
Kingston Black
Lord's Seedling
Lubsk Queen
Macfree
Macoun
Melrose
Minnesota 1734
Mollie's Delicious
Mutsu Crispin
Newtown Pippin
Novamac
Pink Pearl
Pound Sweet
Prairie Spy
Red Baron
Red Jonagold
Ribston Pippin
Richard Delicious
Ross Nonpareil
Sops of Wine
Spartan
Spencer
Splendour
Stayman Winesap
Sutton's Beauty
Sweet Sixteen
Tompkins King
Turley Winesap
Tydeman's Early
Westfield Seek-No-
   Further
Wolf River
Zabergau Reinette

Late Bloom

Baldwin
Ben Davis
Bramley's Seedling
Criterion
Golden Noble
Golden Nugget
Horse
Hubbardston Nonesuch
Keepsake
Lady
Lobo
Mother
Northern Spy
Peck's Pleasant
Ralls Janet
Red Fuji
Rhode Island Greening
Rome Beauty
Simirenko Reinette
Snowdrift Crab
Spigold
Spokane Beauty
Tolman Sweet
Whitney Crab
Winter Banana
York Imperial

Table information adapted
from and reproduced courtesy
of Bear Creek Nursery, Northport, Washington. Used by
permission.

KEPT VERSUS WILD BEES

Agriculture is deeply indebted to the honeybee. Yet there's tragedy brewing in the hives. The gentle honeybee has been bred for profit to the point where it has become easy prey for viruses and parasitic mites that are destroying the species. Pesticides take their toll as well. Rudolf Steiner's prediction in 1923 that mankind would lose the honeybee in eighty years time is looking ominously correct. The Japanese now send schoolchildren and the army out to hand-pollinate fruit blossoms in the spring. A holistic approach is needed to save the honeybee and its invaluable role in the cycle of our lives.

Others of us need to focus on Plan B — the humble bumblebee and its solitary cousins; the wasps and hover flies; and the occasional hummingbird. An orchardist should allow other nectar and pollen sources to grow and flower throughout the season to build up a dependable wild population. Try mowing alternate rows two weeks apart to keep blooms available longer, or planting patches of buckwheat and red clover within the orchard.

Bumblebees will fly out in cold, stormy weather, as well as very early in the morning or late in the evening to gather pollen and nectar. Honeybees are more inclined to keep banker's hours, and then only if the weather is nice. The first bumbles of spring in the orchard are the young queens seeking a nesting site. Boxes filled with upholstery stuffing might entice a young queen, but so will undisturbed compost piles or rotting hay bales. The early brood is critical to fruit blossoms, but the health of the bumblebee population through the summer is what will ensure a cyclical return. Simply put, the more flower sources, the more bumblebees.

Wooden "nesting blocks" can be provided to encourage *Osmia lignaria*, known as the blue orchard mason bee, to claim your orchard as home. "Ozzie" is a very efficient pollinator. As few as two hundred female blue orchard bees are needed to pollinate an acre of fruit trees. The same job given to honeybees requires a full hive consisting of twenty thousand or more bees total. Like bumblebees, *Osmia* are better at reaching the pistil of the fruit blossom than honeybees, resulting in less of those misshapen apples due to incomplete pollination. Retired entomologist Philip Torchio in Utah can supply a starter kit of blocked bees and an instruction sheet. Or, if you'd like, use a 7mm drill bit to make holes six inches deep in the end of a 2x; face the block towards the southeast in the crotch of a fruit tree and secure it at least three feet above the ground; and see if any native solitary bees plug a hole with mud. Holes that are shorter tend to produce mostly male progeny, as do holes drilled in wood that is not protected from soaking rains. Moisture swelling narrows the diameter of the holes, again increasing production of smaller-sized males. The eggs behind this plug will hatch the following spring if parasites don't wreak havoc on them. Bringing nesting blocks into an unheated shed or spare refrigerator for autumn and the ensuing winter increases survival rates. Nesting blocks should be moved out to the orchard ten to fourteen days before anticipated bloom.

Growers in humid areas will be interested in *Osmia cornifrons*. These Japanese hornfaced bees are the samurai of the solitary bee world, pollinating up to 2,400 blossoms a day. Native *Osmia* pollinate 1,600 flowers on a good day, and well back in the pack comes the honeybee at thirty fruit sets (honeybees do not gather nectar and pollen on the same trip, resulting in only 5 percent of flowers visited getting pollinated). The newest Japanese recruit is the shaggy fuzzyfoot. These bees pollinate an astounding 5,600 blossoms a day and will work at temperatures as low as 45°F.

The humble bumblebee is my favorite pollinator.

This version of an orchard mason bee-nesting "condo" utilizes coated paper tubes inside PVC piping.

at the pink bud stage helps strengthen the blossom to germinate pollen grain and produce fruit that stays on the tree.

The tree sheds its undeveloped fruitlets after petal fall. One fruit developing out of every eight blossoms is average. This normal failure in the setting of fruit blossoms is due to three causes: poorly nourished fruit buds the year before, lack of pollination, or winter injury to the pistils that cannot be detected by the eye. Take heart; if the tree actually developed all of its potential fruits, thinning would become a horrendous chore. Complete unfruitfulness, aside from those self-sterile varieties that lack a compatible pollinizer, may be due to excessive wood growth, heavy rain during bloom, attack of fungi on the blossoms, or an untimely spring frost. Young trees generally set little fruit in their first years, although they may blossom fully. This trait shows strongly in the Northern Spy, which can take eight or more years before bearing. Older trees invigorated by radical pruning or excessive nitrogen tend to withhold fruit as well. Prolonged rains can wash pollen from the anthers and destroy its vitality. The common brown-rot fungus often kills peach blossoms. Scab can do the same to apple, but more often a heavy affliction destroys the developing fruit. A blackened pistil is an obvious sign of frost injury.

June drop refers to the tree's final selection of fruits that will be retained to maturity, a hormonal decision not fully understood but possibly related to number of seeds in each fruit and photosynthesized cues. Sawfly and curculio damage into the seeded core can also contribute significantly to the number of aborted fruits.

FROST PROTECTION

You can best protect those tender blossoms before the trees are planted by choosing a hilly site with good air flow (see chapter 2). Cold air settles into the lowlands first. Placing trees on a north-facing slope can delay bloom, perhaps enough to avoid that late spring frost. Chances remain good, however, that someday you still might awake to petals of frozen pink.

Pear buds are slightly hardier than those of apples, and, contrary to what might be expected of the tender peach buds of winter, so are the stone fruits upon resumption of growth in the spring. Prolonged cool weather tends to increase bud hardiness, but beware when the weatherman predicts a deep freeze on the heels of warm days. Preventative measures can make the difference between getting a crop and no crop at all.

CRITICAL BUD TEMPERATURES FOR APPLE

	Silver Tip	Green Tip	Half-inch Green	Tight Cluster	Early Pink	Full Pink	Full Bloom
Temperature (°F) for 10% kill	15	18	23	27	28	28	28
Temperature (°F) for 90% kill	1	10	15	21	24	25	25

Source: Adapted from Melvin N. Westwood, *Temperate Zone Pomology,* 3rd ed. (Timber Press, 1993).

A moist, open soil surface can contribute as much as 3°F to the air temperature within the tree canopy. Mulch, cover crops, or sod, as well as recent tillage retard the upward flow of heat on frosty nights. Overhead irrigation works by coating tender tissues with an insulating layer of water against the ice, keeping the bud within from actually freezing. The risk of severe limb breakage from ice buildup needs to be considered, however. Water protection works best when radiational cooling (rather than an arctic front) on a clear night occurs, and only a few degrees protection are needed. Orchard heat—be it in the form of coal baskets hung from branches, a series of small bonfires down the row, or propane stack heaters—can help on those nights when thermal updrafts are strong. A spray application of kelp is said to impart chill resistance. Biodynamic growers swear by a Valerian foliar tea to gain 5°F of frost protection.

Don't despair of moderately brown blooms the morning after. Buds yet to open may be unscathed; pollinated flowers are believed to be slightly hardier than unpollinated ones. Look to the all-critical pistil to see if the frost damage is complete. Some apples and pears will persist in growing, though no seeds or cores may ever develop. Frost-bitten fruit sets may show russeting or crimping marks at maturity.

THINNING THE FRUIT

You won't bring in a marketable crop without thinning regardless of how good you get at balancing the insect and disease dynamics in your orchard. Let's go back to the eminent Mr. Bailey again: "It has been demonstrated time and time again that no work in fruit-raising is more important than this thinning, if one desires to realize the most from his fruit. It results not only in a much finer product, but it is also a means of destroying the insect-infested and diseased specimens, and of saving the energies and vitality of the tree. . . . The fruit must all be picked sooner or later, and it does not cost very much more to pick it early in the season than to pick it late; in fact, much fruit not worth picking in the fall might have been worth the labor if the trees had been thinned in early summer."

We start thinning when the developing apples reach a half inch in diameter. Cultivars with heavy fruit set are thinned first: an overbearing tree puts less energy into the next year's fruit buds, which begin forming following bloom. We're likely to remove many sawfly and curculio larvae by thinning prior to June drop as well. The largest and best-looking fruit is left in each cluster. Two apples left from one cluster will eventually touch and more likely be favored by the lesser appleworm and leaf-rollers, but it's a judgment call if fruit set was light. Rot is liable to spread in peaches and plums left to grow side by side. Depending on variety, we thin

Certain apple cultivars such as Paulared set a full cluster of fruit.

Head thin every cluster to one fruit, and then some.

to leave an apple every four to eight inches along the branch. This space thinning is best done a second time around, after June drop and new insect damage has laid subsequent claim to the one fruit initially left in each cluster. Work systematically around the tree, then do the top from a ladder. Agile fingers are faster than a pointed snips (which are useful on short-stemmed cultivars). Use a two-handed approach to prevent breaking off entire spurs: grasp the fruiting spur in one hand, remove the apples with the other. All culls are thrown into a hip bag or scattered ground buckets to later be composted or splattered into oblivion by car tires on a country road. Hand-thinning serves two purposes: fruit size and uniformity are increased, and pest larvae and diseased fruit are removed from the orchard.

The sizing value of proper thinning very much relates to getting the job done earlier rather than late. A 100 percent benefit is found if thinning takes place by thirty-five days after full bloom. Twenty days later the benefit shrinks to 85 percent. The potential of strengthening next year's return bloom has passed in apples by this point, though on pears thinning will still be effective for flower bud initiation. Ninety-five days after full bloom the sizing benefit is down to under 60 percent in an irrigated orchard. However, don't rule out late thinning when large fruit commands a premium price.

Annual bearing is important to a commercial grower. A heavy-cropping cultivar like Paulared can fall into a biennial bearing habit if underthinned. Heirloom apples like Ashmead's Kernel can be encouraged to offer a yearly harvest by removing all fruit from alternate spurs, in order that these alternates will produce fruit buds for the otherwise "off" year. Hand-thinning, while laborious, allows the grower to be this selective. This strategy doesn't work for all cultivars, as the fruiting spurs on an apple with an innate biennial tendency are subject to flowering inhibitors produced by the young embryos on nearby twigs. Professor Gourley's work with Baldwin apples in 1915 showed this clearly: "Trees which were thinned to twelve inches apart produced no more blossoms the following spring than did the unthinned trees which had borne an excessive crop." Choice of rootstocks also influences biennial tendencies: Macoun on M26 sets annually for John Bemis in Massachusetts, but the same apple on an M9/MM111 interstem does not.

A thinned tree can produce nearly as many bushels of apples as one that is not thinned, fruit size making up the difference. The percentage of fancy-size fruit can be doubled by thinning. Plus the tree's energy is conserved, as seed production can exhaust nutrient reserves. Removing half the fruit removes half of the potential seeds. The energy saved is put into next year's buds and helps harden-off the tree for winter. In young trees just coming into bearing, this energy is needed for root development . . . leave yourself an apple or two for tasting in that third year, but don't be so eager for an early crop that you set back future bounty. Honeybee hives can be removed when *king blossom pollination*—the center flower in a blossom cluster, which opens first and produces a larger fruitlet—looks good enough to risk the loss of further pollination. Another alternative is to spray garlic after two days of ideal weather to reduce pollinator interest in subsequent bloom. Synthetic sprays used for thinning range from naphthaleneacetic acid and benzyladenine to full-rate applications of carbaryl (an insecticide sold under the trade name Sevin). IPM grower friends tell me these applications can be nerve-wracking—too high a rate when pollination results are as yet uncertain can mean too little crop. Biodynamic orchardists use horn silica spray to thin fruit from an apparent heavy set. Even a modest infestation of curculio can be looked upon as a thinning ally when there's too much fruit.

Here's the advice of Sereno Edwards Todd in 1871: "Do not be chicken-hearted about this job, although it appears terribly destructive to your crop of fruit." Thinning effectively is a matter of timely boldness.

THE GREAT GRASS DEBATE

Some orchards are kept as neatly mowed as a golf course fairway; others are wild pollinator jungles requiring a machete to get to the trees at harvest time. The key question is how to effect a good yield within a diverse fruit-growing environment. The organic ideal favors the wild side, with a few stipulations determined by understory management within the tree row, rodent pressure, and equipment capability.

Hugh Williams, a biodynamic orchardist in Claverack, New York, refers to the first four feet above the soil as the *fungal zone:* "You want a very rich fauna and flora life under the trees. This includes the finer grasses, wildflowers, and legume plants that grow in the understory. This is where the *fungus being* is managed." As applied to apple scab, high grasses in spring make sense. Fungal spores released in a wetting period are trapped by the vegetation from rising up into the air and being dispersed by the wind. Any tree branches left to grow in the more humid air close to the soil, however, can become infected. Secondary infections in the summer months can later spread scab throughout the tree and thus the crop. The air is much drier four feet above the ground, and this is the level at which Hugh feels fruit production should begin. Down beneath the grasses, the living soil is teeming with earthworms and beneficial micro-organisms (including fungi!) that decompose the leaves of the year before where scab would have overwintered. Do understand that, in Hugh's view, the very first application of an elemental fungicide like sulfur or copper is a violation of this whole.

"The ground cover is at the heart of what we're trying to do in the orchard. Mowing influences the richness of the insect life, the fungal life, and soil bacteria. Think about how air passes through the orchard and how leaves get digested. Letting wild plants come into flower provides a home for the parasitical wasps and a continuing food source for pollinators. Close mowing creates a much different situation under the tree," explains Hugh. His new plantings are shallow-hoed within the drip line twice in the spring, followed by a summer of in-row winter squash production (the ultimate living mulch) and then two years of oats as a green manure crop. The oats, like the grasses to come during the bearing years, are mowed down with a side-mounted sickle bar and left to decompose. It's much easier to mow high grasses with a sickle bar than to mow often. This first orchard mowing coincides with the first cutting of hay: cut as a living substance when green, the grasses rapidly decompose to feed the soil once the primary scab season is past. A second sickle-bar mowing follows after

harvest to expose orchard mice to the intense gaze of raptors. Any mulch left piled near the tree trunks is raked back. Mowing the pathways between trees in late summer to facilitate harvesting is optional.

Great-grandfather would likely have stood on turned ground in today's grass debate, clean cultivation of the orchard floor being the recommendation of his day. But even then there were stalwarts of the sod-mulch system, wherein the grass is cut once or twice and the resulting hay spread beneath the trees. These growers emphasized reduced erosion, better fruit color, and, as research showed at the time, better yields than could be gotten from a tillage system. Judge for yourself the influence of cultural treatments on yield from the table below from Gourley's 1923 *Textbook of Pomology*.

Looking at basic assumptions like *grass grows so you mow it* can reveal the connections we need to understand in order to grow fruit ecologically. Conventional texts advise mowing to reduce competition for moisture and nutrients. It's the wind and sun that work to dry out the soil, whereas under a mulch we know that moisture is retained. High grasses and weeds that are left to go to seed can actually conserve soil moisture in the drier months of summer (consider the sheltered ground beneath patches of mature goldenrod). It's the regrowth following frequent mowing that competes

INFLUENCE OF CULTURAL TREATMENTS ON THE YIELD OF TREES

			AVERAGE ANNUAL YIELD TO THE ACRE (IN BUSHELS)		
VARIETIES	PLANTED	DURATION OF EXPERIMENT	TILLAGE AND COVER CROP	SOD MULCH	SOD
Jonathan	1902	1907–1915	85.7	152.6	78.1
Stayman	1901	1908–1915	127.9	147.5	43.7
Baldwin & Spy	1873	1907–1915	398.0	385.2	(no trial)

SOURCE: J. H. Gourley, *Textbook of Pomology*, 1923.

Scything dandelions at blossom time soothes the soul.

with tree roots for precious water. The organic matter content of the tallgrass prairie soil was phenomenal until annual plowing and erosion took its toll. Grasses left to complete their cycle and decompose return more to the soil than ever gets taken out. Organic matter in this situation builds up to 6 percent . . . is that not a nutrient gain for the tree? Such an active soil encourages earthworms, which in turn are a boon to carnivorous shrews. These fierce little mammals also dote on mouse meat . . . is there a balance here that challenges the conventional wisdom that grass cover makes for bad rodent pressure? Or how about the increase in predatory insect populations when wildflowers are allowed to bloom? Again, the transition to balance—not just the highest yield possible—leads us to broader answers.

MOWING OPTIONS

Minimum mowing with maximum results is a good plan no matter how far you take it. Equipment capacity needs to be figured into the equation. Growers with a rotary mower need to mow more frequently so the grass doesn't get so high as to clog the mower. A brush hog gets through the highest and densest growth but disturbs insect life beyond measure. The tarnished plant bug, for one, is generally content to stay in high cover until a mowing aimed at competing bloom in May sends it up into the fruit tree to feed on the pink buds. Cutter bar attachments for two-wheeled tractors (rear-tine tillers with an accessible power shaft) leave tangles of high grass and *rattle you to death*. By contrast, a rotary brush mower works without the vibration and

ALAN EATON

Flail mowing at the Hort Farm at the University of New Hampshire.

shoots a reasonable mulch off to the side. A flail mower has a useful role in destroying scab inoculum in fall: infected leaves are shattered to pieces in the tree row at the point when beneficial insect cycles are mostly completed. The venerable scythe is always available for knocking down ubiquitous dandelions at fruit blossom time and pulling away grasses leaning against the trunk in fall.

Let's put these mowing options into a small-scale context. The faster and more powerful equipment is not likely to be affordable or justified for a limited acreage. Life expectancy spread over the amount of orchard to be worked can be figured into the purchase price to arrive at the annual cost of any piece of equipment on a per acre basis. A $4,000 PTO flail mower used for grass only (chopping brush is that much harder on the machine, shortening its useful life) might last ten years before a major over-

haul is needed. It's amortized cost in a ten-acre orchard would be $40 an acre per year for that period, but it jumps to $133 an acre per year for a three-acre planting. Once net crop return on a bushel basis is figured, the labor saved by a piece of equipment may only prove justified for a larger acreage. A used sickle bar mower on a vintage tractor can look pretty good in this light, provided your mechanical inclinations outweigh the frustrations of inevitable downtime. A garden tractor pulling an independently powered Alamo flail mower on an offset hitch is slow in comparison, but viable for several acres.

Then there's the traditional English cider orchard. Sheep do the mowing in blocks where the height of the bottom scaffold branches are determined by the temptation to browse. Grazing animals in the orchard has had its adherents over the years. Windfalls from June drop on can be consumed before larvae manage to leave the apple. Manure happens in place, but be wary of overfeeding trees between petal fall and leaf fall. Dwarf trees are out of the question with animals, and so are cider drops, which are more likely to be contaminated with E. coli bacteria.

SUMMER CARE

Summer orchard care begins after petal fall while fruit thinning is underway. Sticky traps for sawfly can be removed as eggs are laid and the damage done. A potassium application now can be doubly useful if soil levels are low: the tree is developing next year's fruit buds at this time, and a potassium reserve helps harden-off the trees for winter. If bitter pit has been a problem in the past, include foliar calcium in your spray schedule when fruit sizes to three-quarters of an inch in diameter, again in midsummer, and approximately two weeks before anticipated harvest. Gauge this recommendation to the varieties in your orchard that tend to be most prone to calcium deficiency.

Turn-of-the-century advice to probe borers out of tree trunks at the soil line in May and September needs to be fully heeded. Our reality isn't always this timely, but the first round of borer work absolutely needs to be completed by July 1 here in New Hampshire. The adult beetles invariably emerge by this date and begin a steady succession of egg laying for the next two months. The purpose of the pre-emergent search is to destroy any larvae lurking in cavities that got missed the year before. And no matter how astute you become in grubbing out these damn bugs, some will always be missed. Young trees can be checked in early spring when you remove trunk guards. Mature borers that have a winter of cambium chewing behind them are slightly easier to find—the telltale frass is of greater mass and the enlarged bark depressions more noticeable—allowing these rechecks to be less intense than the final fall probe. Spot searches in August for egg slits aren't a bad idea either, as the minute borer will only just have begun to chew.

Whitewashing the trunks of young trees can help with the borer search by contrasting egg slits and orange frass against the now-white bark. Use a cheap latex paint diluted by a third to a half with water for the whitewash. Wear rubber gloves, whether you choose to use a brush or a sponge. You'll want to whitewash up to the first scaffold branches to prevent southwest injury on the smooth bark of a young tree. Otherwise the darker bark will absorb the sun's warm rays on a winter day enough to thaw, but upon freezing again at nightfall will likely split open. The whitewash reflects this solar heat.

BORER REPELLENT POSSIBILITIES

- An open trunk maintained by renewing a gravel mulch as necessary to suppress sod.
- Wilder's Hot Pepper Wax applied before adult emergence?
- Diatomaceous earth or wood ash used in the trunk whitewash to thicken the crust.
- A light scattering of garlic bulbils planted in the peastone at the tree's base?
- Window screening stapled snugly at the top and buried securely in the soil. Such barriers are best slid up on young trees to check for penetrators early each fall when borer protection needs to be absolute.
- A homeopathic remedy made from borer ashes?
- Biodynamic tree paste with rotenone or tobacco mixed in the clay-covering.

Trunk whitewash on young trees helps avoid southwest injury, and makes borer damage more apparent.

Place apple maggot fly traps to catch the glistening light of the sun yet remain surrounded by nearby fruit.

Traps for emerging apple maggot fly are set out in mid-June. A few yellow sticky cards baited with ammonium (see the Great Lakes IPM catalog) can be used for early monitoring of immature flies if orchard sanitation is not yet up to par. Bait one or two tartar-red spheres with fruit essence along orchard "hot spots" to determine when perimeter trapping should begin in earnest. Sphere traps set out too early get filled with other flies before a full trap-out strategy directed at apple maggot might be needed. Fly emergence can be delayed by a dry spell, but renewed moisture in the ground usually begins AMF activity. Spheres will need to be cleaned of dead flies to maintain an attracting gloss and the sticky renewed every two weeks through the end of August. The brush-on formula of Tangletrap isn't as long-lasting as the paste, but it's much easier to apply and effective given necessary reapplication. Shaping the panel of a plastic milk jug to the radius of your spheres helps tremendously in removing insect bodies and the bulk of the sticky. The wise among us clean their traps in the early fall before the Tangletrap hardens. Yet even next spring, a spurt of WD-40 or Citra-Solv will let you wipe off any remaining goo. Neem, a botanical insecticide, showed promise in repelling apple maggot fly in Massachusetts, which would save all the mess of a trap-out strategy if costs per acre are equivalent. Timely removal of orchard drops come harvest time is essential in either a trapping or repellent approach to reducing the number of pupating flies within the orchard.

Fire blight can show up at any time following bloom if weather conditions have been favorable. Blackened shoots and withered branches need to be removed promptly to prevent further spread of

This "ugly stub cut" for fire blight is flagged with blue marker tape to be properly pruned later in the dormant season.

the bacteria. Make the prescribed "ugly stub" cut when the trees are in leaf (see page 140–41), saving the proper thinning cut for winter when fire blight isn't likely to infect the pruned wood anew. Disinfect your pruning tools between each cut in a 10 percent bleach solution, and burn the infected branches. Flagging tape (I use blue for blight) tied to the remaining branch serves as a good indicator to look for cankered tissue come dormant pruning time.

Pruning actively growing shoots around the time of petal fall may induce higher fruit calcium levels in vigorous varieties—and thereby reduce the incidence of bitter pit—but only if shoot regrowth isn't substantial. You risk reducing fruit size with these earlier cuts, however. Waiting till late July or early August (once terminal bud formation

for the following year is complete) to remove watersprouts allows more light into the interior of the tree to color up the fruit. Pruning too near to harvest may adversely delay winter hardiness.

Evaluate tree structure when in leaf to make mental notes for the dormant pruning season ahead. Have the top branches ballooned out over the lower scaffolds? Are certain droopy branches making mowing a head-whacking ballet? Perhaps it's time to give the central leaders on those rows of Jonathans a convincing crewcut. Look through your trees from the perspective of a developing fruit—yes, lie right down on the ground. You may be surprised how little sunshine filters down through the canopy.

PREPARING FOR WINTER

Getting to Round Two of borer detail during the peak of harvest is an admirable goal, but seldom attainable. September passes, October passes, and it isn't till November that all the replacement trees and young blocks get fully perused. Damage to the trunk tissue happens all this time, so peck away row by row, even tree by tree, during the fruit harvest to be as timely as possible. The adults will have finished any egg-laying by late August. The culprit progeny will be anywhere from egg-slit big to a hefty half-inch of destruction long by the end of autumn. Probe any suspicious spot on the trunk. The egg slits are obvious, and a light scrape will show if a cavity carries beyond. Follow every crooked corner with a sharp pocket knife or awl, until all edges of the damage are revealed. Remember, the tree survived grafting, and it will survive this surgery. Round-headed appletree borer is worse. A flexible copper wire can be pushed into heartwood tunnels—nicking the end of the wire forms rough barbs that might draw the grub out into the light of day. Some cavities will prove empty (search again to be sure), while others will yield a slimy quarry. Don't stop upon finding one larva, as a neighboring borer may have crossed paths. There can easily be several borers in a one-inch trunk, so continue probing diligently. Bigger larvae dating back to early July can obscure smaller brethren laid late in summer. The nuances of trouble are not limited when it comes to borer.

Mulch surrounding any trees should be pulled back several feet from the trunk. Any vole runs will then be abandoned back to the cover of sod. Tunnels that go beneath the peastone can be thoroughly stomped. Tree guards should be installed as a final measure of insurance on young trees. Two-foot-high spiral plastic works well on nursery stock, with snap-on plastic mesh fitting the bill on maturing trunks. Placing guards on as a part of the borer search saves a second stoop; the excavated peastone returned to place serves as an anchor to hold the spiral down. Hardware cloth can be wired loosely around trees of any age, but given that organic growers can't spray or assume borer benevolence, and thus must remove guards annually to inspect trunks, the wire option seems more tedious. Plastic spirals must be taken off early each spring, as the tight guard is conducive to adult borers and codling moth larvae. A thorough fall mowing to reduce rodent cover helps protect ten-year and older trees. So does cross-country skiing: the ski tracks block any runs made in the snow between trees. If rabbits are a girdling concern, Guy Ames in Arkansas suggests eating more rabbit stew.

Scab sanitation begins with a light dusting of lime on the fallen leaves, where the scab ascospore structures will form for the following spring. Plan to alter leaf surface pH to hinder this reproductive stage when two-thirds of the leaves are off the tree (the healthy leaves remaining are less likely to have any scab lesions). Adjust this timing varietally if a greater proportion of early or late cultivars are scab-susceptible. Lime sulfur was used earlier in the century to hasten the fall of unyielding leaves.

It's impossible to cover every fallen leaf in an apple orchard with lime. We target a six-foot swath in the tree row at a maximum rate of half a ton of lime per acre, hand-spreading with coffee cans to target the denser leaf piles. Our soil pH has held steady three years running: no doubt the lime is counterbalanced by our minimal sulfur applications in spring.

Next comes the flail mowing. An offset hitch allows us to get quite near the tree trunks with the flailing knives, which, coupled with the rotary mower on the tractor blowing into the row, stirs up and puts the pathway leaves into the limed swath. (Some growers reverse this plan by using a pinwheel hay rake on an offset to pull the leaves and any missed drops out for aisle mowing.) A handheld string mower can be used to trim any high grass around the trunk and blow back the flailed mulch, if necessary, to reduce rodent cover. Just avoid whipping the bark. Compost is then spread atop the chopped leaves to hasten decomposition of any remaining scab inoculum. The earthworms and micro-organisms carry out the work from this point on until the ground is frozen solid. The trees need to be fully dormant at the time of spreading compost, as fall applications of nitrogen can increase freeze injury. We spread two tons of compost per acre by hand, but it would be more if we had it available.

Deer can quickly put an end to the most diligent orchard work. Bags of human hair, perfumed soap, tankage bars, and taste repellents get a review in the next chapter. Ultimately, the only way to stop deer damage is with either a good fence or dog defenders. All drops that might attract a hungry herd should have been removed long since. Deer are incredibly smart. They remember gaps under fence lines and where to go for tasty browsing. That intelligence can be used to the orchardist's advantage, for they also remember licking peanut butter off a wedge of aluminum pie plate that is

Quasi-protection can be gained, if deer pressure isn't great, by hanging soap bars from the branches.

attached to a hot fence wire. Such becomes a place to avoid, and all the better if next year's fruit buds are never discovered waiting on the other side. Baiting those fence lines at the end of harvest is critical. When all else fails, appeal to your state's Fish and Game Department for a depredation permit to give to a hunting friend.

RESTORING NEGLECTED ORCHARDS

It's tempting to think, looking down rows of overgrown apple trees, that an abandoned orchard can be brought back into full production. The number of years that have passed since a pruner last worked such trees is a big factor, as the need for many large cuts and major topwork is going to ignite a vigorous response in the trees. Two or three growing seasons will pass before the pendulum swings back from vegetative regrowth to fruit bud development. Fungal diseases are likely to be rampant, and only a sanitation effort of similar duration will get such an orchard back to square one. Organic scab control works when inoculum levels from the previous season have been kept low, not when scab spores abound at every turn. Unchecked borers may well be on the way to sapping even a mature tree's vigor. Chemicals used in past spray regimes likely persist in the soil, and organic transition periods aside, what if it's DDT or arsenate of lead? The synergistic effect of more modern chemicals isn't known . . . is a minimum of three years since application enough for your own peace of mind?

WINTER INJURIES

Damage from a freeze varies according to the affected part of the tree: root, trunk, twig, or bud. True winter injury to the trees usually appears in the form of splits or long checks in the trunk, or in the outright death of the ends of branches. Heading-in such branches may help prevent further desiccation in younger trees. Winter-killed trees often have sufficient root reserves to leaf out or even bloom, but when the stored vitality of the plant is gone, the tree goes too. A fruit bud may be killed outright, in which case it turns brown throughout its center. Or only the pistil may be destroyed, in which case the flower may open but fruit cannot set. There is no remedy for winter-injured buds.

NONPOLLINATING VARIETIES (STERILE OR TRIPLOID*)

Arkansas Black	Holstein	Rhode Island Greening	Winesap (diploid, but
Baldwin	Jonagold	Ribston Pippin	quite infertile)
Belle de Boskoop	King	Sir Prize	Zabergau Reinette
Blenheim Orange	Lady	Spigold	
Bramley's Seedling	Mutsu	Stayman Winesap	*Many triploids are self-
Gravenstein	Red Gravenstein	Summer Rambo	fruitful to a very slight ex-
Hibernal	Red Sumbo	Turley Winesap	tent, though they are use-
			less in pollinating another
			variety.

On the other hand, beneficial insect populations are likely high in a neglected orchard. Codling moth and maggot fly pressure may be low if recent crops have been negligible. An isolated orchard, with no wild trees in the immediate hedgerows and woods, offers some hope of gaining ground in a reduced pest-pressure situation. There may be some fantastic heirloom varieties worthy of a comeback, though heavy fruit thinning will be necessary to get some of these bearing annually once again. An orchard on family land or one made available at little or no cost perhaps justifies the tremendous effort of restoration in those first few years, when a marketable harvest is unlikely.

L. H. Bailey's first recommendation for a neglected orchard *with potential* was to till the land. Sod outstrips fruit trees for available nutrients. Rebuilding the soil can be done through cover cropping if the ground is opened up, or by spreading composted manure and mulching if not. A compromise that comes to mind if one's fruiting prospects are intimately tied to restoring such an orchard is to remove every other row of trees. These rows could then be cover-cropped for two years before being replanted with commercially exciting varieties. Meanwhile, the older trees would be undergoing restorative surgery (pruning seems too mild a word for this). Delay fertilizing these trees during this invigorated phase unless annual bud growth is under six inches. A heavy borer infestation would have to be dealt with before any new stock goes in the ground. Apple replant disease, caused by harmful rhizosphere organisms established in the roots of the old trees, would, if present, put a nix to this idea.

Fruit trees do have prime bearing years, and a commercial orchardist is wise not to invest time and money in trees that are in decline. Apples, pears, and cherries have potential here; peaches, apricots, and plums are too short-lived to bother with.

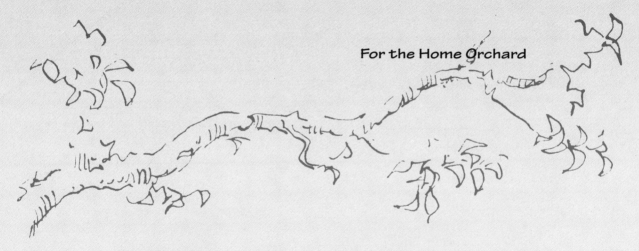

RESTORING AN OLD APPLE TREE

Every cider season two or three people ask me how to care for a long-abandoned apple tree (I've got this one big tree . . ."). The journey back to a manageable-sized tree is doable. The quality of the fruit is another matter, for a chance seedling has about a one in ten thousand chance of being pomologically worthy. However, your tree may be a named variety planted a century ago, or it may be a pasture tree once kept pruned for a cider crop. Put the family detective onto the case of identifying the variety of apple (see "Identifying Lost Varieties," page 44) if your taste test reveals it's an apple with merit. Meanwhile, let's talk about those first big pruning cuts.

The leaf canopy of a tree supports a vast root system, and vice versa. Going in with a pruning saw to undo a decade or more of overgrowth can be disastrous to an old tree. It's far better to approach this task over the course of two or three growing seasons. Year one is the time to think big. All dead and broken branches should be removed first to clarify what's going on in that tumbled confusion of limbs. Seek out three or four cuts either back at the trunk or on major scaffold limbs that follow the guidelines learned in "Pruning 101" (see pages 76–77). Overly tall leaders, crossing branches, and narrow angle crotches will be the chief targets. An overgrown tree likely has a structure of its own that defies orderly notions of a single leader or the old-fashioned open-vase style. Stick to the basic rules in deciding where to make cuts and don't worry yet about being graded on structure. Clean, flush cuts are important, as a stub of dead wood is an entry point for rot-causing organisms.

The year ahead provides plenty of opportunity to ruminate on the shape of your tree. Excessive pruning would have resulted in an abundance of watersprouts that could keep your tree in a non-fruiting mode for several years to come. Most of these suckers can be summer-pruned in early August to stimulate the tree to put more energy into fruit buds the following spring, leaving just a few to provide shade protection from sunscald. Limit your summer cutting to upright shoots less than an inch in diameter. Make your mid-sized pruning cuts when the late-winter dormant season (February through April, depending on your latitude) comes round again. One or two big cuts may still be in order; otherwise focus on those weak crotch angles, excessive growth up high that blocks sunlight to lower limbs, and scaffold branches that don't hold to the horizontal plane. Stop short of removing more than a quarter of a tree's canopy in any one year.

Year three and beyond is the time for moderate thinning cuts. Removing competing shoots towards the end of a branch allows better sunlight penetration and air movement, which in turn results in higher quality fruit. The days of large limb removal should be behind you. Do continue to summer-prune watersprouts to keep the tree's juices flowing in a fruitful direction. Fertilizing a tree during these years of invigorating pruning cuts is usually not advised if terminal bud growth is eight inches or more and the leaves are of a dark-green hue. Composted manure and a sprinkle of Borax (twelve ounces for a large tree) in the spring of year three will get you started with maintaining your now productive and beautiful apple tree.

Before   After

be some remedy discovered to head insects off, but the most reliable one of all will be to catch and kill 'em. . . . Entomologists may pen interesting paragraphs about the origin, hibernation, morphoses, and the habits of noxious insects and worms, and suggest nostrums to repel them and k their ravages; but after all that may be said or written, if we save our trees and fruit, in most nces we must catch 'em and kill 'em. Apple Tree Borers, Peach Tree Borers, Currant Borers, and borers for almost every tree and plant that dares to grow, are incessantly working their gouge-shaped augers night and day. Hence, the only watchword should be: catch 'em and kill 'em. All through the growing season, every employee on the premises should be instructed, whenever he sees a noxious insect at work, to drop all other employment, and catch 'em and kill 'em. We have tried the shoo-fly remedy quite too long, without any satisfactory results. If we fray them away, they are back to their work of devastation before we can return. If we catch 'em and kill 'em, they never have a resurrection.

—SERENO EDWARDS TODD, *The Apple Culturist* (1871)

CHAPTER 6

Apple Pests and Diseases

Every spring the orchard is full of promise at the pink bud stage. Pollination could well be perfect, no insect has yet marred the fruit, the many afflictions of apple haven't begun. Yet such promise is never quite fulfilled. Cool, rainy days during bloom lessen the fruit set. European apple sawfly proves to be rather devastating despite numerous sticky traps. Lots of summer rain means continuous disease pressure. Then again, the Redfree crop packed out over 60 percent. The Macouns have sized nicely thanks to timely thinning. And there are plums, meaning those garlic sprays must have done some good.

Growing apples organically requires a patience measured in years. Observing the intricacies of Nature to find the best approach necessitates the seasons coming round again. And again and again. What we know about orcharding is little compared to all there is to know. Each fruit is an expression

of an underlying spiritual initiative to be. The growth of these cells attracts an entire world of life forms interacting out their parts in an existential plan. We can go on to talk of the life cycle of a specific "pest" and try to comprehend its role in the balance of cosmic and terrestrial forces, yet to start we must simply share in a universal awe that we too are here in the beautiful orchard.

THE BEGINNING OF UNDERSTANDING

Realizing that over five hundred species of insects and a hundred disease organisms have been found in fruit orchards presents an immediate challenge to our understanding. Beneficial insects help with some aspects of fruit production, but admittedly, the perplexity of curculio and fruit flies lies beyond the control of any natural predators alone. On the plus side, modern technology has enabled us to see a microbiology that our great-grandparents would have given their eye teeth to know about. We've learned not only that insects communicate with other members of their species by secreting chemical substances but how to mimic certain sex-attractant pheromones and use them to our advantage. Insects use pheromones as well to mark territories, issue alarms, and to call a gathering to order . . . traits that may prove useful to the biologic orchardist in the future. Researchers are studying the gene path involved in the microevolution of certain insects—for instance, how the maggot flies of hawthorn transformed into a distinct subspecies with a newfound preference for apples—to see if feeding and emergence traits can be directed back on the molecular level. Parasitic nematodes and beneficial fungi have taken us below the surface of the soil in pursuit of pest larvae. Fire blight remains an invasive bacterium that kills far too many apple and pear trees. We've treated for it with doses of aerial antibiotics (a hit-or-miss strategy at best) and massive applications of dormant copper (to the point of turning trees blue), yet only recently have we called in the services of the common honeybee to deliver an antagonistic bacterium that can outcompete *Erwinia amylovora* on the nutrient-rich blossom stigma.

David Gill works at the Geneva Research Station in New York and spends considerable time observing the intricacies of nature in his home orchard. His talks on biodiversity in the orchard are an inspiration. David no longer sprays anything, nor does he mow except in late fall. He leaves wild corridors to carry, as he puts it, "the seeds of life of the native ecosystem. My unsprayed orchard is a classroom where I learn the basics of fruit growing. My feeling is that I don't know enough about the

ORCHARD VOODOO

Inside the little plastic pouch is a damp foam pad containing twenty-five million parasitic nematodes. Cost: $57.32, plus shipping . . . is it any wonder my wife is willing to sell me a similar pouch with supposedly the same invisible contents? And how about pheromones? Here's this rubber nipple saturated with the sex scent of the female Andalusian vigilante moth. Even the notion of apple scab wetting periods can be suspect to a doubting Thomas. Eight hours of wetting have occurred at 55°F and you're telling me ascospores have parachuted onto the apple surface and are just now getting a foothold behind enemy lines? And if I spray sulfur immediately it will inhibit enzymes needed by the spore to attach itself to the leaf?

Bring up the subject of radionics—where wavelength frequencies are used to influence the patterns of plants and animals—and eyes will certainly roll. Yet who is to say that vibrations that are anathema to plum curculio won't be the ultimate wherewithal for growing apples? Rudolph Steiner recognized our need to work in harmony with the ethereal forces of nature when he laid the foundation for Biodynamic agriculture. BD horn manure is prepared by packing cow horns with manure and burying them in fertile soil over the winter months. The formative forces of the earth converge in this potent soil preparation, to later be distilled homeopathically across the field.

Much of what happens in the natural world is both too small to see and of a spiritual influence far beyond our understanding. Today's heretical idea may be standard practice in the 21st century.

natural order of the environment to interfere with it blindly. I believe everything has a purpose and I hold a reverence for all life." Such reverence, more than anything, is the beginning of understanding.

GOODBYE FOLIAR PESTS

Nature is good at achieving diversity. This balance is often knocked out of kilter when we seek higher and higher yields. Nature's aim is healthy plants reproducing themselves by seed; ours is the luscious fruit around the seed. Broad-spectrum sprays aimed at fruit-damaging pests inevitably abet the indirect pests of the trees themselves by reducing beneficial predator populations. The diversity that keeps foliage feeders in check is lost. Thus fruit production manuals are filled with "words of wisdom" on how to control two-spotted mites and white apple leafhoppers and green apple aphids and tentiform leafminers and European red mites and pear psylla and San Jose scale and mealybugs and buffalo treehoppers. Spray strategies are devised that will best protect imported populations of mite predators. High numbers of foliar feeders can substantially weaken the vigor of a tree, leading to early fruit drop, reduced fruit set the following season, and smaller fruit size. Severe scale infestations can even kill a tree. An integrated organic orchard never loses its essential predatory balance. Let's claim bragging rights when we see them: foliage insects are not significant pests in an organic orchard.

Oil sprays smother the overwintering eggs and emerging nymphs of a number of foliar feeders. Use of a highly refined oil is tolerable in an organic orchard, but generally not necessary. Aphid numbers can be overpowering in young trees, where root development hinges on shoot growth, and even though beneficials will eventually rectify any imbalance, leaf damage can be severe. Applying a delayed dormant oil at tight cluster (gauge this by your bearing trees) will smother a good portion of

a potential early aphid problem. Forgoing oil in bearing blocks saves all the worry of overlapping sulfur applications for scab control. Just look upon any aphids you find on watersprouts as your summer pruning crew. Other spray materials are available for soft-bodied insects should leafhoppers blow in from afar. Always remember, however, that there's likely a deeper imbalance behind the immediate need that calls for attention.

INSECT MONITORING AND IDENTIFICATION

We need to know which insects are in our trees if we're to guide the complex interplay of orchard life to a fruitful harvest. Most insects found in the orchard are either innocuous or perform beneficial tasks like pollination or consuming other insect pests. Direct pests damage the fruit; indirect pests feed on the foliage and on the tree itself. IPM manuals available from your Cooperative Extension, are a good beginning reference for learning the life cycles of the major pests in your region. These manuals often provide color photographs of the different life stages of each insect and the types of damage done. Obscure pests that are controlled by broad-spectrum chemicals are likely to fare better in an organic ecosystem. Their identification might well hinge on the old literature and on sharing observations with an enthusiastic entomologist. Lesser appleworm and apple curculio are rarely spoken of in New England, yet we seem to have a plentiful population of both in Lost Nation.

Insect Traps

Traps can be used to ascertain both the presence and date of emergence of many insects. Learning the life patterns peculiar to your orchard site is invaluable in planning repellent and control measures. The damage levels of certain pests like

ALAN EATON

Pheromone traps are placed at eye level within the southeast quadrant of the tree canopy.

European apple sawfly and apple maggot fly can be kept within reasonable limits with an integrated trapping strategy. Spray applications that target a vulnerable point of an insect's life cycle are keyed to a degree-day countdown initiated when the first male is caught. Monitoring is a vital tool for growers tracking economic thresholds: damage to the crop will be less costly than a spray application as long as insect captures per trap remain below a specified tolerance. Such knowledge has cut chemical applications in IPM orchards by a third or more in the past twenty years. Such thresholds, though, have less meaning for organic orchardists, who rely on preventative, cultural, and biological controls (with no broad-spectrum chemicals on the shelf "just in case").

The chemical scent used on a pheromone membrane is specific to the targeted insect. Usually a pheromone imitates the chemical lure given off by the female to attract the male of the species. Fruit moths go for the bait in droves, and, once adhered to the sticky trap bottom, await an ongoing reckoning. A codling moth wing trap placed in the orchard's midst at bloom annually provides the first male capture, upon which first-generation sprays are keyed. I did trap lesser appleworm and redbanded leafroller for several years to cue their generational peaks to my orchard calendar, but now that their pattern is established (in conjunction with seasonal codling moth tracking), I no longer feel compelled to track the flight of other lepidopterous species. Captured moths are removed each time you count to provide a clean slate for the following week. Lures are replaced every two to eight weeks as specified, often along with the wing trap bottom. Unused pheromones can be kept in the

ALAN EATON

Monitoring white card trap for European apple sawfly at the pink bud stage

freezer for four years if a bulk purchase helps the budget.

Visual traps work for tarnished plant bug, European apple sawfly, apple maggot fly, and, to a very limited extent, plum curculio. The trapping details of each are given in the "Bug-by-Bug" descriptions to follow. Sticky surfaces will catch insects in flight, but crawlers usually sense the substance and avoid going further. It's enlightening to understand the thought process by which Ron Prokopy at the University of Massachusetts first developed an effective trap for sawfly:

After observing the behavior of sawfly females on apple trees for many days, we determined that the females spend considerable time visiting the blossoms for feeding and egg-laying, and some time visiting leaves and bark for resting. We decided we would try to create visual models with artificial pigments that mimicked the color of a mass of apple blossoms, a mass of apple leaves, and a mass of apple bark to see if sawfly females might be lured visually to the mimics and trapped there by a thin, clear sticky substance.

Color has three properties: hue, intensity, and purity saturation. Trying to match human perception of color with insect perception of color can be a very deceptive experience for humans. While we can see in the blue, green, yellow, orange, and red parts of the electromagnetic energy spectrum, insects can see in the ultraviolet but not in the red. . . .

Having created visual mimics of masses of apple blossom color, leaf color, and twig color (in other words, having matched rather closely the hue, intensity, and saturation reflectance patterns of natural plant tissues with mixtures of synthetic pigments), we proceeded to test the response of sawfly females to our mimics. To our joy, we discovered a very high response to the white pigment containing titanium dioxide.

You Shall Know Them by Their Scars

Most of us learn which insect is attacking our fruit or foliage by the distinctive damage done. A walk through the orchard can reveal which pest you're up against, even though the adult might not be seen. A white sticky trap for European apple sawfly catches many different insects, but until you develop your "bug sense," any one of them could be your targeted candidate. The winding, russetted trail on an apple's skin, however, can only be credited to the first instar stage of sawfly.

Plum curculio leaves the most distinctive scar of all, biting a crescent moon over each egg oviposition to prevent fruit growth from crushing its young. The emerging larvae chew an oval-shaped exit hole on the underside of a June-dropped apple. First-generation codling moth often choose to enter the fruitlet through the calyx end, an opening marked by brownish frass. Sawfly leave a similar poopy entrance on the side of the apple. The only sure way to identify A from B is by cutting out the worm and (using a 10× hand lens) counting the legless segments between the three pairs of true legs and the false prolegs on the rear abdominal segments: codling larvae have two such segments between, sawfly have one legless segment. A feeding puncture can be attributed to either plum or apple curculio, but the latter reveals itself with certainty

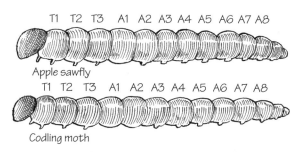
Apple sawfly
Codling moth

Codling moth larvae have two legless segments, while European apple sawfly have only one, between the true legs and the false prolegs on the rear abdominal segments.

not too long after June drop. "Feeding-frenzy" apples are subject to repeated punctures, to such a degree that the underlying tissues collapse. Missing large hunks out of your developing fruit? Credit the green fruitworm.

Summer "leps" damage can vary, but it is always attributable to successive-generation larvae of the lepidopterous moth family. Red-banded leafroller makes winding feeding depressions on the skin of the apple, always where a leaf covers the fruit or two apples hang side by side. Lesser appleworm might work an exposed surface as well, but generally limits its feeding to shallow tunneling around the calyx end of the fruit. Oblique-banded leafroller damage results in deep sunken areas of light corky tissue on misshapen fruit. Codling moth, being an internal feeder, is the proverbial worm inside

The crescent moon scar of plum curculio.

WORMY INTUITION

As a 1907 spray bulletin from New Hampshire College put it: "What small boy does not know the wormy apple almost by intuition? And, if he fail to announce to his companion that *there ain't going to be no core*, it is probably because the codling moth has already devoured that toothsome morsel."

the apple. Entry stings appear when these larvae have had a brief start on the fruit before dying from spray. Oriental fruit moth larvae burrow into succulent shoot tips as well as the apple, but they do not feed on the seeds like their codling cousins do. A cluster of tiny circular excavations on the fruit beneath a touching leaf is either the work of the eye-spotted bud moth or the tufted apple bud moth.

Apple maggot long ago earned the name "railroad worm" for its meandering tunnels beneath the apple's skin and eventually throughout the flesh. A fine eye can pick out the puncture where the fly laid its egg by catching the slightly depressed sting mark in the right light. Superficial dimples and conical depressions on the fruit are the result of tarnished plant bug feeding on the young fruit. Rosy apple aphids cause clusters of stunted fruit. We'll leave the description of foliage damage to the chemical handbooks. Nor is much description needed down low on the trunk—borers alone lay claim to this devastation.

BUG-BY-BUG PROFILES

Knowing an insect's behavior is key to understanding how to manage it. We identify points of vulnerability in a pest's life cycle to apply integrated practices that will limit its damage to the fruit. An *ecology approach* looks at ways insects move within their habitat. Perimeter trapping and border row sprays are based on the "gradual movement inward" trait of curculio and apple maggot. Applying sticky to trunk bands to stop ants from herding aphids throughout the tree recognizes where to set the roadblock. Mating disruption keys into the mechanism by which moths find each other to mate. A *biocontrol approach* ignores insect behavior, focusing instead on applying beneficial organisms at the location of the pest, often when it is in its larval or pupal stages. *Physical intercepts* detour insects from

the usual feeding and egg-laying routine: sawfly with a blossom-like trap, roundheaded borer with a screen-covered trunk, and the whole gang (hopefully) with a neem/garlic repellent spray. Inspirations like hanging suet in a few trees to attract woodpeckers that rat-a-tat on pests hiding beneath bark suggest themselves.

Each of us has differing levels of pest pressure in our orchards that determine our priorities. Here in New England, Ron Prokopy has tracked the whodunits in wild apple trees for twenty years. Plum curculio and apple maggot fly afflict 90 percent of the fruit, with codling moth getting its digs into about half of these. All other insect damage tallies up below 10 percent. Managing this situation to get marketable fruit can radically alter the pest profile. An organophosphate spray that eliminates one pest may induce others to significant proportion. Nature is not necessarily disposed to our plans; repercussions always follow. Keeping this bigger picture in mind means knowing how any step we take is designed to work, as well as what collateral effects our actions may have on the whole orchard ecology.

Tarnished Plant Bug

Plant bugs have marred the surface finish on as much as 35 percent of past Lost Nation crops, but never to the point of having to downgrade apples from select grade. White sticky cards can be hung at knee height in the tree to monitor for TPB if a chemical spray is planned. The adults become abundant from green tip through petal fall. They feed by inserting their mouth parts into developing buds and fruitlets. Such damage at tight cluster causes the buds to abscise; later feeding results in the conical-shaped russetting usually seen on the calyx end. TPB are generally content to feed and lay eggs on legumes and other broadleaf weeds on the orchard floor. Mowing just before the blossoms come out will drive many of these insects up into

A ROGUE'S GALLERY

Identifying the insects in your orchard is step one in figuring out what to do about them. The Cornell Tree Fact Sheets show the life-cycle stages (with the aid of silhouette sizing charts) and the types of injury caused by each major apple pest. Fourteen of the five hundred or so species of insects you may encounter in the orchard are briefly described here.

- **Tarnished Plant Bug.** Adults are 6–7 mm long, angular bugs, somewhat flattened and brown in color; each forewing sports a black-tipped yellow triangle.
- **European Apple Sawfly.** These fly-like insects are 8 mm long, dark brown above with a distinctive orange belly and legs, with clear smoky wings.
- **Green Fruitworm.** This caterpillar is a robust fellow, in varying shades of green with white or yellow longitudinal stripes, that turns into a mottled, grayish brown moth with a 40 mm wingspan.
- **Red-Banded Leafroller.** This small moth, about 10 mm long when resting, is brown with reddish brown bands across the forewings; its larvae are yellowish green with similarly colored heads and thoracic shields.
- **Plum Curculio.** Picture the Hunchback of Notre Dame (bad case of back warts actually) with a curved snout on a 5–6 mm long, grayish brown weevil and you're face-to-face with our most wanted felon.

ALAN EATON

Adult plum curculio.

- **Apple Curculio.** Think *red-hued* Hunchback of Notre Dame, and just slightly smaller than Cousin Plum despite its considerably longer snout.
- **Codling Moth.** Adults are about 12 mm long with wings folded, grayish striped overall, with coppery brown patches at the pale-fringed wing tips; the mature larvae reach 20 mm long and are pink to creamy white, with brown heads.
- **Lesser Appleworm.** These small moths, about 8 mm long at rest, have multicolored wings with shining pale blue and grayish orange markings on black.
- **Round-Headed Appletree Borer.** The beetle that inflicts the nefarious white, footless grub upon our trunks is yellowish brown with white stripes, about 18–20 mm long exclusive of its antennae.
- **Oriental Fruit Moth.** The internal-feeding larvae of this smallish moth are white to pinkish gray; the adults are about 9 mm long when their mottled gray wings are folded.
- **Oblique-banded Leafroller.** These light brown moths are 14 mm long at rest with a banded pattern in the forewing; larvae are large and robust with a green body and dark head.
- **Apple Maggot Fly.** These black flies are 6 mm long with dark bands resembling a "W" in clear wings, a bright white spot in the small of the back, and light stripes across the abdomen.
- **Tufted Bud Moth.** The tufted scales on the forewings give this inconspicuous gray moth its name.
- **Woolly Apple Aphid.** These pinkish gray aphids are usually hidden under a white, cottony secretion.

the trees. The tarnished plant bug parasite, *Peristenus digoneutis,* recently introduced from Europe in the Mid-Atlantic States, is gradually becoming established elsewhere. No doubt soldier bugs and spiders will welcome the beneficial assist.

European Apple Sawfly

The pesky sawfly emerges from the soil in spring to lay its eggs in blossom clusters on the outside of the tree canopy. A larva in the first instar stage bores barely beneath the skin of a fruitlet which, given a chance to mature, has that distinctive winding sawfly scar. The greater damage results after larvae molt and then tunnel to the core of additional fruit, often ruining each apple as far back as six feet along the branch. Timely fruit thinning can be helpful in this regard, but EAS devastation can strip a good 20 percent of a dwarf tree crop if left unchecked. After feeding and completing its development, the larva drops to the ground to pupate in the top few inches of soil. There it remains till next spring beckons with showy blossoms.

White sticky cards are used to capture adult sawflies who mistake these for blossoms. These trap cards, placed just above eye level on the south side of the tree canopy, won't catch every sawfly but can stick a hefty majority. Researchers in Switzerland (where EAS is a native pest of long standing) hope to improve results by developing synthetic odor attractants for EAS adults. The pollinators—including European apple sawfly!—that inevitably get lodged in the sticky coating are a tradeoff of this trapping method. The thirty or so 5-by-8-inch cards we hang per acre at pink average sixty-odd sawfly captures per trap in a bad sawfly year. That adds up to some significant non-egglaying. EAS traps are removed at petal fall as adult activity ceases. By motivating yourself to do some early thinning of infested fruit—before the second instar stage larvae drop to the ground—you can make a dent in next year's population. Few adults emerging from ground outside the orchard are likely to fly through a hundred-yard buffer zone.

A garlic repellent strategy won't prove as effective against sawfly. Insects, in order to be repelled, need somewhere else desirable to go. Your orchard is "home sweet home" to any EAS overwintering in the ground beneath the trees. The egg-laying urge won't be denied if no other blossom options present themselves. A neem spray at petal fall could theoretically help by inhibiting instar molting. Pupating adult numbers the following spring can definitely be checked by parasitic nematodes. A soil application rate of twenty-five million per acre unleashed *beneath the trees* on a showery day not long after petal fall should match the 80 percent larval promise found in Quebec. Timing is important, as EAS larvae are much more susceptible than pupae. Vincent and Bélair also showed that evening application of Steinernematid nematodes to the fruitlet clusters at petal fall can significantly reduce the percentage of fruit showing secondary damage.

Fruitworms and Leafrollers

We make an application of Dipel DF as a matter of course at the pink bud stage. Most tent caterpillars, first-generation leafrollers, and green fruitworms get a fatal "stomach bug" as a result. A follow-up spray at petal fall presents an equal opportunity if larval numbers still seem high.

Oblique-banded leafrollers (the half-grown larvae overwinter on the tree) tie bud leaves together and hide in the resulting chamber to pupate. Feeding excursions to the developing apples often cause the fruitlets to drop. The characteristic corking damage results from second-generation feeding in July and August on apples either shaded by a leaf or touching fruit-to-fruit. Variegated leafroller larvae do their "spring thing" in the ground cover, with adult moths emerging shortly after petal fall. Eggs laid on the apple leaves hatch in late June through July. The larvae often use dead leaves to build a

(top left) European apple sawfly. (top right) Sawfly work the blossoms much like any pollinator. (lower left) Full-grown sawfly larvae in fallen fruitlet. (lower right) The distinctive winding scar of European apple sawfly

feeding shelter beneath the apple. Red-banded leaf-rollers overwinter as pupae and so first appear as adults from green tip through bloom. The first-generation larvae begin feeding after petal fall, with round two coming in late July and August in Lost Nation. Such dates shift ahead to earlier in the summer in warmer climates. Apple pandemis in California has a similar pattern to OBLR, but orange tortrix confounds matters with generational overlap all year long. Fruit-tree leafrollers are more akin to the humped green fruitworm in that both overwinter as eggs laid on twigs. The speckled green

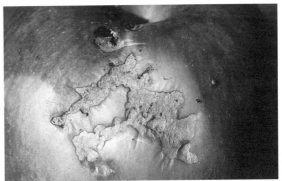

(left) Red-banded leafrollers caught in a pheromone trap. (right) Fruit injury from second generation RBLR.

fruitworm emerges from the soil as an adult to lay its eggs when buds start growing. Fruitworms have one generation per year, with fruit damage limited to early in the season.

Males of most of these species can be monitored by pheromone traps to determine peak flight activity. Early season "flags" of leaves webbed together are easy to spot when walking through the orchard. Codling moth sprays serve to keep many of these pests from getting out of hand in subsequent generations. Beneficials play a major role in keeping summer leafroller damage tolerable. Proper fruit thinning leaves few apples touching on which these characters can hide. Mating disruption products for the more widespread leafroller species are coming, including sprayable pheromones.

Curculio

Plum curculio is the most challenging pest an organic fruit grower faces. A number of my grower friends spray Imidan once or twice during the course of the season because of this one insect. Most of their crop can be lost at June drop otherwise.

Catching curculio on framed sheets in a Georgian peach orchard. Note the padded stick used to jar the tree limbs. (*Source:* The Plum Curculio, *by A. L. Quaintance and E. L. Jenne, USDA Bulletin 103, 1912.*)

Plums and peaches are next to impossible to grow organically unless one exercises daily vigilance. Curculio wounds in these stone fruits are often colonized by brown rot, and much of the fruit spoils before it's ready to eat. Growers with just a few trees can fare the worst, as the odds are proportionately stacked against a limited crop.

The plum curculio has rightfully been dubbed our "Achilles heel." Botanical sprays like rotenone can wreak more damage on beneficial populations than the half-gain achieved against this snout beetle is probably worth. Turn-of-the-century advice was to jar each tree every morning for two to three weeks after petal fall to cause the little buggers to fall onto sheets held beneath the tree, to then be gathered and killed. The drawback here is the scale of an orchard-wide effort, and the inevitable insects that remain hidden in the ground cover. Each curculio female can lay four or five eggs per day in those few weeks. Both males and females are busy all the while feeding. New adults emerging in late summer riddle calyx ends with feeding punctures that appear as small, rotting craters. Natural enemies exist, but none has yet been proved to provide sufficient control. All told, high curculio populations left unchecked equal a fruit disaster.

Curculios move into the orchard as early as the pink bud stage, both flying and crawling to reach the trees. Temperature and humidity influence this movement inward, but not in a way that can be reliably pinpointed by degree-day tracking. The first scouts forage under the trees while awaiting fruit set, crawling back and forth between blossoms and ground cover. Granny Smith apples can be hung high in border row trees to monitor for initial oviposition punctures before petal fall. Come the first *curculio night*—an evening with temperatures above 70°F coinciding with early fruit set—the bulk of the party can move in from hedgerows within a matter of hours to commence a nocturnal egg-laying disaster. A Quebec study found 83 per-

ALAN EATON

(top left) Plum curculio feeding on fruitlet. (top right) Oozing punctures from plum curculio on a Gala apple. (above) Curculio larvae before exiting a dropped apple to pupate in the soil.

cent of curculio activity in the tree takes place at night. The threat wanes three weeks after petal fall, though adult activity can be prolonged by cool, wet weather. Growers who use synthetic chemicals can generally assume that a last organophosphate spray at 340 degree days (above a 50°F base) after petal fall will keep curculio under wraps. Egg incubation averages five to six days, after which the larvae feed within the fruit for two to three weeks. The legless larvae lack the ability to go very deep into the soil, where they pupate for approximately one month.

Mortality of larvae in fruit results from the rapid growth of surrounding tissues. Apples punctured while still small (less than the diameter of a nickel) soon fall to the ground, as damage to the seeded core triggers a hormonal abscission. Fallen fruitlets provide a far greater survival rate for larvae than those in apples that continue to grow on the tree. Firm-textured fruitlets usually crush the newly hatched grubs. Certain varieties like Melrose and Northern Spy limit the curculio's reproductive success for this reason. Unlike apples, pears dry up quickly once fallen, and the stony tissue on the ground becomes just as implacable for the hapless larvae as a fruit still growing on the tree. Ants and ground beetles claim quite a few of the vulnerable grubs during their move from fruitlet to soil.

The detailed life-cycle information contained in a 1912 USDA bulletin on plum curculio was the result of exhaustive research efforts across the country. Still, glaring questions remained: Where exactly did curculio go for the winter? How far can the insect effectively migrate? How high do they fly? Work in Quebec has recently provided some answers by marking adult curculios with radioactive isotopes: Geiger counters can be effective bloodhounds. Plum curculios were found to migrate out of the orchard to seek wintering grounds at the base of hardwood trees perceived at twilight in a southwesterly direction. But they'll return to the orchard if the leaf litter proves too thin. Come spring, PC gather on the forest or hedgerow edge for as long as three weeks, presumably to mate. Their willingness to crawl afield ended at less than 200 meters out, but flight behavior couldn't be as readily tracked. One interesting sidenote on this

1849 CURCULIO UPDATE

At the regular meeting of the St. Louis Horticultural Society, held on the 7th of May, 1849, the curculio was the subject of some interesting remarks; an abstract of which we publish from the minutes.

The president stated that his attention had been called to the various recommendations of remedies or preventatives of the ravages of curculio, one of the most nefarious pests of the orchard in this part of the country. This insect invariably takes our entire crop of apricots, nectarines, and plums, and injures the cherries, and even peaches. He has determined to try every practicable proposed remedy of which he could avail himself the present season. The following were among those suggested:

- Horse stable manure. This was believed to be ineffectual.
- Spreading sheets under the trees, and tapping the body and branches with a mallet.
- Placing iron hoops, or pieces of iron, in the branches of the tree. He had seen at his mother's residence, last fall, a greengage tree having an iron hoop entwined among its branches, and from which a crop of fruit was always obtained, whilst the fruit of other plum trees nearby, without the iron, was destroyed.
- The insects may be fenced out by a tight board fence eight to ten feet high. A gentleman on Long Island succeeds perfectly with his, but he also paves the ground.
- Placing a coat of salt under the trees. This is believed to be ineffectual, as he had partly tried it, but without success.
- Washing the trees, and even the fruit with the strongest decoction of tobacco and whale oil soapsuds will have no effect.
- Swine and poultry, running daily among the trees, during the fruit season, as a permanent annual practice, will ultimately drive away or destroy the insect. The poultry, however, are not alone sufficient.

Captain Bissel said he had tried horse manure and salt without any effect. He was inclined to try swine.

General Milburn said that a Mr. Price, of this county, kept off the insects by tying a band of sheep's wool around his plum trees.

Mr. Clark said that the insect would not attack the fruit upon a tree standing along a frequented walk.

SOURCE: *The Plum Curculio*, by A. L. Quaintance, U.S. Dept. of Agriculture, Bulletin No. 103, 1912.

research is the alliance we should all be seeking with the common American toad—one amphibian had the Geiger counter going bonkers until a couple curcs were removed from his stomach.

Ron Prokopy in Massachusetts is looking into effective ways to monitor plum curculio behavior in the orchard. The Tedder trap (originally designed for pecan weevils), which simulates the dark vertical silhouette of a tree trunk, has limited use with curculio without a strong odor attractant. Volatile chemicals found at fruit set in plums and favored apple varieties have potential, as does an

ALAN EATON

Counting curculio to evaluate spray trials in Lost Nation Orchard.

unidentified pheromone produced by female PC when feeding. Chemical mimics must match molecular shift patterns when exposed to light, making them rather involved to develop. The lack of research funding more often than not holds up such work. Ron suspects curculios can fly many hundreds of yards, in stop-and-go spurts, to reach the orchard. He picks up the June drops in his home orchard, which, though buffered by two hundred yards of open fields, still attracts an immigrant hoard annually. Much of the inward flight takes place in the daytime when temperatures are warmer, though once in the tree canopy, curculios get around by crawling almost exclusively. Fliers can entirely bypass funnel traps elevated a few feet off the ground. Flying height is somewhat suggested by the observation that dwarf trees in border rows get skipped in favor of a taller canopy a few rows back. Despite

the odds, with the right scent lure, we may yet be able to perimeter-trap curculios. Waiting to prune border row trees until after half-inch green tip may increase the draw to the perimeter because of odors released from newly cut branches.

Human sound and movement cause curculio to drop to the ground. This "playing possum" behavior more likely than not evolved as a protection mechanism from birds and explains why limb-jarring works to trap the fallen curculios onto ground sheets. The nuances of jarring must be observed to knock down the greatest number of captures. Merely shaking the branch leaves other curculios still ensconced; these only become unseated when the limb is struck with a padded hardwood pole. Such jarring makes further inroads if an exposed limb stump (about one inch in diameter) or an iron pin prepositioned in the trunk is struck with two sharp ax-head blows in quick succession. Nails will work in younger trees, but the pin should have a square end to prevent its being driven further into the wood. Our great-grandparents rigged up encircling tarps on wheelbarrows to efficiently move from tree to tree. The time of day for gathering matters too. First light in the morning finds curculio sluggish and likely still in the tree after a cool night. A greater percentage may have dropped below to hide again in the ground cover by twilight. This back-and-forth tendency is more apparent from pink through early petal fall. Evening gathering can be just as effective once the nights have warmed. Twice a day jarring over this two-week period leads to moderate success where curc pressure is extreme. The scale of the effort and potential fruitlet loss are other matters.

Back in the 1860s another mode of catching plum curculio was devised worthy of mention. Growers found that smoothing cultivated earth beneath the trees takes away the weevil's hiding places. Here they propped pieces of oak bark (smooth side down) or cedar shingles, three pieces to each tree a foot or so from the trunk. The curculios crawled under these for shelter, and a significant proportion could be taken each morning after having dropped from their nocturnal frolic up above. Jarring the branches allowed for a subsequent late-afternoon gathering as curculios retreating back towards the dark trunk often hid beneath the shingles. One Michigan peach orchard reported as many as twenty thousand curculios taken by this so-called Ransom method.

Not everyone suffers plum curculio injury to the same degree. Here in Lost Nation, plum curculio overwinters poorly, and we recognize what little damage there is as a reverse blessing. Our bugger of buggers is the apple curculio. This PC cousin leaves similar egg-laying scars and feeding punctures on the developing fruit, only without the characteristic crescent shape. My partner David and I get into a little friendly competition when hand-thinning our apple crop in June, stacking each of our crushed curc count against the other. We seem to average up to twenty finds a day. Apple curculio damages some 10 to 40 percent of our crop, and, though cosmetically regrettable, it's nowhere near the devastation others experience with *curculio de la plum*. The primary difference AC has from PC is its habit of pupating within the larval feeding cavity of the fruit—emerging as a young buckaroo in five to nine days—rather than going into the soil for a few weeks. Apple curculio are less timid than plum curculio, and thus more readily observed at feeding and oviposition.

A 1928 Iowa bulletin concluded that immature stages of AC can be killed by allowing the fallen fruit to shrivel in the sunlight on bare ground, but that cleanly cultivating the orchard floor was not a complete answer, as some adults still emerged if buried two or more inches down. Which is why the researchers recommended running five young hogs —on the hungry side—to the acre at the time of June drop to eat the immature fruit and thus the all-too-smug apple curculio. The folks at the Rodale Institute have demonstrated that foraging chickens can reduce PC damage from 53 percent down to 33 percent in a small plot. Turkey Ridge Orchard in Wisconsin had decent success with roving flocks of border bantams until coyotes had even greater success with the tasty birds. The problem with chickens is effective control requires almost "more birds than apples," or at any rate more birds than most commercial orchardists will want to manage. Nor do ground foragers such as chickens help on those warm nights of massive damage when curculio flies in en masse. Still, the home orchardist has a fighting chance against curculio in the chicken yard, particularly if following 19th century advice to sprinkle the ground under each tree with cornmeal. This induces the chickens to scratch, search, and pick up curculios with the meal. Bluebird and

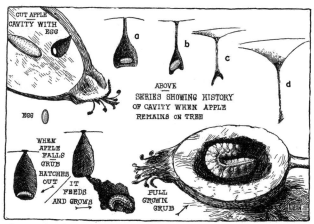

Cut apples showing development of apple curculio grub in fallen apples and history of egg cavities in growing apples.

Source: The Apple Curculio and Its Control by Hogs, *B. B. Fulton, Journal of Agricultural Research, Vol. 36, No. 3, 1928.*

The all-too-smug apple curculio pupa.

Source: The Apple Curculio and Its Control by Hogs, *B. B. Fulton, Journal of Agricultural Research, Vol. 36, No. 3, 1928.*

wren houses placed around the orchard attract additional feathered allies.

As organic orchardists, we're called to resume the cultural approaches of our great-grandparents, albeit with a few modern twists. Trap trees are early-blooming varieties with that lush, leafy foliage curculio tends to favor. Melba, Early Mac, Chestnut Crab, Liberty, and Freedom apples along with the Brandy pear are all noted for attracting curc attention, but early-blooming plums are a proven vote-getter. A cluster of plum trees placed towards the hardwood edge of an orchard should be a surefire draw for curculios on the move. Clean cultivation could be practiced here to allow Ransom trapping, but growers might actually find "wall-to-wall carpeting" a cheaper solution to achieving a smooth orchard floor. Any adults that wiggle into the soil to hide could no longer, and those cryptically lurking on the trunk might fall victim to a basal rotenone spray. Check with a local rug installer for a used deal (possibly free for the hauling) in a tightly woven commercial carpet. Six-foot-wide runners can be laid out at tight cluster and removed again in midsummer to limit vole habitat.

Practicing "border intelligence" helps a lot with curculio. A conifer forest edging an orchard provides unsuitable duff in which the overwintering adults can hide. Winter mortality rates run as high as 85 percent for those curcs forced to stay in the orchard. Hidden deep in maple leaves, however, survival rates are nearly reversed. Brush that has been bulldozed along the forest edge of cleared ground provides shelter too suitable to leave. A pocket of wild plums can perhaps be turned to advantage with an Imidan spray before adults move towards the apple orchard. Brian Caldwell in New York planted a hedgerow of serviceberries (*Amelanchier* spp.) and plums to the south and west of his orchard. Chickens could patrol such a border, birds might eat infested serviceberries, and the ground could be tilled to break fragile pupal chambers. Deer undid the hedge, unfortunately, before its effectiveness could be measured. Apple cultivars inhospitable to curculio reproduction (because fruit growth outpaces the larvae's development) could be planted on orchard border rows to further limit next year's returning mob. Pruning these after bud break heightens curc interest in the recently-cut branches

Unfortunately, no beneficial parasites have followed plum curculio from the native plum thickets since it added apple to its menu in the mid-1800s. Picking up June drops in orchards of an acre or more is a daunting task. A spray made with crushed seeds of the neem tree failed the efficacy test alone, but appears to offer greater repellent promise when enhanced with garlic as a synergist. The integrated trapping plan for curculio laid out in the next chapter ties these pieces of the puzzle into one coherent approach. Organic growers need to be satisfied with knocking the *screaming roar* of plum curculio down to a *dull murmur*.

Codling Moth and Lesser Appleworm

Researchers of yore got as far as recognizing the vulnerability of codling moth larvae when crawling and eating their way from leaf to fruit, but we'll leave their subsequent recommendations to spray lead arsenate behind. Organic orchardists use a wide variety of approaches today to control CM damage. Foremost is removing every wild apple tree within one hundred yards of an orchard. Even fifty yards has proved adequate on leeward edges. Managed moth populations dwindle without a renewed influx of immigrants. Mating disruption lures work by saturating the orchard air with female scent to prevent the male from ever finding his nuptial mate. Codling Moth Granulosis Virus works in much the same way as the more familiar *Bacillis thuringiensis* (Bt). My own preference for a spray material is ryania, a botanical insecticide made from the ground wood of a tropical shrub. It selectively acts as a stomach poison as well as on contact against most Lepidoptera. Since larvae only surface-feed for twenty-four to forty-eight hours before burrowing into the fruit, the odds of ingesting Bt or granulosis virus are half those of crossing a leaf with longer-lasting ryania coverage. Summer oils that smother both eggs and larvae have a place in defending orchard borders. Growers using Imidan against curculio find the timing of a second application effective with codling moth as well.

The timing of sprays is an exact science thanks to research on degree-day (DD) tracking. The countdown of CM degree days begins with the capture of the first moth in a pheromone wing trap, hung out when the blossoms open. Traps are hung at eye level within the southeast quadrant of two centrally located trees. Degree days are calculated by subtracting a 50°F base temperature from the mean daily temperature (add the daily high and low, then divide by 2). Mating doesn't begin until twilight temperatures stay above 60°F. Can you picture the male moths hanging out after petal fall? *"Hey, Joe, what temperature you got now? . . . Only 58, huh? She-it!"* The first expected egg hatch occurs when 243 DD have accumulated, and that's the day I make my first application of ryania. Fifty percent of the first generation of eggs will have hatched at 465 DD, which point marks a second spray. Rate of application is six pounds of ryania per acre per spray with a feeding attractant and fish oil. Three weekly

CODLING MOTH TRACKING

Degree-Day Monitoring of First CM Generation in Lost Nation Orchard, 1996

Date	Max/Min	DD (50°F Base)	Accumulated DD	Notes
				Full bloom on May 28
				Petal fall began June 4
June 5	74/50	12	12	First male moth captured in trap
June 6	78/52	15	27	
June 7	76/54	15	42	
June 8	72/56	14	56	
June 9	76/56	16	72	
June 10	79/57	18	90	
June 11	82/59	20	110	
June 12	92/60	26	136	
June 13	84/56	20	156	
June 14	80/42	11	167	Traditional first cover spray
June 15	81/51	16	183	
June 16	80/48	14	197	
June 17	87/53	20	217	
June 18	85/49	17	234	
June 19	84/52	18	252	CM egg hatch begins @ 243 DD
June 20	85/58	22	274	
June 21	85/52	18	292	Ryania spray (delayed due to rain)
June 22	70/50	10	302	
June 23	78/57	17	319	
June 24	76/47	12	331	Traditional second cover spray
June 25	70/46	8	339	
June 26	72/42	7	346	
June 27	80/49	15	361	
June 28	84/53	19	380	
June 29	82/56	19	399	
June 30	76/58	17	416	
July 1	88/60	24	440	
July 2	92/61	26	466	50 percent egg hatch @ 465 DD
				Second ryania spray

applications of granulosis virus covers this same period, and Bt might best be applied at five-day intervals if moth populations are high. Get good coverage up high, as codling moths fly towards the light of the moon.

We achieve near-total codling moth control with two ryania sprays. Growers in regions with multiple-generations should continue to monitor pheromone traps after the first emergence flight has peaked. Poor abatement of the first generation results in a continuing worry to the tune of thirty to forty eggs per subsequent female. When an average of five or more codling moths per trap per week are captured again, begin a 175 DD countdown to initiate successive-generation sprays. Summer target dates come closer together, as growth and development is most rapid in the warmest weather. I apply ryania one last time in early August (at a rate of four pounds per acre) to target a second generation of the lesser appleworm. This smaller cousin of the codling moth is one of those forgotten pests of apples rarely seen in conventional orchards. LAW cycles of egg hatch and fruit burrowing run two to five days ahead of that of the codling moth. Timely removal of drops, especially beneath early-ripening cultivars, will lessen LAW buildup in your orchard.

The ropes of twisted hay tied around trees a century ago were intended as a *preferred hiding place* on the trunk for the moth pupae. CM larvae ordinarily crawl out of the fallen fruit to seek seclusion beneath the rough bark found on the lower trunk. Some larvae enter hibernation for the following year, while others return in the next summer generation. The hay twists were burned before the succeeding moths took flight, just as we burn corrugated cardboard sheets wrapped around trunks today. Bottle traps containing molasses and cider vinegar were once hung in branches and were great-grandfather's main defense against fruit moths. A kerosene lamp lit over a shallow pan of sweetened water for a few hours each evening attracted moths to the light to drown. Those black light zappers found in backyards work similarly, but they are indiscriminate and may kill many beneficial insects as well as the target species.

Other Fruit Moths

The Oriental fruit moth is kin to codling moth and lesser appleworm in that all three are internal feeders. The moths pupate on ground debris and the trunks of host trees in early spring and emerge in May to mid-June. Each female can lay as many as 200 eggs. The young larvae bore into green twigs where they pupate. Round Two focuses more often on the developing fruit, be it apple, pear, peach, or cherry. The third generation of larvae that arrives by the end of August in northern zones (as far north as peaches can be grown) affects apple aesthetics by boring into the stem or calyx end of mature fruit. Mating disruption is a control option in appropriate-sized orchards; otherwise, look to summer sprays of Bt. Codling moth larvae are an interesting OFM nemesis: *one worm to the apple* is apparently a family rule backed by cannibalism.

Eye-spotted bud moths and tufted bud moths overwinter in a larval case found in the crotch of fruiting spurs and in bark crevices. The larvae emerge in spring and burrow into the unfolding buds to first feed. Any resulting leaf growth turns brown and curls up. Other leaves are webbed together at the tips to form a feeding chamber used beyond fruit set. A nearby rolled leaf, lined with silk, often serves as a pupation chamber, with adult moths emerging over the course of the next four to six weeks. These lay eggs on the leaves to initiate a second generation. Come August, new larvae are actively beginning to web together their feeding shelters. Pitting damage to the apple takes place where leaves get webbed directly to the fruit. Larvae feeding behind the protection of such shelter are difficult to effectively reach with Bt. Spray applications need to be targeted at earlier stages, when the leaves first unfurl in spring and in late July. Bud moths appear in a cyclic fashion because they are killed by temperatures below minus 20°F and by a nuclear polyhedrosis virus disease, as well as being preyed upon by many natural predators. Don't work up too much of a sweat worrying about a few odd fellows unless their numbers swell.

Western tussock moth has one generation per year. Overwintered eggs hatch when spring growth begins. The larvae are black with long bristles and red and yellow spotting. A heavy infestation can destroy all the opening buds in a newly planted orchard and consume the majority of leaves in established trees. A dormant oil spray answers best. If egg sacs are numerous in only a few trees, spot-spray Bt as necessary. Tent caterpillars and red-humped caterpillars offer a similar scenario elsewhere.

Aphids

Aphids are often held in check by beneficials, yet occasions arise even in organic orchards that may require attention. The rosy apple aphid can be the most damaging to fruit, particularly Cortland, Golden Delicious, Idared, and Gravenstein varieties. Its saliva, injected while feeding on bud clusters, causes leaf curling and severely stunted apples. RAA spends the summer on narrow-leaf plantain on the orchard floor, after which winged adults return to the fruit tree to lay eggs for the following year. English grain aphids are an innocuous green presence early in the season that soon migrate to grass crops for the summer. Woolly apple aphid (WAA) feeding on roots can go unnoticed until galls diminish root vigor and the tree becomes stunted. Above ground, any crawlers dispersing from below settle in around wounds and sucker shoots in June. Green apple aphids usually do not become abundant until July and August, and then primarily on the succulent foliage of shoot tips.

Young trees can be set back by as many as ten generations if beneficials are slow in righting the balance.

All aphids overwinter in the egg stage on twigs, around bud scales, and in bark crevices. A delayed dormant application of 2 percent oil emulsion smothers most eggs. Female aphids can give birth to live nymphs parthenogenetically, that is, without mating. Such rapid reproduction can get out of hand. Rosy apple aphids are active well before any predators, and once leaves curl around a cluster colony, they become harder to treat effectively. Spot applications of insecticidal soap can help, provided coverage is thorough. Fermented nettle tea slightly changes the makeup of the plant sap, causing the biodynamic tree to no longer be quite so palatable to the aphid. A rotenone soak can be directed at below-ground woolies. Semi-standard rootstocks of Spy parentage—the Malling-Merton series—are resistant to WAA.

Wood Borers

The insect that promises to discourage the most ardent apple grower is the borer. If your young trees have died and can readily be snapped off at the base, the round-headed appletree borer has your number. I was completely naive about borer possibilities when I first planted trees on our home farm. Certain lessons sank in twenty replacement trees later. *Obsessive diligence* is everything when it comes to eradicating borers from the orchard.

Borers come in three shades of concern: the round-headed appletree borer, the flat-headed apple-tree borer, and the dogwood borer. RHAB attacks at ground level and merits a detailed look. FHAB search out sunburned areas on limbs or trunks on which to lay their eggs. The hatching larvae bore through the bottom of the eggs directly into the damaged bark, where little gum is produced to repel the attack. The winding, raised trails—visible without digging into the bark—end a year later in an oval exit hole. Pacific flathead borers have been found to be attracted to severely drought-stricken trees by sound due to broken capillaries in the tree. The beetle then attacks the "crying" tree. Dogwood borers are the progeny of a moth, not a beetle. Their damage is limited to burr knots, and, though not fatal to the tree, can considerably weaken it. A crusty coating of latex paint (mixed with diatomaceous earth) can help on such aerial knot growth.

"Round heads" lay anywhere from one to seven eggs in the tender bark found at the soil line. The female beetle uses her jaws to make a short, curved slit in the bark. Turning around, she then places an egg beneath the cut edge with her ovipositor. The larvae hatch fifteen to twenty days later and eat the cambium and inner bark. A tree in good vigor expresses sap to smother invading larvae. The grubs thrust their castings of reddish, stringy wood out through small holes made in the bark. Beware these reddish castings! The grubs are closest to the ground surface during the first months, then work downward amongst the root unions. RHAB will be in the base of the tree for two to three years before emerging early in summer from a pupation chamber "drilled" up through the trunk a foot or so above the ground. A round emergence hole is a sure sign that trouble has begun again.

Here's what *The Apple Insects of Maine* had to say about the "vulnerable points and remedies" for round-headed appletree borer back in 1899: "The adult insect may be prevented from depositing eggs by the application of repellents to the trunk of the tree . . . soft soap or whitewash to be applied in late June. The trees should be examined twice each year, in May and September, and the young larvae removed. Should any escape, and penetrate deeply into the wood, they may be destroyed by probing with a sharp wire."

That's the gist of what we do today. We paint the base of young trees with a diluted white latex paint.

Perhaps this helps repel the borer, but it sure makes egg-laying slits and castings that much easier to see. Borers prefer the seclusion offered by high grasses growing up against the tree. I've been spreading a mulch of peastone several inches thick in a three-foot diameter around each vulnerable sapling. This makes searching for borer damage that much easier, as I can push aside the pebble surface to look closely at a clean soil line. When I see egg slits or meandering cavities in progress, I don't hesitate to cut open the bark to reveal the damage behind. It's radical surgery, but borers are radical bastards. Full probing details are given in chapter 5. A hypodermic syringe filled with either rotenone spray or vegetable oil can be squirted into an unsuccessful probe hole. Dig up any trees that die and follow the roots to the cause. That way, whether death was caused by borer, fungal decay, or pine voles, you'll

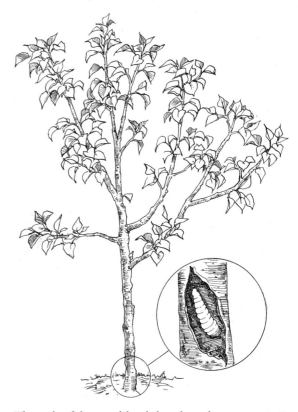

The grubs of the round-headed appletree borer cause significant damage within the tree trunk.

know for sure and can act accordingly. Each failure is an opportunity to learn.

Mark Fulford in Maine has designed a "lazy-grower's borer guard": ⅛-inch mesh cylinders are wired around each trunk and embedded in the soil. Adult beetles can get through ¼-inch mesh. A tight-fitting foam donut seals the top. This can be coated with sticky to further deter borers crawling down from the tree above, who might be tempted to oviposit above the barrier. Grass must be kept from growing into such a year-round collar; otherwise, moist conditions might lead to collar rot. Bob Sewall in Maine successfully uses window screening, buried at the bottom and stapled anew each spring to allow for trunk expansion. However, I've become too paranoid not to be able to see my trunks each and every time I pass by to check for damage. The one year I tried using screening, egg slits appeared above the protection.

Eventually, two things will happen. My trees will get large enough that limited borer damage will be tolerable. Ryania sprays applied to fruiting trees might also help, as the adult borer lands in the tree to nibble on leaves and twig wood before

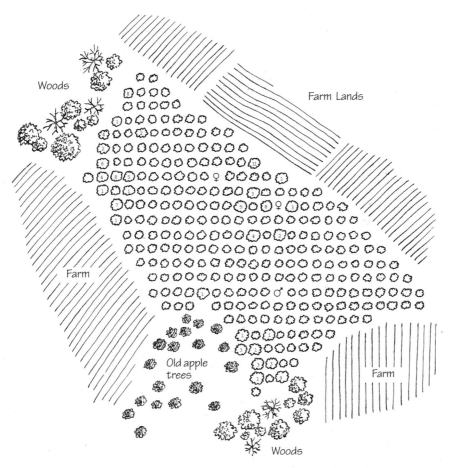

Schematic of orchard showing the tendency of adult female round-headed appletree borers to group their eggs (indicated by number count) about the trees where they developed. Alternate host trees in neighboring woodlots are the other source of borer infestation. (Source: The Roundheaded Apple-Tree Borer, *by Fred E. Brooks, USDA Farmer's Bulletin 675, 1915.)*

IT'S A SMALL, SMALL WORLD

The bugs and diseases we deal with in the orchard are not necessarily the same ones our great-grandparents knew. Apples were first introduced to the North American continent by the European settlers. Certain insect species migrated from other plant hosts in the 19th century in ever-expanding severity: plum curculio, apple maggot fly, red-banded leafroller, and tarnished plant bug are all native species. Fire blight and cedar apple rust constitute native-born diseases that made the transition. Meanwhile, international commerce brought codling moth, San Jose scale, European red mite, and apple scab to our shores. Diseases like powdery mildew, the fruit rots, sooty blotch, and flyspeck presumably evolved with apple trees in Eurasia. European apple sawfly began its American odyssey less than fifty years ago.

Is there more to come? Can it get worse? Check in next week to see if curculio gets over the Continental Divide and changes the happy tune of West Coast growers.

crawling down the trunk to deposit eggs. Secondly, adult borers tend to lay eggs within a short radius of their pupation tree. An orchard schematic from 1914 clearly showed the borer's egg-laying pattern. Removing alternate hosts—mountain ash, dogwood, serviceberry/shadbush, hawthorn, cotoneaster, and flowering crab apple—from nearby woods is equally important. I'm seeing cleaner trunks as my yearly surgery lessens the borer population.

Apple Maggot Fly

Southern growers mostly miss out on the "pure fun" of cleaning the fly-encrusted spheres used to trap apple maggot flies. Some researchers have speculated that the milder temperatures in the southern states are not sufficiently low for the flies to "chill out" as pupae. This pest really becomes serious, though, north of a latitude of forty degrees, from Illinois and Pennsylvania on up. Growers in Northern California, Oregon, and Washington have only recently begun to contend with AMF, and geez boys, they aren't pleased.

The apple maggot overwinters in the soil beneath wild apple trees outside a "drop-maintained" orchard (see page 130). Adults emerge in June and July, but females cannot lay eggs until reproductively mature, seven to fourteen days after emergence. Young flies feed on bird droppings and the honeydew of aphids. Both sexes arrive in the orchard by mid-July, drawn by the odor of fruit. Summer apples such as Red Astrachan, Quinte, and Paulared produce ripening volatiles earlier and so are targeted first. Eggs are oviposited just under the skin of the apple. The first two weeks of August mark peak activity on midseason varieties. Each female can be counted on for 180 eggs on average. Winter varieties of apples are too low in sugar content at this point to attract AMF interest, though late arrivals can be found on the keepers through September. Larvae tunnel throughout stung apples, leaving brown winding trails, until emerging to pupate in the earth.

Trapping immigrant flies on baited sticky spheres at the orchard perimeter protects the crop. The so-called Ladd trap—a red sphere bisected with a yellow sheet to increase trap visibility—appears to be more effective at drawing in greater numbers of flies than a solid red sphere. Border spacing with Ladd traps can be stretched from the original fifteen-foot recommendation to a hundred feet, reducing the number of traps needed to be maintained by a

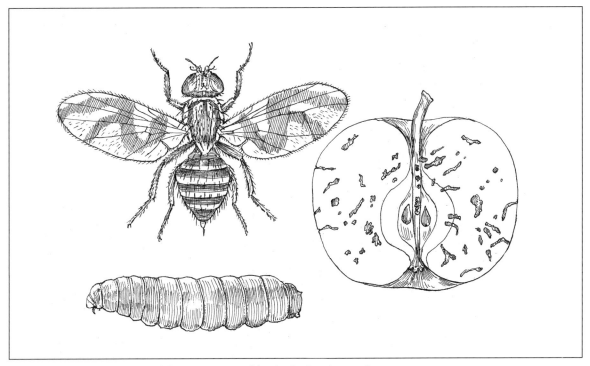

The apple maggot fly adult, and fruit injury caused by the "railroad worm."

ALAN EATON

An ovipositing apple maggot fly.

Ladd trap for apple maggot fly.

factor of six. Jim Gallot of West Meadows Orchard in Vermont uses just eighty traps to successfully protect thirty acres of fruit without any chemical intervention. His trap spacing is reduced to fifty feet wherever a known "hot spot" for AMF entry occurs. The recommended bait to attract mature flies is butyl hexanoate, available in slow-release vials from Gempler's.

Placement of traps is integral in attracting the maggot fly. Traps are hung at least shoulder-high about eighteen inches into the canopy facing the world beyond the orchard. Developing apples need to be growing nearby since the flies can only see about three feet and flit from fruit to fruit. A foot or so of unobstructed space beneath and to the sides of the trap creates good visual access. The odor lure

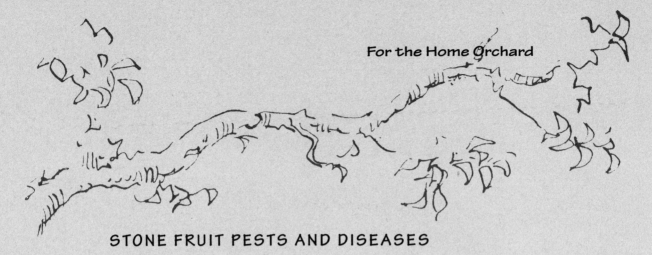

STONE FRUIT PESTS AND DISEASES

The good Lord created a handful of unique pests for plums, peaches, cherries, nectarines, and apricots to show us that stone fruits are indeed different from apples. But not to worry . . . our familiar friend the plum curculio is still here to keep us company.

- *Peach twig borer* prefers weaker trees. If you see wilting and a gummy exudate from twigs, snip off shoots just below the entry hole and destroy. For larger branches, slide a wire into the hole to kill the borer. This moth is readily controlled with Bt sprayed at pink and again at petal fall.

- *Oriental fruit moth* has a preference for peaches over apple. Its most noticeable damage also occurs to shoot tips. Larvae tunnel several inches into new twig growth, causing it to wilt and die back. The second generation makes a rotting mess of late-maturing varieties. Try rigging vinegar-molasses bottle traps or a timely spraying of Bt.

- *Cherry fruit fly* is akin to apple maggot fly. Sticky traps hung out in late May are effective. Red balls can be used with a pheromone lure, but, even better, paint plastic soda bottle tops bright yellow and coat with sticky. Beneath these hang screen-covered jars containing equal parts ammonia and water. Clean traps of dead flies and renew bait weekly up until harvest.

- *Peachtree borer* is a blue-black moth with an orange band across its midsection. Its larvae can girdle any of the stone fruits, much as round-headed borer does to apple. However, being a moth, eggs are laid in crevices in the trunk within a few inches of the soil line rather than oviposited beneath the bark. Add some diatomaceous earth to thicken latex paint and smooth over any bark roughness by early summer; otherwise, reach for that wire probe to grub out larvae in early fall.

- *American brown rot* is the fungal challenge of stone fruits in the humid East, attack-

ing blossoms, spurs, shoots, and fruit. It is spread from blighted twigs and "mummies" (the dried-up, brown-rotted fruit from the year before either hanging or fallen beneath disregarded trees). Good sanitation often needs to be accompanied with sulfur sprays at first bloom and petal fall, and again three weeks before harvest. Insect injury promotes secondary infections on immature fruit.

- *Black knot* is a perfect description for this affliction of plum and cherry trees. Microscopic spores produced by the fungus on one- and two-year-old knots provides the inoculum for the disease to spread in spring. Prune out and burn these grotesque galls growing on the twigs and branches in late winter on both your home orchard trees and surrounding wild fruit hosts.

- *Valsa cankers* form on the trunks and branches of most fruits and increase in size until they girdle and kill the affected part. Vigorously growing trees are less susceptible to this fungus. Prune out infected branches during dry weather.

- *Shot-hole disease* causes small purple spotting on cherry and plum leaves. The centers of these spots often enlarge to about $1/4$ inch and then fall out. You can't cure this fungus during the growing season, but a dormant copper spray will help the cause.

- *Peach leaf curl* is a fungal disease with a window of opportunity. A lime-sulfur application made in late fall and/or before the buds swell will eradicate the overwintering fungus on the bud scales. Otherwise, the fungus enters the unfurling leaves, which later curl, yellow, and drop. Monthly kelp sprays from bud swell on have been found effective by some Southern growers.

- *Bacterial leaf spot* spreads from oozing leaf scars in the spring. Leaves develop dark, angular spots, and the sunken spots on fruit are soon followed by cracking in the skin. A dormant copper application can help with this Eastern disease, but planting resistant varieties is the better choice.

(tied within six to twelve inches of the trap) brings them into the vicinity. Unbaited spheres positioned in the middle of the orchard serve as a check that perimeter trapping is doing the job. Left unattended, spheres lose about 25 percent of their fly-trapping power each week as they become obscured by dead insects. Clean traps of fly bodies and renew sticky every two weeks through the end of August. Research underway to develop a biodegradable sphere that incorporates insecticide into the red paint—thus eliminating the need for sticking agent—could merit "quasi-organic" consideration if traps are disposed of at season's end.

BENEFICIAL INSECTS

Insect predators of many apple pests abound in an orchard ecosystem untouched by chemical pesticides and heavy-hitting botanicals like rotenone. A balance is achieved when the "good guys" find enough "bad guys" to prey upon in a diverse habitat that supports each stage of their life cycle. Take note here: modest numbers of the bugs deemed pests are necessary to support an ongoing balance. Trichogramma wasps, for instance, parasitize the eggs of most fruit moths with their own young. The adults feed upon umbelliferous flowers like Queen Anne's lace, dill, and caraway. Any remaining storage carrots in the root cellar planted in the orchard the following spring are a sure-flowering delight for Trichogramma. Both the targeted moth eggs and adult flower habitat are needed for the wasp population to naturalize. The larvae of syrphid flies feast on aphids, but without buckwheat and other wildflowers, the adults won't be around to hover and feed.

Orchard diversity happens when you don't mow excessively or spray chemical pesticides. The second-level IPM strategy of using only biological and cultural controls after June cover sprays (aimed primarily at curculio) is based on letting beneficial

Syrphid fly larva enjoying an aphid feast.

populations rebuild themselves each summer. Some IPM orchardists leave abandoned pockets of trees within their orchards to serve as beneficial nurseries. Others purchase ladybugs and predatory mites from insectaries to reintroduce in their trees after the chemical "smoke" clears. Organic orchardists have no need to make such purchases unless the orchard is in its first years of transition from chemical management.

Cecidomyids (pronounced SEH-sid-oh-my-ids) are those brightly colored orange maggots that can be found eating green apple aphids on the leaf surface throughout the summer. Small grains of "rice" laid singly in leaf clusters are the eggs of syrphid flies. Syrphid larvae suck the fluids from aphids and caterpillars, leaving behind blackened bodies.

Ladybird beetles, more generally known as ladybugs, are the ambassadors of organic farming. The all-black *Stethorus punctum* is a voracious predator of European red mites in the Mid-Atlantic States. Ladybugs range in color from bright red to black, some with spots, some without. Their eggs are typically yellow, spindle-shaped, and standing on end. The black-and-orange larvae resemble miniature alligators and can be found consuming aphids at a forty-per-hour pace. Lacewing larvae feed on aphids, leafhoppers, and the eggs of moths—look for single white eggs attached to the leaf on a long, threadlike stalk. The larvae stage of parasitic miniwasps and tachinid flies feed on the tissues of other insects, consuming most if not all of their host before emerging as adults in search of new prey.

In Nova Scotia—where ryania use was first advocated because moth damage increased unexpectedly with DDT sprays—the braconid parasite, *Ascogaster quadidentata*, of codling moth still thrives. Red-banded leafroller, however, became an induced pest of apple in the U.S. only after the DDT cloud settled. Sadly, the beneficial that once kept the red-banded leafroller in balance was never even identified. The lesson for us as growers is to understand the ramifications of whatever we do before we do it. I take this creed to heart in the orchard, never destroying unknown eggs or insects that may well help the fruit-growing cause. For years I wondered what unknown havoc I was allowing to take place by not removing certain dark reddish egg clusters that I found on the undersides of leaves when thinning . . . until our extension entomologist, Alan Eaton, delighted me by nonchalantly pointing out the just-hatching eggs of the spined soldier bug (the egg case is rimmed with spines and barrel-shaped). Coupled with the many spiders in our trees, we have a very visible one-two punch on the beneficial front.

Parasitic nematodes have shown promise in reducing certain pest larvae that eventually pupate in the orchard soil. These microscopic beneficials destroy a soil-dwelling insect by penetrating its body, and then releasing a pathogenic bacterium inside, killing it within sixteen to seventy-two hours. *Heterorhabditis bacteriophora* nematodes hunt for a host in the two- to six-inch soil depth range; *Steinernema carpocapsae* prefers to ambush its potential host from the surface on down to about three inches deep. Both will reproduce up to three times in the host and produce as many as two hundred thousand offspring. Although these beneficial nematodes are native worldwide, targeted releases are used in the orchard to insure sufficient results. A soil application timed just before the massive June drop would target European apple sawfly and possibly plum curculio. Mike Cherim at The Green Spot is a very knowledgeable supplier who can suggest how and when to most effectively use the nematode police force.

GOOD SANITATION

The most important pest-management practice in an organic orchard is sanitation. Preventative and repellent sprays are effective only in a *clean* orchard. Broad-spectrum insecticides and eradicant fungicides allow chemical growers to manage enormous orchards without the bother of decomposing leaves and picking up every fallen apple. Organic growers prioritize the latter.

Be on the lookout for cankered tissue as you prune your trees. Any blue flagging tied to a limb can provide a vivid reminder of where fire blight struck the year before. All dead and diseased branches should be taken directly from the orchard and burned along with any "mummified" fruit still hanging in the tree. Other prunings can be thrown in the aisle to be gathered when all the cutting is done. Volunteers dragging plastic tarps to a truck or wagon can make quick work of a rather tedious chore. We pile our prunings in a distant field to dry out before burning. Such a pile left on the edge of the orchard would be a source of rot spores for several years to come.

Spring is a good time to seek out wild fruit trees and other alternate hosts of fruit pests. The blossoms stand out now against forest foliage. Being on good terms with neighbors helps in getting permission to remove such trees from their hedgerows as well. Old laws in some states once directed incorrigible landowners to care for such trees or else local tree wardens would cut them down at the owner's expense. A buffer zone of one hundred yards is effective against codling moth migration. European apple sawfly is also not a strong flier. Apple maggot flies, however, can easily travel a full mile. Extending this border to three hundred yards keeps round-headed appletree borer further afield. Scour surrounding red cedar trees (if you lack removal permission) of the gelatinous yellow spore masses that spread cedar apple rust disease.

Removing larvae-infected fruit when thinning substantially reduces curculio and sawfly pressure for the following year. Most of these larvae will either have "parachuted" to the ground or exited the fallen fruitlets soon after June drop. Picking up countless fruitlets is a daunting task if you have more than a few trees. Great-grandfather found that raking the June drops into the sunshine worked to shrivel up both the fruitlets and the curculio dwelling inside.

Begin picking up dropped fruit as the early varieties begin to ripen. Scythe down a mulch carpet to make windfalls that much easier to find. The first drops often are those damaged by the worm of codling moth penetrating into the core. Apple maggot fly larvae exit the fruit fairly quickly once the apple has fallen. Researchers at the University of Massachusetts have determined that drops need to be gathered weekly beginning a month before harvest to prevent most emerging maggots from reaching the soil. These numbers for Golden Delicious reflect a typical varietal pattern: 13 percent emergence four weeks before harvest; 55 percent emergence two weeks before harvest; and 32 percent emergence at harvest. Picking up drops after harvest only helps in deterring voles and deer. All Lost Nation drops end up in the digestive tracts of my sheep, as ad hoc compost piles often don't heat up enough to destroy the pest larvae in fallen fruit.

You won't control apple scab without entirely too many sulfur sprays unless you do some major leaf work each fall. The spores of next year's woes overwinter on the fallen leaves beneath the trees. Backyard growers have the option of raking up these leaves; commercial growers are better off applying the lime/flail mowing/compost plan (see page 97). Earthworms are a proven ally in decomposing leaf litter. Rub loose bark off anytime you're under the tree (when pulling mulch back from the trunks, for instance), as pupating caterpillars are then left exposed to the elements and vigilant woodpeckers.

FUNGAL DISEASES

As with insects, understanding the annual cycles of a given disease is integral to reducing crop loss. Controlling the first round of infection eliminates the need to worry about secondary infection with scab and powdery mildew. A preventative approach relies foremost on orchard sanitation. Elemental fungicides make up the difference when blown-in inoculum and favorable conditions make infection likely. We need to fully understand the mode of action of any treatment used if we're to apply it effectively and in the least harmful manner. Our actions (and reactions) always bear upon the balance of life forces at play in the orchard ecosystem. Foliage pest escalation can be caused by fungicides as well as insecticides. Specific advice on timing sprays and phytotoxic cautions are mentioned in the disease descriptions or in the spray materials section of the next chapter.

Entire books are written on the diseases of tree fruits. The *Compendium of Apple and Pear Diseases* (for one), listed in the appendix, provides a depth of detail and color photographs this manual can't begin to offer. What follows are some of the "better bits" about each disease and the current state of the art of organic management.

Apple Scab

I came into organic orcharding with the expectation that a dozen to twenty sulfur sprays were a requisite for apple scab control. The apple scab fungus releases its spores in spring rains, with those ascospores getting a foothold on the leaf surface when the wetting period lasts long enough. Conventional wisdom has always said sulfur applications need to be in place before the rain begins to prevent the ascospores from getting that foothold. Bordeaux mixture (a mixture of copper sulfate, lime, and water) was used at the turn of the century for the same purpose, though the copper in the formulation often caused fruit russeting after the green tip stage of apple growth.

Dr. W. D. Mills at Cornell University charted scab infection periods in the 1920s through the 1940s to show the relationship between average temperature and length of wetting period for primary infection to occur. IPM growers use an updated version of this chart every spring in determining if fungicide applications are necessary. The beauty of this lies in determining if the leaf surface has dried soon enough to naturally prevent scab infection. If sulfur indeed needs to be applied before each rain, we'd be unable to take advantage of the wetting period chart. Other than one protectant spray to start the primary discharge season, I now apply sulfur (with an exceedingly tenacious sticker) only at the end of a possible infection period. We have very minimal

scab in Lost Nation Orchard, but only in part because of the timing of our sulfur applications.

Much of the credit belongs to Dr. William Mac-Hardy at the University of New Hampshire. The first discovery of his that came to my attention was that nighttime release of scab ascospores was negligible in well-managed orchards. Thus, if a rain begins during the night, you consider the leaves to have been wet only from sunrise when using the wetting chart. Long-wavelength red light plus wetness are necessary to trigger spore release. We track degree days for scab (beginning at earliest green tip with a 32°F base temperature) to predict the percentage of ascospores mature and thus available to infect our trees. I'm much more concerned with sulfur coverage during the accelerated phase of ascospore maturity (from approximately 300 DD to 700 DD) than I am earlier in the season. The odds of infection correlate to the amount of surface showing as buds unfold and leaves grow, to plant tissues becoming less susceptible in time, and to the maturation of the inoculum. The variation in spore maturity is reflected between the upper and

Apple scab injury on fruit.

GAUGING SEVERITY OF POTENTIAL SCAB INFECTIONS

Table 1: Percentage of available ascospores that will be discharged under various
environmental conditions

TYPE OF RAIN EVENT	PERCENTAGES OF AVAILABLE ASCOSPORES RELEASED
Night rain only	5%
Day rain, temperature ‹ 50°F, rain ‹ 0.10 inches	25%
Day rain, temperature ‹ 50°F, rain › 0.10 inches	50%
Day rain, temperature › 50°F, rain ‹ 0.10 inches	50%
Day rain, temperature › 50°F, rain › 0.10 inches	90%

Table 2: Revised criteria for leaf infection by ascospores of *Venturia inaequalis*.
Times represent the minimum hours of continuous leaf wetness required
for infection at each temperature.

TEMPERATURE (°F)	HOURS*
34	41
36	35
37	30
39	28
41	21
43	18
45	15
46	13
48	12
50	11
52	9
54	8
55	8
57	7
59	7
61–75	6
77	8
79	11

*When rain begins after sunset, leaf wetness should be assumed to begin at sunrise. For all other events, times should be computed from the start of rain.

SOURCE: David Gadoury, Robert Seem, Arne Stensvand, Stuart Falk; New York State Agricultural Experiment Station at Geneva.

lower DD curves: fungal fruiting bodies (pseudo-thecia) in the leaf litter, though all in the same orchard, are subject to a wide range of micro-ecological conditions that cause them to ripen at different rates. The severity of the odds goes sky-high when the potential ascospore dose (PAD)

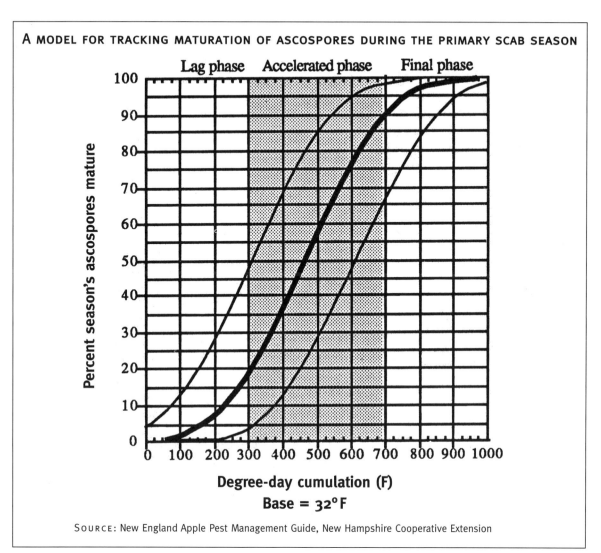

A MODEL FOR TRACKING MATURATION OF ASCOSPORES DURING THE PRIMARY SCAB SEASON

Lag phase   Accelerated phase   Final phase

Percent season's ascospores mature

Degree-day cumulation (F)
Base = 32°F

SOURCE: New England Apple Pest Management Guide, New Hampshire Cooperative Extension

from the year before is high. Dr. MacHardy has worked out a procedure for predicting this PAD, but for organic purposes, good sanitation should simply be counted on to make the PAD low. If it is, experience has shown that the first protectant spray can be delayed until early pink or until after three infection periods, whichever comes first. Degree-day tracking also tells us when the primary discharge season ends—the first daytime rain after 760 DD—after which we can stop tracking wetness periods to determine if a sulfur spray is necessary.

I'm resolute about renewing sulfur coverage in those two weeks following open cluster. Any wetting periods now require action whether there are open blossoms or not. Geneva researchers have determined the percentage of ascospore release based on amount of rain and temperature, which helps in judging severity of these wetting periods. How to handle a "split wetting period"—when drying occurs in between rains or the next morning's dew—is a judgment call. West Coast growers consider six hours of dryness enough separation to consider the first round of spores *goners*. The conservative Yan-

LOST NATION ORCHARD SCAB LOG 1996

Date	Time Leaves Wet	Temp.	Time Leaves Dry	Temp.	Elapsed Wetness Time	Average Temp.	Bud Stage	Predict Infection	Degree-Day Count	Treatment
May 3		36°F min		66°F max			Green tip	No	162 / 5 to 20% ascospore maturity	Good sanitation in place
May 9	late copper application russeting concern						Half-inch green			Kocide 10 lbs. per acre (primarily for fire blight)
May 10	8 AM	45°F		55°F max						
May 11		30°F min					Tight cluster		315	
May 12			Noon		52 hrs.	42°F		High	5 to 45%	
May 16	6 PM	52°F	9 AM	42°F	15 hrs. thru night	47°F	Opening cluster	Low	372	Relying on low potential ascospore dose (PAD)
May 18	first spray application for predicted rain						Now in Accelerated Phase			Sulfur 8 pints per acre as protectant
May 19	8 AM	48°F	10 AM	60°F	2 hrs.	54°F	Open cluster			
May 20	1 AM	56°F	9 AM	66°F	Add 8	61°F		Possible	452 / 20 to 75%	
May 21	8 AM	64°F	5 PM	72°F	9 hrs.	68°F	Early pink	Moderate to High		Sulfur @ 3 PM, 8 pints per acre as eradicant
May 29	8 AM	44°F	6 PM	60°F	10 hrs.	52°F	Bloom	Low		
May 30	4 AM	35°F							682	Sulfur @ 6 PM, 8 pints per acre as both
May 31			10 AM	55°F	Add 30	45°F	Petal	High	67 to 98%	
June 3	6 PM	60°F								
June 4		51°F min	4 PM	75°F	22 hrs.	63°F	Fall	High	838 / 85 to 100%	Sulfur @ 3 PM, 8 pints per acre
							Now in Final Phase			
June 7	Three days of rain at 65°F average temp.							High	968	Good coverage still in place

Primary Scab Season now over!

The disease cycle of the apple scab fungus.

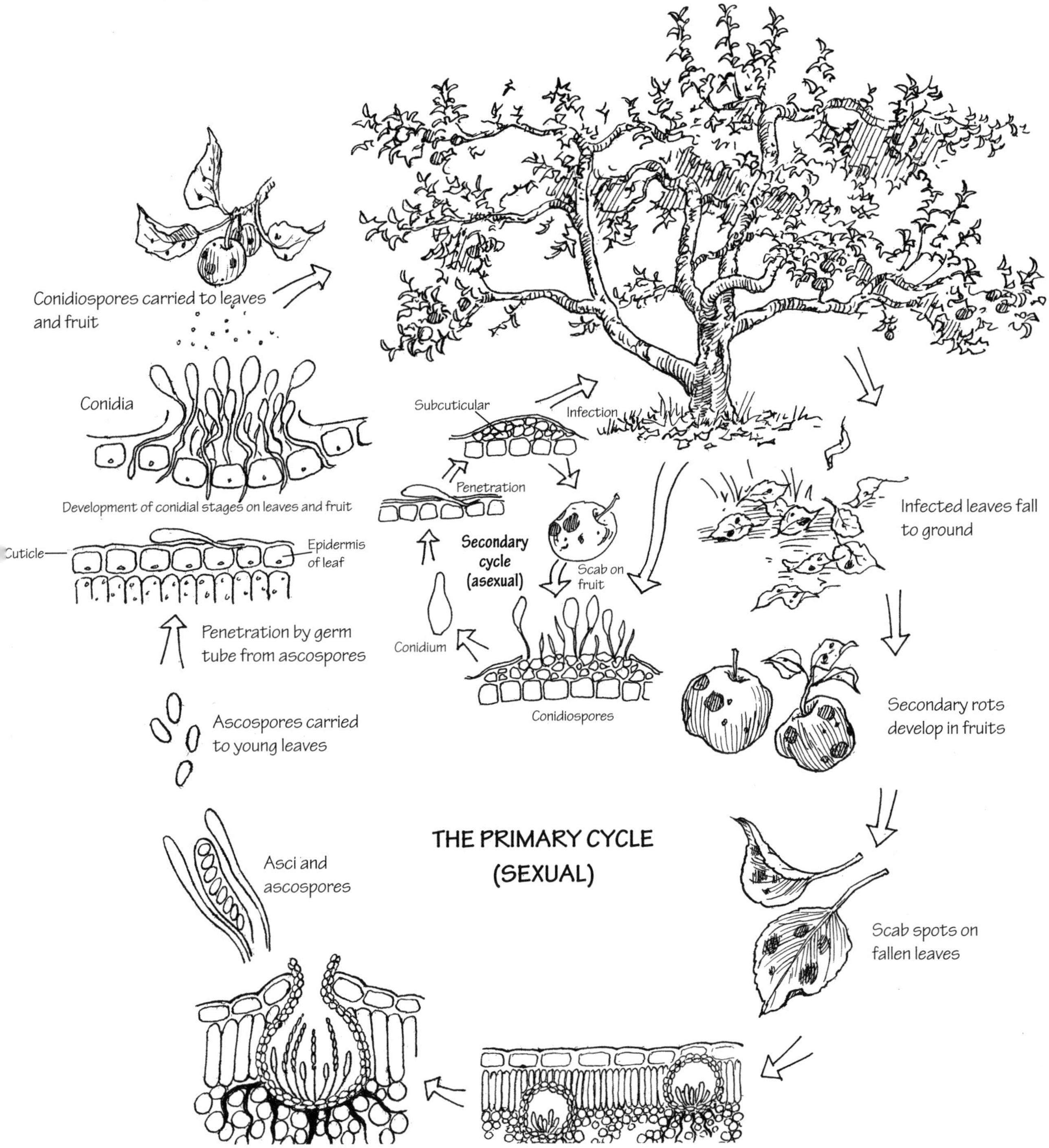

Conidiospores carried to leaves and fruit

Conidia

Development of conidial stages on leaves and fruit

Cuticle

Epidermis of leaf

Penetration by germ tube from ascospores

Ascospores carried to young leaves

Asci and ascospores

THE PRIMARY CYCLE (SEXUAL)

Subcuticular

Infection

Penetration

Secondary cycle (asexual)

Scab on fruit

Conidium

Conidiospores

Infected leaves fall to ground

Secondary rots develop in fruits

Scab spots on fallen leaves

kee approach is to add only the additional hours of wetness (but not the dry hours) from the second wetting as a continuation of the first if the intervening dry period is twenty-four hours or less. Later, after petal fall, high grasses help to entrap any ascospores that weren't yet done in by earthworms and other micro-organisms consuming the decaying leaves.

A further revelation about scab is perhaps the most exciting of all. The scab fungus has male and female aspects that mate on the fallen apple leaves soon after leaf fall to create the spore-fruiting structures for the coming spring. Spreading lime on the fallen leaves after harvest has been found to hinder the scab reproductive act. One study out of Oregon on pear scab reports 50 to 90 percent inoculum reduction. This is comparable to flail mowing results or what unhindered earthworm populations can do. Our fall sanitation regimen consists of liming the fallen leaves, flail-mowing the works, and then spreading compost (see "Preparing for Winter" in the preceding chapter, page 96 for details). Perhaps in the years to come organic growers will be able to achieve good scab control without spring sulfur sprays. One integrated proposal is to water-release any waiting mature spores on a dry day—four hours of ground wetting in the late morning would do it—to force their discharge. The forecast for the next two days should also be for dry weather if attempting water release. Controlling the potential inoculum on the orchard floor in late fall by a choice of sanitation practices is the key to the success of any plan. Any ascospores blown in from outside the orchard are usually too few to cause noticeable economic loss.

Each primary scab lesion becomes a problem in the life cycle of *Venturia inaequalis* (apple scab) because it produces as many as one hundred thousand conidia (asexually produced fungal spores). These secondary spores splash on the susceptible leaves and fruit within the infected tree throughout the summer months. Each scab lesion can produce conidia for four to six weeks, repeating that damning inner loop in the cycle of scab several times. High heat in southern regions often kills off secondary inoculum, thereby reducing spore loading for the next spring. Secondary scab is what downgrades the fruit come harvest time. All the emphasis on checkmating the ascospores is to avoid getting involved in a second game, one in which the fungus almost always wins.

Powdery Mildew

Podosphaera leucotricha is a major fungus affecting apples and pears in semiarid regions, but can occur to some extent wherever apples grow. Like scab, powdery mildew is an early-season disease with a primary infection period that has substantial ramifications for the next phase. It overwinters as fungal strands (collectively called *mycelium*) in leaf and fruit buds which were infected the previous season. Temperatures below minus 18°F kill a majority of mildew-infected buds and the fungus within them. As buds break dormancy, the fungus colonizes developing shoots. The powdery white appearance on infected shoots consists of many thousands of spores, which are responsible for causing secondary infections. These usually develop on leaves and next year's buds prior to terminal bud set and may reduce the vigor of the tree. Severely infected leaves are narrow and folded longitudinally, become brittle with age, and sometimes abscise by midseason. Fruit infection results in a netlike russetting on the surface of the fruit. Infections occur when the relative humidity is greater than 90 percent and the temperature is between 50° and 77°F. The tree needs to be almost damp, but not wet, as the spores won't germinate in water. Non-germinated spores can wait out hot dry spells.

The critical period for powdery mildew control is between tight cluster through three weeks after bloom. Leaves are susceptible for only a few days after they emerge, though they may be infected at any time if damaged. Sulfur applied every seven days during the stages of rapid leaf development (up through petal fall) is an effective fungicide. M-Pede soap has achieved good control in Oregon test plots. Summer temperatures in many regions suppress the growth of powdery mildew, so treatments are not necessary after new leaf growth ceases. Terminal shoots with white, flattened, pointed buds can be removed in the dormant pruning season to reduce inoculum loading.

Certain varieties are much more susceptible than others, particularly Yellow Newton, Braeburn, Jonathan, Gravenstein, and Rome Beauty. Several scab-resistant varieties have similar resistance to powdery mildew. Interestingly, in pear orchards located more than two hundred yards from susceptible apple cultivars, no infection occurs. All inoculum that infects pears appears to come from apples.

Rusts Diseases

Cedar apple rust, quince rust, and hawthorn rust are three related fungi that spend part of their life cycle on red cedar trees. Cedar apple rust fungi overwinter as galls on the cedar branches. When these galls become wet in spring rains, gelatinous spore horns are formed that release basidiospores.

Cedar apple rust gall.

The wind carries these spores as much as a half mile to the leaves and fruit of the apple. Leaves are most susceptible when they are four to eight days old; thus the timing of sulfur sprays is most critical between pink through three weeks after bloom. All rust fungi require moisture on the leaf or fruit surface to take hold. There is no secondary cycle of infection on the fruit tree. Any cedar apple rust lesions produce aeciospores during July and August, which are carried back to the cedar trees to begin a two-year gall phase. The MacIntosh family of apples (including Cortland, Macoun, and Empire) are not affected by cedar apple rust.

Canker and Dieback Diseases

Apple trees are susceptible to many wood-rotting fungi which follow in the footpaths of more invasive pathogens (like fire blight) and environmental stress from cold or drought. Silver leaf is a condition caused by *Stereum* fungi. Affected leaves show a white metallic luster and are often found on only one branch of the tree. Two years of double-dose compost cured this in one of our young Jonafree trees. Trees that are nutritionally healthy recover best from environmental stress. Black rot cankers should be pruned out when first seen so that no discolored wood remains.

Root, Crown, and Collar Rots

These diseases are caused by soil fungi that favor poorly drained sites. Different rootstocks show varying susceptibility to these rots: MM106 is very susceptible to crown rot, M9 and seedling rootstock are resistant. Afflicted trees show symptoms of reduced vigor, sparse foliage, and premature fruit coloring. Underneath the bark, infected tissue is reddish brown. Severely infected trees die. Periods of soil saturation promote these diseases by enabling movement of infective fungal spores. The lack of oxygen in a drowning soil inhibits any root growth, making it hard for the tree to "grow beyond" a non-fatal attack. Decay at the base of the trunk (the crown) blocks the flow of carbohydrates from the leaves to the starving roots. Good drainage and site selection cannot be emphasized enough.

Summer Fruit Rots

Fruit rots are caused by many different fungi. Bitter rot appears as brown, slightly sunken spots that expand rapidly at temperatures over 80°F. Spore-producing structures develop in concentric rings and become a further inoculum source that same growing season. White rot is most severe in the Southeast, where fruit losses of 50 percent have been reported. Fruit lesions are similar to bitter rot but with cylindrical rather than V-shaped decay. Black rot has a leaf-spot phase of the disease, known as frog-eye leaf spot. Leaf lesions appear a few weeks after petal fall as small purple flecks that enlarge to 5 millimeters across with tan centers. Fruit affliction ranges from rot in the seed cavity to pimplelike lesions that do not enlarge rapidly until right before harvest.

Rotted fruit usually drop, but some mummify in the tree. Limbs and twigs can harbor mycelium and spore structures in dead shoots and cankers. Current-season fire blight strikes often become colonized by rot fungi. Good sanitation is essential for control.

Sooty Blotch and Fly Speck

These summer disease twins (in that they almost always occur together) present an aesthetic dilemma. Sooty blotch and fly speck do little or no actual damage to the fruit, but their presence on the apple's surface lowers visual quality and thus market value. Both diseases occur throughout the East, but are most severe where humidity runs high. Their common names aptly describe the superficial blemishes on the fruit.

Both pathogens overwinter on the bark and twigs of over a hundred woody plants with waxy cuticles (including blackberry canes). Sooty blotch is spread by waterborne conidia and fly speck by airborne ascospores. Fruit infection can occur anytime from bloom on, but is most prevalent later in summer. Warm humid nights, dense fog, and abundant rainfall contribute to the 200 to 250 hours of accumulated wetting both diseases require before becoming visible. The big hope of eliminating fungicide use on scab-resistant varieties fell short at the far end of the growing season with sooty blotch and fly speck: all apple cultivars are susceptible. Both fungi feed on the wax that covers most apples. Dark red varieties show less sooty blotch and fly speck, as do early season apples that are harvested before enough wetting has accumulated.

The conventional recommendation is to be very aggressive about summer diseases by applying sulfur every two weeks beginning in mid-June. However, Arthur Tuttle at the University of Massachusetts suggests that we're just as well off putting time and energy into summer pruning to increase air flow to dry things out quicker. Sulfur should be reserved for more serious fungi, where its effectiveness is better known. Equisetum (horsetail) spray, being rich in silica, enhances light energy to dry off leaves within the biodynamic tree. Blackberries, being a preferred host, can be removed within fifty yards of the orchard.

Sooty blotch and fly speck can be washed off apples. Chilling fruit overnight and then bringing it out in the morning to sweat for an hour or two helps loosen the fungal grip. Chlorine can be used in the bath water, but the physical action of brushing often does the bulk of the job. Yellow apples admittedly look worse—and often prove unmarketable—once blackened with summer disease, but this reject perception should not go unchallenged. Wager a bet with customers on a sooty blotch rubdown contest (Hint: you won't lose if you use spit) if they don't quite get the point that the beauty of an organic apple defies surface

DISEASE-RESISTANT CULTIVARS

Much of the breeding work in developing disease-resistant apple varieties focuses on immunity to the scab fungus. Additional resistance to cedar rust, powdery mildew, and fire blight — or adverse susceptibility — are generally listed in the varietal description. These apples can save the home orchardist the bother of sulfur applications in controlling common apple diseases. If sooty blotch and fly speck are a problem in late summer, give affected apples a good rubbing to get back to a clean look.

- **William's Pride** — A longer-lasting summer apple than most. Crisp, very juicy, and slightly spicy. Quite hardy, vigorous annual bearer that seems to train itself. Long ripening period needs two or three pickings. Scab-immune with high resistance to cedar apple rust.
- **Redfree** — A crisp late-summer apple. Medium size with 90 percent bright red color (despite its name!). Waxy skin, juicy, excellent flavor. Tree bears annually and does best in northern orchards. Resistant to all major diseases.
- **Dayton** — Ripens in early fall before McIntosh. Bright cherry red with high dessert quality and mild flavor. Consistent bearer of moderate vigor. Fruit hangs for almost two weeks without losing firmness. Does well in the Midwest and Northwest. Scab-immune but moderately susceptible to cedar rust.
- **Nova Easygro** — Super-disease-resistant introduction from Nova Scotia. Very cold-hardy. Similar to Cortland with a sprightly flavor. Stores well into March. Tree is moderately productive.
- **Liberty** — One of the most disease-resistant apples ever developed. Crisp, juicy, and flavorful, with McIntosh aroma. Good as dessert or cooking apple. Requires heavy thinning. Good choice across the middle growing zones. The tree is spreading and develops numerous fruiting spurs.
- **NY 75413-30** — Now is as good a time as any to introduce you to numbered selections. This Delicious x Liberty hybrid is a research apple with promising commercial potential. A large, attractive, dark red apple that does well as far south as the Virginias. It'll get a name once it shows its market mettle.
- **Enterprise** — A good, all-purpose, late-fall apple. Very spicy, rich flavor; tart at harvest but mellows in time. Quality holds six months in common storage. Moderate to good annual bearing. This super-disease-resistant apple comes highly touted for commercial planting.
- **Gold Rush** — A high-quality, yellow winter apple. Its pleasant tart flavor at harvest soon develops into a very rich, well-balanced flavor in storage. Moderately vigorous, semi-spur tree. Late maturity may limit its northern adaptability.

Disease-resistant apples like these have a place in a home orchard, particularly for folks who run perpetually behind with preventative measures. Yet for all the ballyhoo, apple lovers really don't need to forego great old varieties like Cox's Orange Pippin or current favorites like Macoun or Honeycrisp. Organic scab control is effective and really not that difficult to achieve. The prevalence of other diseases varies with the climate of your locale.

aesthetics. They may yet come to see a moderate touch of "summer earthiness" as a token of Nature's esteem.

OTHER DISEASES

Disease possibilities in the orchard do not end with fungus. An orchard doctor needs to reckon with fruit tree viruses and bacterial outbreaks as well. Now if only the remedy was as simple as grandma's advice to "feed a cold and starve a fever."

Fire Blight

One way to gauge the seriousness of a disease is by seeing when chemicals can't provide a "quick fix." Whatever your particular orcharding philosophy—from conventional spraying to Biodynamics—*Erwinia amylovora* bacteria are a challenging bunch. Pruning sanitation is of paramount importance, and planting less susceptible varieties (particularly with pears) almost a must in fire-blight-prone regions. Go light on the nitrogen feeding, whether the source is a synthetic or organic fertilizer. Dormant copper is effective at reducing infection risk, but there are valid concerns about earthworm health after years of heavy copper use. Such a copper barrier must be sprayed on all trees in a treated block, not just on susceptible varieties. Otherwise, the blight bacteria find a safe harbor in which to colonize before bees disperse the pathogen back to the open flowers of the once-protected susceptible varieties. Spraying antibiotics every few days through the blooming period is preventive medicine overapplied—resistant strains of the bacterium develop in response. Computer predictions of high infection risk have helped growers pinpoint only those times deemed crucial to spray streptomycin. Still, when temperatures rise above 80°F and humidity is high, fervent prayer may be the best bet going.

Fire blight can strike in one of five ways. Shoot blight bends succulent shoots over to form the typical "shepherd's crook" of burnt appearance that gives the disease its name. Blossom blight is usually the first symptom seen during spring when open flowers wilt and turn brown to black. The bacteria may have been dispersed by insects and wind weeks before conditions warrant an *explosive* epidemic. The entire fruiting spur ends up infected and can lead to a cankerous girdling of the branch. Renewal of bacterial activity in the spring can extend the margins of such bark cankers further along the trunk as well as ooze new inoculum. Such is canker blight. Trauma blight works much the same as blossom blight, except now the opening into the tree's vascular system is caused by hail or a true idiot pruning in a warm rain. Rootstock blight is the end of the line for the tree. Many dwarfing rootstocks have little resistance when blight infection is passed down through the bark phloem from scion injury above. The resulting canker girdles the trunk just below the graft union.

Many pear cultivars are especially susceptible to fire blight, perhaps in part because a greater number of blossoms stay open longer than those on apple trees. Full bloom on pears finds 80 to 100 percent of the blossoms open, whereas on apple 65 to 70 percent is the maximum. Bacteria first colonize the blossom and then await proper conditions. Warm days during bloom preceding a wetting period exponentially increase the chances of disaster. Sherman Thomson at Utah State University, noting how honeybees play a key role in distributing the blight pathogen to the nutrient-rich stigma, came up with the idea of having the bees introduce an antagonistic bacteria instead. Bees crawl through a spore-laced pollen insert in exiting the hive, then sally forth to make site-specific delivery of the *Pseudomonas fluorescens* bacteria in their search for nectar. The race is on, with fire blight the loser 90 percent of the time when the weather favors pollination. Such biocontrol looks promising, making the possible loss of the honeybee that much sadder. Blight Ban is a spray version of this strategy.

Fire blight sanitation begins in the dormant pruning season. Let your motto be "a visible canker is a gone canker." Heavy pruning that invokes vigorous regrowth favors blight, as does excessive nitrogen: the resulting succulent growth, pierced by aphid and leafhopper feeding, is more prone to shoot blight. Conversely, more mature trees tend to be less susceptible to bacterial infection once early vigor runs its course. Blight symptoms begin to show up after bloom. Making a weekly tour of duty in June to remove all infected twigs and limbs is prudent. The "ugly stub" is a strategic summer cut devised by Paul Steiner (the man to credit for most of our understanding of this disease) of the University of Maryland. Cutting at least eight inches behind the infected tissue—but not quite all the way back to the point of a branch intersection—recognizes that wound tissue is likely to become reinfected. The "horticulturally correct" pruning cut can then be safely made in the dormant season. If faced with multiple blossom injury throughout a tree, breaking off the infected spurs by hand is an expedient.

Streptomycin works best in limiting the multiplication of bacteria, not in killing large populations. Sprays that are applied too early do not protect flowers opening after treatment; sprays that are applied too late do not stop infections already in progress. Only applications made the evening before or the day of infection provide preventative control of blossom blight. Streptomycin serves no purpose whatsoever against shoot blight.

Dennis Mackey in Germantown, Wisconsin, tells of his realization about copper's effectiveness against fire blight: "A number of years ago, my cousin bought a new sprayer. While trying to figure out the calibration, he applied copper on a Jonathan block at an extreme rate by mistake. This block always seemed to have a considerable amount of fire blight. After a few years without blight in this block, we considered the implications of his miscalculation. The C-O-C-S label states two to four pounds per acre for fire blight control, applied dormant. I had a thirty-acre Idared (on MM106 rootstock) block that had a terrible time with fire blight. I lost almost a thousand trees in the third leaf to this disease. I applied thirty pounds of C-O-C-S dormant in 125 gallons of water per acre. I also used two gallons per acre of spray oil for a sticker and to increase copper penetration into the bark. This Idared block has been fire-blight-free the last eight years. That single dose of copper worked so well that I stopped using streptomycin completely. . . . If you apply copper to turn dormant trees Smurf-blue, fire blight will cease to be a problem. Hopefully, research can be done with copper sprays at higher than label rates."

Applying such a high amount of copper is illegal, of course, and *bad, bad, bad* for the soil and those earthworms we so cherish. Yet it's indicative of the spray tradeoff faced in broaching a disease dilemma like fire blight. Is the highest rate allowed for a given formulation of copper, applied dormant, on susceptible varieties worth potentially years of soil damage? Or is it better to lose such fruit trees and plant more resistant cultivars?

Bacterial Blossom Blast

Here's a West Coast disease that sounds almost fun. Frost or freezing temperatures and available moisture are required for *Pseudomanas syringae* infection to occur. Flower symptoms resemble fire blight but without any bacterial ooze. Blast blackens fruitlets and leaves, but rarely moves beyond the base of the fruit cluster. Antibiotics can help from green tip through bloom if these bacteria are present in your orchard and a freeze is imminent.

Apple Mosaic

This virus is spread by grafting infected tissue onto healthy stock. The growth and yield of severely affected trees is reduced by as much as 50 percent. Leaves of sensitive varieties turn pale yellow or white along the veins and eventually turn brown and fall off. You shouldn't get apple mosaic from a nursery that certifies its stock as virus-free.

Apple Measles

Internal bark necrosis affects Red Delicious, Jonathan, and Stayman Winesap the most. The appearance of small, red measles on the smooth bark of young twigs is the first symptom caused by such manganese toxicity. These lesions eventually thicken, crack, and slough off large areas of bark. Applying lime may alleviate measle symptoms, but properly adjusting soil pH before planting prevents the condition entirely.

Bitter Pit

If late-season spotting shows on your apples, suspect this disorder, which is attributed to calcium imbalance. The spots appear first on the blossom end of the fruit and eventually darken and become slightly sunken. Bitter pit continues to worsen in storage, so even clean-looking fruit may become pitted after a month or two. Certain varieties of apples exhibit bitter pit more than others, but all cultivars can be affected. Yellow Newton and Gravenstein are highly susceptible, with Cortland, Jonathan, and Northern Spy not far behind.

Soil levels of calcium may well be adequate. It's the calcium uptake by the leaves and fruit that can be negatively influenced by weather and orchard management. Incidence of bitter pit tends to be higher in years when good rains either come too often or infrequently. A light crop load worsens the situation, so be wary of overthinning. This rela-

tionship to a high leaf/fruit ratio also appears in tree canopies left too dense. High levels of potassium and magnesium in the soil act to hinder the availability of calcium. Excessive tree vigor (resulting from massive dormant pruning or heavy applications of nitrogen) diverts calcium from the fruit to the rapidly growing leaves. Fruit on upright, vigorous branches are more likely to show pitting than those on horizontal wood, as are the large apples from trees just coming into bearing. Hot days lead to greater rates of transpiration from the leaves. Calcium moves in the xylem along with the flow of root water to the leaves. Once in the leaf tissue, calcium is thought to be immobile and will not move back to the fruit.

Most of the calcium contained in apples and pears moves into the fruit in the four to six weeks following bloom, when fruit cells are actively dividing. Thus, early summer pruning (before terminal bud set) to remove vigorous shoots improves fruit calcium levels, provided significant regrowth doesn't occur. Later summer pruning meets other horticultural goals, but not increased calcium uptake. When calcium base saturation on soil test results is less than 60 percent and the pH is above 7, an application of gypsum can help dramatically with bitter pit.

Many growers rely on summer foliar sprays to get more calcium into the fruit. Bitter pit incidence is typically reduced with calcium chloride applications, but there is a risk of leaf burn. Three sprays are made one month apart at minimum, starting when the fruit is the diameter of a nickel. Good coverage is essential, as the spray must contact the fruit to be absorbed. Bio-Gard's Calcium-25 contains natural plant waxes, which, when mixed to an exact proportion with water alone, "fools" the leaf into absorbing additional calcium into the vascular system. Apparently the fruit benefits from the calcium being translocated within the tree, as bitter pit reduction is on a par with calcium chloride.

Chelated forms of calcium have the advantage of being compatible with most other spray materials.

FOUR-LEGGED CONSIDERATIONS

Is Bambi an orchard pest? And those cuddly bunnies? Can an innocent meadow mouse possibly harm an apple tree? You better believe it!

The Bark Nibblers

Pine voles and meadow voles are the two principal rodents to watch out for in the orchard. The pine vole lives underground and feeds on fruit, tubers, and the roots of certain trees (such as apple) in their burrows. The extensive burrow systems radiate out from the trunk to the dripline of the tree,

with the tunnel runs averaging one to three inches deep. A large root being gnawed by these rodents will send up a row of suckers. Thick surface litter prevents tunnels from collapsing, so don't mulch if pine voles are a serious problem. The meadow vole prefers to construct networks of runways in thick grass, though some soil tunnels may be found near the trunk. It feeds on grasses, legumes, seeds, and tubers; but when these are scarce, look out for the cambium layers on the trunk. Much of the girdling damage by these "meadow mice" occurs under the cover of snow.

There are other small rodents in the orchard that get confused with these two. Moles are earthworm carnivores that love to dig—they'll aerate your soil but rarely damage tree roots. Another potential ally is the short-tail shrew, which devours other small rodents along with insect delicacies. Deer mice and their white-footed cousins might nest in surface litter but rarely cause problems.

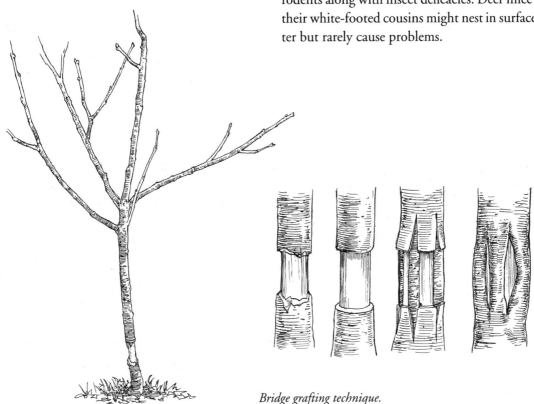

Bridge grafting technique.

Voles enjoy fallen apples, so clean the orchard floor of all drops. A fall mowing reduces run cover, as does pulling back the mulch from around the trunks. The peastone mulch at the base of young trees helps keep the immediate area of concern open throughout the growing season. Galvanized hardware cloth secured around the trunk offers year-round insurance against any lower bark nibbling, but it is very time-consuming to remove if borers plague your site. Quarter-inch plastic mesh in a twenty-four-inch width, cut large enough to allow room for ten or more years of growth, is more economical and comes with readily removed button snaps. Spiral plastic guards serve on young saplings for the winter months, when girdling is most likely. Try putting up perching posts for sharp-eyed hawks, who will watch for any sign of prey movement. The orchardist with a resident fox is lucky indeed. Rampage mouse bait, which has vitamin D3 as its active ingredient, is the only acceptable organic poison option.

Recently planted trees that get girdled are usually replaced. A bearing tree with large areas of wintertime chewing can sometimes be saved by bridge grafting. Watersprout scions are wedged into the cambium layer both above and below the damage in early spring. Be sure to insert the new wood so that upward sap flow continues in that direction. Several scions can be used to bridge around the trunk—saving a completely girdled tree is akin to adding an interstem between the varietal wood above and the rootstock below. The grafts that take will grow rapidly and, being of such succulent growth, will likely be sought out by voles again if left unprotected.

Rabbits can be quite harmful in a high-density planting where scaffold shoots are trained low. Once such branches get snipped off in feeding, replacements that are overshadowed by the upper tree structure are never quite as productive. A mixture of seven pounds of tree rosin in one gallon of denatured alcohol painted on the trunk and lower branches is said to repel Peter Cottontail.

When Wings Count as Legs

Birds can wreak great devastation on the fruit crop. As much as 15 percent of the harvest can be pecked with holes in August and September. The scare-eye balloon—a round, plastic balloon with oversized eyes printed on it—is a quiet deterrent. These are hung from a pole above the topmost foliage to make birds think a large owl or hawk is flying above the orchard. One balloon is effective over a radius of 20 yards. Large growers rely on timed cannon blasts (powered by propane gas) to disturb birds and the neighborhood alike. A sound system rigged to play bird distress calls keeps your neighbors less distressed.

The Bud Browsers

I remember leaving certain wild apple trees for the deer when we first moved to our farm. Other areas I cleared for new apple plantings. The vision was one of peaceful coexistence. Deer are admittedly beautiful and graceful animals in the woods, but, loosed on an apple farm, there can be no peace.

Deer devastate apple trees. Bearing blocks can be completely stripped of all fruit buds on the lower scaffolds to the tune of a bushel of fruit (or more) per tree. The desired structure of young trees can be permanently lost when the growing tips of shoots are browsed year after year. Summer shoot injury is conducive to fire blight. Bucks in rut snap developing trunks in two with their antler rubbing. Fruit trees are a sure investment loss where deer pressure is high if you don't have an effective plan to keep these animals at bay.

Spray repellents work by putting a bad taste in the deer's mouth. I've used two of the commercial preparations available. Hinder is the ammoniated soap of a fatty acid that can be applied directly to the foliage, but it needs to be reapplied following

The deer that bit off these shoot buds didn't realize that "soap effectively repels deer within a radius of three feet."

becoming immune to one consistently used deterrent. Garlic oil dispensers add a third scent to the mix. Place one repellent per nonbearing tree, or one every three feet around the circumference of a mature tree, but realize that when deer are hungry, browse is inevitable. One fall we scattered several tankage bars throughout a young planting. Damned if that didn't piss off a certain buck who found each one, bit the bar, and then proceeded to thrash those trees with his antlers till each snapped. The soaped trees were left alone until after the chickadees ate each bar of Dial. *Cést la vie!*

Deer can smell dropped apples even under a blanket of snow. A clean orchard floor removes the

a heavy rain unless NuFilm sticker is used. Deer-Away is Weyerhaeuser's answer to protecting replanted conifers: these putrescent egg solids are equally effective on the dormant buds of fruit trees for two months at a time. Homemade concoctions can save much expense, however. One brew that has worked for me included three aged eggs (six weeks in a sunny window made them bad but not gross beyond measure), half a pint of Safer soap, and several tablespoons of cayenne pepper to five gallons of water, all applied with a backpack sprayer. Only the bottom six feet of the tree needs to be protected. In a small planting of standard trees, young whips can be encircled with broken lengths of snow fence until the leading shoot gets above this deer-browsing height.

Odor repellents may work when deer pressure is light to moderate. Highly perfumed bars of soap (Cashmere Bouquet and Irish Spring get high ratings) and the Green Screen bags of meat meal can be rotated every few months to keep the deer from

Eight-foot-high fence posts on this Lost Nation planting provide a ready option for adding higher wires if needed. The sweeping corner of posts in the background works best on such sloping terrain.

The ideal hi-tensile deer fence.

temptation that might cause the deer to jump all but the tallest fence. Once we left a bushel of Cortland apples unpicked above a ground hornet's nest. The deer polished off the apples in two nights after they fell but kept coming back to that spot all winter in hopes of more. Each visit meant more browse damage. Hanging scare-eye balloons or tin can lids (bent at a forty-five degree angle to flutter in the wind) makes deer more apprehensive about returning.

A Good Deer Fence

A fence can never be high enough the morning after deer have devastated the growing tips of a new planting. Some growers claim success with a single, baited electric strand suspended thirty inches off the ground. Once the deer get their noses shocked from sniffing the peanut butter on aluminum foil strips, the theory goes, they shy away. Simple plans like this, however, don't work as well when there are many hungry deer in the neighborhood.

A solar-powered fence charger protects a remote orchard planting in Lost Nation.

The ultimate deer fence consists of three rolls of woven wire installed to a height of twelve feet. The deer cannot go under this, they can't go through it, and they can't go over it. Nor can anyone afford it. A good fence needs to be a compromise on expense based on the penetration habits of most deer. Hi-tensile electric fencing is cost-effective because line posts separated by sixty feet are fewer in number, low-impedance chargers reduce the need to trim grass as often, and the intensity of the shock is long remembered by deer. Only fearful deer will not jump a fence. The basic design calls for six wires spaced ten inches apart. We installed eight-foot (above ground) posts around our new Thayer block

to give us the option of adding higher wires later. Total material costs with a solar charger ran just under a dollar per linear foot. Advocates of the so-called Penn State fence—where slanting struts on each post hold the hi-tensile wires on a diagonal plane—have found that deer are spooked by the funnel effect of the wires "descending" overhead when they go looking for openings down low. Supposedly, deer cannot gauge the actual height of such a multiple-strand fence either, but that may well be so much bunkum. We opted for a vertical fence primarily to ease mowing requirements around the orchard perimeter. Ask your local Premier Fence distributor for the scoop on properly installing a hi-tensile fence.

Surprisingly, given that these animals can vertically jump eight feet with ease, both bucks and does first look for a way to go under or through a fence. This includes the dips and vales of hilly country as well as widely spaced electric wires. Our undulating terrain precluded using the hi-tensile woven wire available from Langley Industries for the bottom half of our fence. Deer share a determined intelligence to get to the other side. Once one figures out that diving through two hot wires results in no shock (being airborne, they're not grounded), it quickly teaches others in the herd to take the plunge. Wintertime adjustments are necessary on an electric fence where snow cover insulates the animal from the ground: take the second and fourth wires off the circuit to provide parallel grounds down low. A bipolar charger is necessary to provide enough shocking power under such poor grounding conditions. Electric fences need to be charged at all times from the day the first wire goes up. A cleared lane of four feet or more outside the fence reduces the tendency of deer to jump. Scorching the grass beneath the fence line with a portable flame weeder (check the Snow Pond Farm Supply catalog, see appendix 2) can be maintenance time well spent.

THE STORY OF BABS

She started off like most deer, shyly exploring the edges of the orchard and garden. The bone tar repellent didn't seem offensive to her nose, as often she'd stand by the oil-soaked rag tied to a perimeter stake. Under cover of nightfall she discovered the garden. The beets disappeared, then the beans. The tips of young apple trees were an appetizer on the way in and out. No rain fell for six weeks, making our irrigated plots that much more lush. She began to appear at the height of the day to graze the buckwheat in the stream garden.

Enough was enough. I got out my Dad's old .22, loaded some blanks, and gave chase. Bang! She leapt the fence, then paused at the top of the pasture. Was that a bemused smile at the raving madman panting up the slope? Bang! Off into the woods we went. She'd stop every hundred yards or so to make sure I could keep up. Bang! Now she was out of sight, yet here the forest thinned around one giant pine thirty feet ahead. Silently she peered around the pine, craning her neck to keep her body out of sight. She saw me, dropped back, then peered around the other side. The gun in my hand was silly. I knew it, she knew it. It was simply time to talk.

"Babs, about the garden. Those plants are our food. Someday the apple trees will bear lots of fruit for both of us if you let them grow. It seems there's plenty of other things for you to eat in the woods. Could you please leave our plantings be?"

She listened, then turned and ran out of sight. The next day she was back, in the lower gardens, eating oats and clover. The sheep seemed to flock round her, but on this side of the fence. I crept down in the fading light to a grove of trees, a borrowed shotgun in hand, loaded with a special scare shell provided by the Fish'n'Game boys. The sheep moved away towards the stream, Babs grazed uphill towards me. I'd been told these scare shells travel quietly for a hundred yards, then explode like an M80 in the midst of a fireball. The distance seemed right; I fired. Boom! Babs looked up and walked off into the swamplands.

Nancy suggests setting up our tent on the far side of the main garden and sleeping out. The Swiss chard and second planting of beans are likely to be Babs' next nighttime feed. Sadie, our golden retriever, looks sad-eyed at pulling guard dog duty. Her barking wakes us and I fly out of the tent. Babs is in the orchard, heading for her favorite salad bar. Boom! It no longer matters what the neighbors think — we're at war down here in the hollow. Sadie barks a few times a night, I get up to patrol, shotgun in hand. The stars are brilliant and often we see meteors, but Babs seems to have recognized the persistence of our defensive effort. We stop sleeping out ten days later and enjoy a side dish of steamed chard.

There's a high-pitched screaming in the lower pasture. I run down and see a lanky fawn caught in the portable netting attached to our solar charger. Babs is there too, a look of grave concern in her eyes. I run to help the little fellow but he breaks free on his own. There's a rustling behind Babs and another fawn emerges. It's both beautiful and devastating: two young deer learning not to fear humans (me anyway) and seeking out my apple trees. All this time Babs has been a mother and suddenly its clear why she's been sticking around. Nancy tells me, "She needed those beet greens for the iron to nurse her babies."   (continued)

Babs and her fawns disappear after that day for the rest of summer. One late fall weekend I discover her and a son browsing in the orchard at dawn. I decide to shoot that last scare shell and this time place myself an exact hundred yards away. Boom! Perfect placement and the deer run to my shouts of good riddance. Later we hear the tale of our friend Simon and his new girlfriend from the city. Unknown to us, they arrived the night before to sleep at the family cabin in the woods above our farm. But Simon lost the key, so they slept out in a tent. They awoke at dawn to the sounds of a gunshot and belligerent raving. Simon, being of an active mind, panics, drives to town, and calls our nearest neighbor to announce my murder. Simon's girlfriend determines never to come North again. Somewhere deep in the woods Babs is smiling.

Dogs are the latest rage in keeping deer out of the orchard. Off Limits Crop Protection Systems offers the buried wire and radio shock collars that keep a pair of dogs within the boundary of the orchard. The dogs quickly learn how far they can roam in search of deer: an audible warning signal in the collar tells them the wire is approaching. A mild shock occurs if the dogs go further. Deer, too, learn the limits and graze just beyond the line in taunting defiance of the dogs who relentlessly protect the apple buds. Dogs help keep vole populations in check as well.

Heavy deer pressure is a result of deliberate Fish and Game Department management in many states. There are more deer today than when this wooded country was first settled. High populations are encouraged at the expense of farmers to provide plenty of fall targets for the hunters who pay licensing fees. Growers in Michigan have brought a damage suit against their state in rightful response. Decades ago, fencing costs were paid from hunting revenues. Orchardists need to work together to make game managers and state legislatures more responsible for their policies.

With the development of chemically synthesized pesticides, man had a shot-gun that he could use to destroy virtually all pests in one blast. But these pesticides began to migrate into his food chain and destroyed much of the natural balances, hence creating even more severe problems affecting the very basis for his own life. Pests became immune to the poisons and new ones were developed. We are now at that point when the health of people is on a collision course with catastrophe.

—A. P. THOMSON, *Your Apple Orchard* (1982)

CHAPTER 7

Spray Options

Growing tree fruit today for a living involves spraying, whether we choose an "organic" approach or this past century's "conventional" chemical approach. A wide spectrum of options exists between these seemingly polar perspectives, from "almost organic" to "IPM" to the "all-purpose spray mix" used by ill-advised home orchardists. A certain naiveté in the early Rodale Press literature did little to boost organic prospects in the minds of commercial growers, given the broad-spectrum effects (killing many species of insects, whether the targeted pest or completely innocent bystanders) of so-called "natural" materials like copper and rotenone. Choice of allowable spray materials for a certified organic orchard continues to merit legitimate debate as we shall see.

The control garnered by an organic spray program needs to be taken in context. Two dictums of modern fruit production don't necessarily mesh with the public's desire for apples free of chemical residues: an economic mandate for an exception-ally high packout of dessert-quality fruit can only be met with the near-total pest control of synthetic chemical applications. What I do in Lost Nation often falls short of both precepts. Changing the "rules of the game" suits me fine. A value-added organic packout will be detailed in chapter 9; spray effectiveness often lies in integrating two or three organic practices to balance pest dynamics at acceptable levels.

THE COMPLEXITIES OF NATURE

The practice of the Western mind has always been to logically and rationally break apart the whole into its constituent parts. Given this way of thinking, it's no surprise that the litany of pest management reads this way: here's damage on the fruit, here's the pest that did it, here's a spray that kills the pest. Organic growers for the most part have attended the same service as growers of a chemical spray persuasion. The only real difference is that the botanical insecticides we've been using haven't proven nearly as effective as synthetic organophosphates in producing profits. Great-grandfather was equally eager to embrace lead arsenate and go heavy on the Bordeaux mixture at the turn of the century in response to an increasing array of insect and disease pressures on the fruit. As small diversified farms and home orchards were abandoned, the economics of large-scale production drove this mindset to the fore. Studies of cultural and biological pest vulnerability had ended by the time the great god DDT arrived on the scene. Yet today our desire to understand and work with nature has come full circle, as a chemically dependent agriculture reveals numerous shortcomings both in the orchard (high costs, resistant species, induced pests) and in the long-term genetics and health of our children.

Turns of events we never anticipated are frightening. Researchers at Tulane-Xavier Center for Bio-Environmental Research in New Orleans published results in 1996 showing that two petrochemicals combined to become one thousand times more dangerous than either used alone. Such *synergistic chemicals* can disrupt the human endocrine system, causing unprecedented levels of breast cancer and lowered sperm counts. Farmers have a higher risk for certain cancers, particularly cancers of the blood and the immune system ("Occupational Risk of Cancer from Pesticides: Farmer Studies," National Cancer Institute, 1991). It seems we all know more friends and family stricken by this disease than we did a generation ago. *Something* has gone seriously awry.

Our food system need not be linked to such fears. Stepping back to examine the context of past choices reveals broader outlooks. It has been a mistake to separate insect and disease pressures from soil health and enduring diversity. These are exciting times to embrace the challenge of growing fruit that is both safe and profitable. Orcharding becomes that much more a delight when we can meet our needs within the complexities of the natural world.

Consider that some apple maggot flies and codling moths pupate over two or more winters, thus ensuring their own continuity on a site should a cropless year break the fruiting (and supposedly the insect) cycle. In other words, those creatures we call pests belong in the ecosystem, which in turn suggests that our own answers lie not in spray annihilation, but in a balance of many natural factors. The science of IPM has rekindled old ways of thinking that pre-date our lethal arsenal of synthetic chemicals. At the same time, microbiology has opened our eyes to a world that has always been there. We're aware of *Beauveria bassiana*, a soil fungus that penetrates through an insect's skin with its "roots" to claim the host's nutrients for its own. An open mind observes the critical details: the fungus establishes itself on contact and requires moist conditions. Then assesses the possibilities: weevils pupating in the soil would be reached by a fungal application in a steady rain. And goes on to a promising scenario: plum curculio is a weevil with an essential life stage in the soil beneath the tree. And if *Beauveria* fungus naturalizes? And if we're now able to accept a reduced curculio population as a reminder of a more hapless time?

ALL THE ANSWERS AREN'T KNOWN, BUT WE'RE GAINING

Clearly, new research is needed to form such thoughts into workable practice. It may be that clusters of plum trees within the apple orchard (never sprayed with elemental fungicides) get renewed applications of *Beauveria* yearly. Parasitic nematodes may better serve on such targeted ground, although Brian Caldwell has postulated a potential soil predator more sensitive to nematode attack may account for a replicated curculio increase in his New York orchard. The expense associated with either approach is greatly reduced from an orchard-wide application. Perhaps the ground beneath these trees is kept open to (1) limit curculio cover going into bloom for trapping purposes, and (2) practice shallow cultivation following June drop as great-grandfather once did. Perhaps old carpeting spread beneath these trees makes the gathering of infested June drops a cinch. A garlic repellent spray on the other fruits would help funnel curculio to these early-blooming trap trees. Keith Kozub in River Falls, Wisconsin, reports that most of the curculios in his four-acre orchard tend to gravitate to the same twenty trees (mostly early-variety apples) year after year, where he daily shakes them out onto tarps.

An integrated orchard approach gets involved. But without the willingness to undertake replicated trials based on a thorough understanding of pest dynamics—and without forums, like this book, where growers can share what's being learned—we're not going to figure out an economically acceptable management plan anytime soon. There are relatively few orchardists poised to get beyond the economic damage of an insect like curculio without chemical intervention. University researchers look at organic methods and materials on a component basis, rarely integrating such trials into a holistic orchard setting. Thus, for example, the sole use of garlic spray (with no soil-building, no unmowed diversity, no mating disruption, no foliar

BUFFERING AGENTS AND SPRAY ADJUVANTS

Enhanced effectiveness is the name of the game when spray materials cost as much as they do. Organic growers generally have not embraced the science of proper tank pH and leaf ionization as have the better chemical growers. However, a sound understanding of spray chemistry applies to organic materials, which are equally subject to alkaline hydrolysis and in need of a surfactant boost. We research long and hard what to spray but rarely consider application technique. Yet the results we seek depend on both.

Buffering agents adjust the pH of the tank mix to prevent the alkaline breakdown of a spray formulation in water. Neem requires a pH between 3 and 7 to be effective, garlic extracts stay potent below pH 6, and Bt is stable up to pH 8. Use pH test strips (available from Forestry Suppliers) to assess spray water. A cup measure of cider vinegar to a hundred gallons of water is a buffering rule of thumb to acceptably lower pH. Using rainwater gets around a high mineral content problem.

Spray adjuvants are those mysterious "inert ingredients" that are never disclosed in a spray formulation. The more innocuous ones improve compatibility of tank mixes, help "wet" dry powders, and act as either a sticker or a spreader. A *sticker* provides greater adhesion to the leaf. NuFilm 17 has been found to increase the amount of spray material initially deposited during spraying by 30 percent or more. The real virtue of this pine resin product is its tenacity in adhering sulfur to the leaf through a full-fledged wetting period. A *spreader* (also called a *surfactant*) reduces surface tension in the spray liquid to increase coverage and penetration on the leaf surface. Plain vegetable oil always serves in a pinch. Some surfactants provide longer residual life via their ultraviolet-screening properties. Nutrient-rich fish oil augments ryania, Bt, and granulosis virus beneath a varnish-like coating that resists weathering. Manufactured formulations usually specify when a supplemental sticker or spreader is needed.

enhancement) can be "conclusively demonstrated" by harvest assessments to stack up nowhere near the standards of chemical dependency. Research from an integrated organic perspective doesn't fit the going philosophy. Notwithstanding, we are deeply indebted to university research on the IPM front. These discoveries aren't always directly applicable to organic growers, but, with a bit of thought, we can pick up the ball and run with it.

Open-minded researchers are working towards the goal of organic fruit production. Often they can tell you what has been done to date and add pertinent details to your understanding. Call the manufacturer of any spray product to talk to the technical rep about concerns and trial possibilities. Extension literature and conventional fruit grower magazines often contain tidbits of organic interest. Ultimately, though, our best connections are with each other. Growers share a special slant when it comes to analyzing the feasibility of a new approach. The farmer-to-farmer exchanges held here in the Northeast among ecological and organic apple growers are always more eye-opening than any conference.

We each have our own ideas about what works. Every orchard has localized effects . . . my answers may well not be your answers. Higher humidity may make summer disease a vexing frustration for you, just as lesser appleworm teaming up with codling moth rules out mating disruption for me. Yet we share the basics. A spray material works by a specified mode, which affects the disease or insect in a known way. It is wrong to apply materials without understanding the full spectrum of anticipated effects. The pest's life cycle reveals points of vulnerability. Other insects and pathogens lend a beneficial balance to these affairs. Good soil nutrition results in good tree health, which in turn results in greater pest resistance. We each have a part of the puzzle to share. Together we're proving that an integrated organic approach is a viable way to grow fruit.

A spider captures a tarnished plant bug in the tall grass beneath an apple tree.

TIMING IS EVERYTHING

People are amazed that much of the work of protecting the apple takes place long before they notice the fruit sizing on the tree. Organic fungicides are protectants that need to be on the unfolding leaves before conditions warrant disease infection. Spray repellents only have potential if the pest has not yet made itself at home. You can't trap apple maggot flies if they're not active, nor is there any point in being behind the times. Microbial insecticides have a short residual of effectiveness, often geared towards the most vulnerable stage of an insect's cycle.

Bud development and insect activity don't coincide from year to year with the precise dates of the astronomical calendar. In other words, don't plan on the grand arrival of plum curculio on May 20 year after year whatever the weather. The biological calendar is based on solar revolutions of a different kind—degree days accumulated from the continual return of longer days each spring. You can establish pest-specific benchmarks for your orchard, but the basic ones already determined set the orchard alarm clock nicely. Apple buds, averaged across cultivars, will show pink after 300 degree days (above 40°F), and the whole pollination shebang will end when the blossom petals fall to the ground another 240 degree days later. This schedule holds true regardless of where you're located on the continent (provided chilling requirements have been met to break dormancy). And, both these orchard "dates" signal that it's time to commence well-planned pest management strategies.

Timeliness relates equally to watching the weather. An orchardist is on call in primary scab season just like any doctor scheduled for emergency-room duty. A warm rain counsels action that won't be effective a day or two later. Make that sulfur spray first and then go golfing. Conditions right for widespread fire blight? Streptomycin's potency as an arboreal antibiotic on the open blossoms is strongest just before an infection begins, making timely application vital. A prediction of temps down in the teens at the other end of the season is a clarion call to pick fruit like mad, since tomorrow it will be hard as a rock.

DEGREE DAYS

Tracking degree days allows us to accurately predict many orchard events: scab ascospore maturity, the rapidity of bud growth, and codling moth egg hatch, to name a few. Accumulated warmth is the driving force of spring. Insects are *exothermic*, meaning they remain at the same temperature as their environment. Being unable to generate heat, they wait for ambient temperatures that allow life-stage development. An insect's developmental threshold is the minimum temperature at which activity resumes, and thus the base temperature chosen for that insect's degree day countdown.

Calculate the mean daily temperature from the minimum and maximum readings taken in the orchard. A specified base temperature is subtracted from this average to obtain the total number of degree days garnered each day. Researchers have correlated the cycles of nature to these accumulated degree days from an identified starting point. Bud stages are tracked on the basis of temperatures above 40°F as the days lengthen. In the case of codling moth, capture of the first male in a pheromone-baited wing trap marks the beginning of the countdown to egg hatch. Two hundred and forty-three degree days later (above a 50°F base), a first spray of either Bt or ryania will prove effective as emerging larvae crawl to the fruit.

Our great-grandparents relied upon folk wisdom rather than this scientific accounting. The observation of events was keyed to signs of spring rather than the thermometer. Gardening advice on waiting to set out cabbage transplants until the apple blossoms opened was more than a superstitious gesture: cabbage root maggot flies are finished laying eggs about the time of fruit bloom. "Plant corn when oak leaves are the size of a squirrel's ear" means that the soil is now warm enough to ensure kernel germination.

Taken as lore, or taken as science, degree days really work.

THE ORCHARD CALENDAR

Orchardists share a common language to describe the season at hand. The trees are at rest in the dormant season. Bud stages distinguish tree awakening and associated pest activity nicely. Silver tip, green tip, quarter-inch green, half-inch green, tight cluster, open cluster, pink, first bloom, and full bloom are very observable benchmarks of the apple's spring. This progression varies slightly in other tree fruits that blossom without spur leaves. (Peaches, for example, start at first swell and proceed through calyx green, calyx red, and first pink into full bloom.) Petal fall indicates that delightful "rain" of blossom petals to the ground. It's an anxious time as we await the visible result of pollination: good fruit set. Unfertilized ovaries soon yellow and fall away. "June drop" is the tree's response to an overabundance of developing fruitlets and early-season insect damage. The concept of cover sprays goes back to the era when spray applications were made every ten days as a matter of course to provide continued protection after the petal fall spray. Thus first cover, second cover, third

cover, and so on until harvest time. Terminal bud set in late summer marks the end of growth and subsequent hardening off of buds in preparation for winter's cold.

Augmenting the orchard calendar with the pest particularities for your region helps you focus on the tasks at hand. Primary scab season extends approximately fourteen days on either side of pink—sulfur vigilance needs to be unwavering if the orchard is to be free of secondary infection risk for the remainder of the summer. Fire blight danger peaks when the open blossoms offer a pandemic point of entry for infection. The three weeks following petal fall is curculio control time, though repellence and trapping can begin as early as pink. The "calyx spray" of yore was timed at petal fall to fill the calyx cup of the exposed fruitlet with arsenate poisons before it closed to await any end-tunneling larvae. The time-honored notion of a petal-fall application isn't quite the same when your intentions are to renew a systemic repellent rather than "blast" the pests away (whether by chemical or botanical means) after honeybees have safely moved on. Our two applications of ryania

(left) Half-inch green tip on apple. (center) That magical moment known as "pink." (right) Full bloom.

for codling moth based on degree-day countdowns curiously fall between the traditional first three cover sprays. Here the first of July marks two tactical undertakings: plan A for round-headed apple-tree borer and plan B for apple maggot flies. The latter part of summer is "second-generation Leps season," when trapping patterns determine any need to act.

The Orchard Almanac by Steve Page and Joe Smillie outlines the orchard calendar on a monthly basis for growers. The compendium of orchard tasks found in the appendices of this book lists *what we do when* here in northern New Hampshire. This includes ever-evolving spray schedules as well as trapping needs, sanitation practice, foliar enhancements, and other seasonal notes. Overemphasis has been given to spray schedules alone in the past: the art of orcharding needs to be understood as much more than obligatory spraying. Compiling such a compendium for your own orchard will prove eye-opening.

BOTANICALS, ELEMENTALS, AND FORBIDDEN FRUIT

Organic orchardists generally take on one pest bug at a time. What might work for codling moth won't necessarily help with plum curculio. Curculio is the reason many organic-at-heart apple growers become *ecological growers* who choose limited chemical insecticide use over a devastated crop. This Faustian bargain to use Imidan is based on its track record of apparent safety and reasonable effectiveness. Botanicals are not the solution to our curculio dilemma, but synergistic repellents hold out promise in conjunction with an integrated trapping plan. Elemental sprays of copper and sulfur provide disease control, and the good news is these don't need to be applied to excess if your cultural sanitation is topnotch.

Any decision to spray should be well thought out long before a crisis erupts. Winter months are for researching new options, talking to other growers, pricing products, and drawing up orchard budgets. Most organic spray materials are not available at the local farm supply store—although some incredibly toxic synthetic ones are—so you need to place orders ahead, preferably before buds break dormancy and the intensity of the growing year begins.

My personal goal is to do as few sprays as possible in order to achieve satisfactory results. Not spraying saves time, expense, and in most cases, biological diversity. Monitoring with traps gives you some sense of pest cycles. Deciding if a sulfur application for scab is essential requires experienced use of the wetting period chart (see page 132). Setting up trials in different sections of your orchard to determine what works may enable you to forgo a spray in future years.

Rotenone and Pyrethrum

Botanicals are natural insecticides derived from toxic plant materials. Rotenone occurs in more than sixty-five species of plants, but most commercial supplies are derived from Peruvian cubé or Malaysian derris plants. Pyrethrum refers to the dried, powdered flower heads of certain *Chrysanthemum* daisies (pyrethrin products are the extracted active ingredients). Yet "natural" doesn't mean that these materials are safe or environmentally benign: these botanicals are "heavy hitters" with the power to upset ecological balance like the worst chemical sprays. Beneficial insects are at risk as much as the targeted pest. Pyrethrin insecticides are moderately toxic to mammals, but do not appear to be harmful to bees. Rotenone is one of the most powerful fish poisons known, kills birds, and is a strong respiratory inhibitor. Humans are wise to avoid the rotenone dusts altogether, but if you're resolved to use the wettable-powder formulation, wear full protective

ORGANIC SPRAY MATERIALS

The spray formulations used by orchardists are tools for balancing pest dynamics in favor of better-looking fruit. Organic materials are naturally derived and therefore supposedly safer; chemical options are synthetic and therefore (to an organic purist) supposedly anathema. This rather blunt differentiation irritates many growers, who take into consideration whether a spray is broad-spectrum or specific to the targeted pest, its acute toxicity, and how rapidly the material breaks down into benign elements. I might add economic effectiveness here as well, for part of the struggle faced in the organic orchard is the labor issue: consumers wanting organically grown fruit really have no idea of the many work hours that synthetic chemicals replace in the pursuit of unmarred fruit.

Yet this point of spray definition is a beginning for those of us with concerns about long-term health issues, both human health and that of the soil. We do take into consideration how rapidly and completely a spray material breaks down. The integrated organic approach requires us to consider the ramifications of our choices on the orchard ecology as a whole: bad bugs have a place just as much as the good fellows. There may be instances where a manmade material might be preferred — azoxystrobin (synthesized from a naturally occurring fungicide found in strobilurin mushrooms) may well prove to be a more ecological fungicide than sulfur. Human technology is not in and of itself evil: an organic grower sitting atop a diesel-fueled tractor or cruising the orchard with a plastic backpack sprayer should face up to that fact.

Few of us are "long-term chemists" who can understand the really important issues of what we're doing to our bodies and our planet. Organic sprays may or may not be acceptable in the big picture, but it's a responsibility I'm willing to bear.

gear and a snug-fitting respirator. Commercial products of either botanical may contain the synergistic agent piperonyl butoxide (PBO) to enhance the effects of the active ingredients. Sesame-derived PBO may affect the human nervous system . . . don't use it.

Botanicals do have positive attributes worth mentioning. Both rotenone and pyrethrum have a short residual once applied, meaning they break down quickly in sunlight. There is no long-term persistence in the environment with either, unlike most chemicals. Rotenone acts as a contact and stomach poison on insects with chewing mouth parts: curculio and apple maggot fly are listed on the label, but its effect is modest at best. Pyrethrum acts as a paralytic nerve poison on aphids, most

moth larvae, leafhoppers, adult ladybugs, and other beneficials. You can grow pyrethrum daisies and extract a pyrethrin concentrate by packing fresh flowers overnight in isopropyl alcohol to make a homegrown spray.

A few years back I attended a fruit growers meeting where a university researcher gave a talk on his environmental impact quotient. The EIQ is an assessment tool that is used to rate the adverse impact any one pesticide has on the environment. A good idea on the whole, but one that fell short in the bias of the assumptions behind it. Suffice it to say that, at this meeting, organic fruit growing was "mathematically proven" to be far more harmful than a chemical IPM approach. The other growers gave the presenter a resounding ovation while I kept a

ROTENONE REBUTTAL

One steadfast advocate for the use of rotenone in the orchard is Brian Caldwell, a certified organic grower near Ithaca, New York. "Because of rotenone's quick degradation, it will only kill beneficials if it hits them. I spray this botanical in the evening and have not had the outbreaks of aphids or mites that would be associated with heavy beneficial kill." Plum curculio is subject to this same hit or miss strategy, however, and accordingly, a rotenone spray schedule features up to four applications over the three weeks following petal fall to get noticeable results. "We added a trunk application of rotenone at the pink bud stage to our curculio strategy in 1997. These insects tend to hide near the base of the tree when first moving into the orchard," Brian explains, "so we flamed the grass beneath the trees and relied on rotenone at the base of the trunk. Coupled with our usual petal fall sprays, we had our best crop yet."

The conventional wisdom outlined in this book has been to avoid orchard-wide applications of rotenone. Brian's take on it is different than mine. Thank goodness we all have our own ideas! Using rotenone within a very targeted radius at the base of the tree when curculio tends to congregate there has "frontier potential" for us all.

particularly humble profile. But a valid point was made about relying solely on botanicals and elementals to produce an apple crop: rotenone and sulfur applied every five to seven days throughout the growing season has a tremendously negative impact on the environment. Fortunately, an *integrated organic approach* to growing fruit produces an entirely different effect.

Ryania

Ryania is a selective botanical I've used with great success on codling moth and lesser appleworm. Other growers report similar results with oriental fruit moth. These three lepidopterous cousins are particularly susceptible to this contact and stomach poison as larvae, provided the worm has not deeply penetrated the fruit. Adult moths and eggs succumb to a lesser degree. Ryania is generally assumed to be harmless to beneficials and mite predators (however, European red mite populations did increase in ryania trials done forty years ago, but lead arsenate was being used at petal fall and first cover). This botanical consists of the ground stems of *Ryania speciosa*, a shrub native to Trinidad, and works on certain insects by paralyzing muscle tissue. It has an active residual period of several days, which can be enhanced by mixing it with fish oil and a feeding attractant such as blackstrap molasses. Ryania toxicity may be slightly lessened in a mixed application with sulfur.

The bad news about ryania for American growers is that it is no longer registered for sale with the Environmental Protection Agency (EPA). Registration costs begin in the tens of thousands of dollars, and can go up to tens of millions for broad-spectrum chemicals. It takes a substantial profit margin for companies to recoup that kind of investment. The organic fruit market at this time is simply too small to justify the registration costs for a relatively narrow-use botanical like ryania. Something is seriously wrong when we have a pesticide-regulation system that makes more toxic chemicals readily available while discouraging even the possibility of those in lower risk categories.

Other Botanicals

Nicotine is a highly poisonous alkaloid extracted from tobacco. Concentrations of 0.05 to 0.1 percent will kill most soft-bodied insects like aphids and spider mites and remain toxic on the leaf surface for several weeks. We have no call to use it in an organic ecosystem. Yet I have this one notion about using shredded tobacco in a basal tree paste specifically targeted at the round-headed appletree borer. Just tell it Joe Camel says hello.

Quassia is a bitter substance found in the bark and wood of the Jamaican bitterwood tree. It has a long history of medicinal use (natural food stores may carry quassia wood chips) and was once substituted for hops in making beer. Yet it acts as a narcotic poison on some insects if infused into a tea with "a spoonful of sugar to help the medicine go down." Sawflies are reported to be affected, suggesting its use in a hanging jug trap at blossom time.

Sabadilla is made from the seeds of a lily-like plant found in Venezuela, which can be soaked to make a spray solution. It is moderately toxic to mammals but does not seem to harm beneficials. Aphids, stink bugs, leafhoppers, and tarnished plant bugs can be targeted on fruit trees.

Cryolite is a mineral insecticide from a naturally occurring deposit of sodium aluminofluoride found in Greenland. Its label at one time listed plum curculio on apple. The pure deposits have long since been mined, so it now must be refined by chemical means. Cryolite is very persistent in the soil.

Citrus peel extracts contain insecticidal compounds that cause massive overstimulation of insect motor nerves, which leads to convulsion and death. Fruit flies are definitely immobilized. No specific orchard use is yet approved, but one can't help but wonder if the Florida Orange Juice Commission doesn't owe apple growers something for convincing so many people that orange is the essential breakfast juice.

Neem

Azadirachtin is extracted from the seeds of the neem tree (*Azadirachta indica*), which is common throughout most of Africa and India. The chinaberry tree (*Melia azedarach*) in the southeastern United States is a closely related species. While neem works as an insecticide, it is of greater use as a broad-spectrum repellent and growth regulator. It deters both feeding and oviposition by insects, and should they persist, neem interferes with the key insect molting hormone ecdysone. Larvae prevented from molting from one life stage to the next do not survive to become reproductive adults. Azadirachtin kills pest pupae as well, but adults and eggs are rarely affected. Many lepidopteran larvae are listed on the label, along with sawfly. Adult beneficials are not harmed by a botanical growth regulator aimed at plant feeders.

Neem oil extracts have fungicidal properties due to the smothering effect of any oil formulation. Trilogy is one such spray product listing anthracnose, alternaria, powdery mildew, and scab on its pome label. Work needs to be done to see if there is any applicability to summer diseases. Sulfur is phytotoxic in hot weather and its control of sooty blotch and flyspeck variable, leaving a wide opening for an organic summer fungicide.

John Bemis had hoped that an earlier formulation of neem would solve his plum curculio problem in Massachusetts, but he found little difference from the untreated control. Apple maggot fly, however, was somewhat rebuffed by weekly summer applications. Dennis Mackey in Wisconsin considers neem in combination with garlic extracts to be a credible replacement for Imidan against plum curculio.

Copper

The primary organic fungicides are elemental metals. Copper in its various formulations can be caustic—causing chlorosis in leaves and russeting

THE IMIDAN DEBATE

Phosmet, known best by the trade name Imidan, is not an organic spray material. Many growers who otherwise could be considered "organic" use this chemical once or twice after petal fall to control plum curculio. There's little room to compromise when as much as 90 percent of a crop can be devastated and on the ground by the end of June. Imidan is the forbidden fruit of the organic orchard. Yet growers with valid concerns about making a living and the impact of harsher botanicals on beneficial insects have savored its results. It's a decision each one of us needs to make for ourselves. Here's what is known and unknown about using Imidan in the Orchard of Eden.

Imidan is a broad-spectrum organophosphate insecticide that poisons insects through cholinesterase inhibition of the autonomic nervous system. My doctor described this phosphorylation of acetylcholinesterase at the nerve endings as a "one-way ticket out" for fish, birds, insects, and mammals. While considered not to be particularly harmful to predatory mites at the recommended rates of application, it is toxic to bees, so hives must be removed from the orchard before spraying. Imidan has a desirably short residual, as it breaks down in sunlight. Plum curculio, codling moth, red-banded leafroller, and apple maggot fly are all listed on the label as target species. Its oral LD50 (lethal dose which has been found to kill 50 percent of a large number of test animals) puts Imidan in the "warning" category. Most organic spray options get a milder "caution" rating, but, to be fair, both Kocide DF (copper hydroxide) and lime sulfur have the higher "danger" label. Phosmet is not a chemical yet listed as having reproductive and endocrine-disrupting effects.[1] Phosmet has been classified as a "tentative" Category C (possible human) carcinogen, due to significantly elevated incidence of liver tumors in mice.[2] It isn't scheduled for a more stringent review by the EPA until 1998 at the earliest.

1. T. Colburn, F. S. Vom Saal, and A. M. Soto, 1993. "Developmental effects of endocrine-disrupting chemicals in wildlife and humans," *Environmental Health Perspectives* 101:378–384.
2. "Guidance for the Reregistration of Pesticide Products Containing Phosmet as the Active Ingredient," CAS Registry Number 732–11–6, 1986, Environmental Protection Agency, Office of Pesticide Programs.

on fruit—yet it has a place when used properly. Delayed-dormant copper sprays are applied mid to late morning in dry, bright weather. Phytotoxicity results when free copper ions in solution penetrate plant tissues, but once dry, copper forms a fungicidal shield that is effective against leaf spot, black rot, powdery mildew, and peach leaf curl. Copper is considered a broad-spectrum biocide with a mode of action, as Dave Gadoury of Cornell University aptly puts, "not unlike having a piano dropped on you." The availability of copper ions inactivates many enzymes and other proteins essential to vital cell membrane function.

Different formulations list different diseases, but invariably all include fire blight. This antibacterial attribute is copper's outstanding virtue. Overwintering blight bacteria on the bark and buds may be killed, and the inoculum produced by cankerous lesions will be suppressed by applications of copper in high concentrations made between bud swell and quarter-inch green tip. Fruit russeting is likely if copper is applied any later than this.

Copper's primary role in controlling fire blight is to provide an inhibitory barrier over all bark and bud surfaces in the orchard. Only then will the bacteria be prevented from colonizing these areas. Coverage from a high-volume spray must be thorough. Blight-susceptible pear varieties are often sprayed out of necessity during bloom with a tribasic copper sulfate (the micronized sulfur helps release the "fixed" copper without damaging tissue as severely). The enhanced coverage of Kocide DF is due to its extremely small particles of copper, which adhere to coarse bark surfaces. Phyton 27 is a patented copper polymer that's *leaf safe* for summer application but still awaiting registration on food crops.

You become part of a "blue, blue world" whenever copper is applied. Use a full-face respirator to avoid a severe headache, as copper can irritate the eyes and the skin. The restricted entry interval mandated after a Kocide (cupric hydroxide) application is forty-eight hours. Persistent use of copper over the years may cause metal toxicity, as elements don't break down. Earthworm populations—a vital ally in the organic orchard—are drastically reduced by moderate concentrations of copper near the surface of the soil, even as little as 260 parts per million of copper sulfate. Elementals, like drugs, are medical tools not to be used indiscriminately.

Bordeaux Mixture

Copper's caustic effects can be reduced when mixed with hydrated lime, a historic combination that makes possible its use after the tree is in full leaf. Even so, Bordeaux mixture can be phytotoxically brutal, to some varieties more than others (Jonathan, Wealthy, and Gravenstein come to mind). Bordeaux mixture was the primary fungicide at the turn of the century, when some fruit russeting was tolerated over no disease control. Today's formulations of sulfur are a safer bet should a particularly wet growing season find your orchard in need of continued fungal protection. Bordeaux's compatibility with 1 percent oil makes it useful for a half-inch green application where smothering pest eggs and early-season disease control are mutual goals. Still, this is best done only in a clean orchard where the use of sulfur can be delayed two weeks (or more) till early bloom. A better use of Bordeaux correlates to copper's bactericidal ability in a bad fire blight year: post-bloom applications to help protect susceptible trees might be worth the russeting tradeoff.

Making your own Bordeaux mixture is fairly straightforward. Copper sulfate (also called blue vitriol) and hydrated lime are each stirred separately into two-and-a-half gallons of warm water as slurry concentrates. The lime slows the release of free copper ions by combining them into soluble copper hydroxide. L. H. Bailey regarded the 5–5–50 formula as standard: the first number refers to pounds of copper sulfate, the second to pounds of hydrated lime, and the last to total gallons of water. A 2–2–50 dilute formulation is less likely to injure leaf tissues. It's critical with this concoction to first mix the vitriol slurry with the other forty-five gallons of water in the spray tank before adding the lime slurry.

Sulfur

Elemental fungicides work primarily as protectants—they need to be in place on the leaf surface before the fungal spores land. Sulfur is an effective fungicide, though its short persistence on the leaf surface makes many applications necessary when disease pressure is high. A combined chemical approach (where a sterol inhibitor is used to eradicate infections up to four days after occurrence and an EBDC protectant provides reliable coverage seven days ahead) looks much simpler in comparison. Yet we've had equivalent scab control in a wet spring with just four applications of liquid sulfur in the primary infection season. The integrated organic approach to apple scab requires a persistent sticker in the sulfur tank mix; thorough understanding of the parameters for deciding when to spray; and, especially, reduced inoculum loading as a result of good sanitation the previous fall.

Sulfur works as a fungicide in one of three ways. Hydrosulfide gas is toxic to the fungal spore on the leaf surface when high temperatures establish its volatile stage. Sulfur acts as an enzyme inhibitor when in solution: the ascospore needs to produce certain enzymes to degrade the waxy layer on the leaf in order to take hold. This is generally the case —sulfur gets dissolved into solution by rain—and why we emphasize its nature as a protectant fungicide. Lastly, a direct hit on a germinating spore by

A tenacious sticker helps adhere sulfur to the leaf surface, even after a heavy downpour.

a grain of sulfur is evidently poisonous to the fungus as well. The suspected eradicant ability of sulfur (as evidenced in lime sulfur) exists, but it is entirely hit or miss unless we can learn a way to transpose the element throughout the waxy cuticle.

The liquid formulations that contain 52 percent sulfur are much easier to work with than the original wettable powders. Thiolux is a micronized dry mix with similar effectiveness. The range of rates each brand recommends varies with the tenacity of the sticker used in the formulation. Adding Nu-Film 17 to a less expensive sulfur blend (available at your local farm supply store) has proven more cost-effective for us than shipping in the well-known THAT Flowable Sulfur. Eight pints of Sulfur 6L per acre is an effective rate during the accelerated phase of ascospore maturity, and this gets cut back to four pints per acre for any secondary applications (if necessary). NuFilm 17 is made from the resins of pine sap and keeps sulfur in place through most wetting periods. Such staying power is the key to being able to make the next sulfur application immediately *after* an infection period has actually occurred rather than every time potential rain threatens. Only the first sulfur spray of the season (delayed till early pink if the potential ascospore density is known to be low) is put on as a traditional protectant before it rains. Good coverage in the top branches is doubly useful: scab lesions up high become a later source of secondary conidia, and sulfur washed to lower leaves in a rain still serves its purpose. The maximum interval between primary applications cannot exceed seven days despite no wetting period occurring: even "tenacious sulfur" degrades in sunlight or loses its mobility in solution once incorporated into the waxy leaf surface. Primary scab season ends approximately fourteen days after pink, ending the need for more sulfur directed at scab, *provided* you've done it all right. Secondary infections throughout the summer months are an entirely different ball game.

HOME ORCHARD SOURCE LISTINGS

Source listings for the commercial orchardist are given in the appendix. You might be willing to stock up with what amounts to a ten-year home supply of spray materials and soil amendments to save a few bucks buying in bulk. However, the following mail-order companies may be better suited to your backyard growing needs.

Planet Natural
P.O. Box 3146
Bozeman, MT 59772
(406) 587–5891

Catalog features the whole gamut of soil amendments, insect traps, garlic spray, liquid sulfur, and beneficial insects.

Gardener's Supply Company
128 Intervale Road
Burlington, VT 05401
1–800–863–1700

Felco pruners, backpack sprayers, AMF red sphere traps, some spray and fertilizer products, and, yes, even hammocks!

ARBICO Environmentals
P.O. Box 4247
Tucson, AZ 85738
(520) 825–9785

Beneficial insects and lots of organic spray options.

DeerBusters
9735A Bethel Road
Frederick, MD 21702
(301) 694–8209

You'll be amazed at all the ways to repel deer.

Sulfur provides moderate control of powdery mildew, brown rot, and cedar apple rust. It also has some insecticidal properties: sulfur dusts are especially toxic to mites of every variety (including the predatory ones), thrips, newly hatched scale insects, and as a stomach poison for some caterpillars. Its phytotoxic effects are greatly increased at temperatures over 85°F and when used within fourteen days of oil. Excessive amounts of sulfur reduce the ability of the leaves to photosynthesize and so can reduce harvest yields. Be particularly mindful of fruit finish on more sensitive yellow apple varieties. High levels of sulfur in the soil may inhibit beneficial fungi that colonize on the roots and help the tree obtain nutrients.

Lime Sulfur

Calcium polysulfide is a mixture of quicklime and sulfur, thus the more common name *lime sulfur*. The lime causes a chemical change that allows the sulfur to actually penetrate the leaf tissue. The sulfur now acts as a short-term eradicant that can kill germinated spores. This kickback ability lasts about six hours after an infection has occurred. Apply after the rain stops but before the leaves dry out. Lime sulfur belongs in our fungal arsenal for those occasions when wetness periods be damned (when life has that tendency to thwart even the best-laid plans).

Such strength means more risk of damaging the plant tissues—avoid using lime sulfur when temperatures will exceed 85°F to avoid serious plant injury. Wait three weeks after a delayed dormant oil application to play this kickback card, though prior to green tip the two are compatible. Besides scab, lime sulfur is effective against brown rot, leaf spot, and powdery mildew. While it kills mites and scales, numerous beneficials also fall victim. Beware that foliar pests will be on the upswing in any orchard relying too heavily on lime sulfur for scab control. Peach trees in full leaf might also be defoliated.

Lime sulfur is toxic to mammals and can cause severe eye damage and skin irritation.

GENTLER SPRAYS

The problem with sprays is that we often create new problems in our attempt to solve an initial pest or disease situation. The chemical approach keeps getting deeper and deeper into a mire of failing complexity. Our natural botanicals and elementals often fall short of the mark as well. L. H. Bailey summed this up a century ago: "We must look to the day when effective materials of a less poisonous nature shall be discovered for [fruit growing] and also when greater reliance than now shall be placed on securing the proper balance in nature." That day has come, dear professor laureate.

Bacillus Thuringiensis (Bt)

The spores of this microbial insecticide attack the digestive tract of lepidopterous caterpillars. Beneficials, bees, and orchardists are not harmed. Moth larvae must eat the *Bacillus thuringiensis* var. *kurstaki* spore, which gets broken down by the gastric juices of the caterpillar's highly alkaline stomach. A protein crystal is then exposed within the Bt spore that neutralizes the enzymes protecting the stomach lining from its own digestive juices. Holes are quickly eaten through the target organism's stomach wall, with a resulting poisoning of the bloodstream. The caterpillar stops feeding within hours of ingesting the Bt and dies within a day or three.

The challenge is getting the larvae to ingest the toxic bacterium. Codling moth larvae need only cross a leaf or two before reaching a fruit in which to tunnel. Egg hatch is ongoing over a four-week period. Cryptic pests like Oriental fruit moth hide inside shoot tips, and leafrollers curl the leaf around themselves to feed as first-generation larvae. Bt breaks down rapidly in sunlight (those ultraviolet rays will get you every time!) leaving gaps in a weekly coverage plan. Feeding attractants like dried milk powder or warmed molasses can help. A half-pint of fish oil (per acre of coverage) helps to adhere the bacterium to the leaf surface and has UV-screening properties.

Dipel DF is a wettable powder formulation registered for use in fruit orchards with 6.4 percent active ingredient. Integrated Fertility Management in Washington has bulk prices on Dipel DF that beat all mail-order sources. Encapsulated forms of the bacterium prolong protection beyond the typical three-day residual; however, there is evidence that the cell cap passes through some insects before dissolving.

Can pests develop an innate resistance to Bt as has happened with numerous insecticides? Such immunity is unlikely for two reasons. The complex killing mechanism of Bt can't readily be turned off by one enzyme change in the offspring of surviving pests, as is the case with the single-step mechanism of many chemicals. Secondly, most small orchards are located close enough to wild refuges, where original gene pools are kept intact and crossbreeding is inevitable. Moderate use of any one toxin limits the chance of resistance developing in the first place.

Garlic

The repellent qualities of garlic have been known to the home gardener for a long time. But only recently have we begun to seriously explore its commercial potential. Garlic's reported mode of action is that of a systemic repellent. The rules of stomatic uptake are fairly simple: the leaf absorbs the extracted garlic juice through its cell walls, where the garlic essence becomes part of the nature of the tree. Repeated applications every ten to fourteen days compound the effect. Insects sense the difference and look elsewhere for their preferred host plant on which to feed and reproduce. It's a good theory, but very much dependent on the consistency of the ex-

tract, the use of a spre[...] tion. Cal Crop's ga[...] achieved what the othe[...] the "recipe-tweaking" o[...] "Keeping garlic juice b[...] tion of consistent proce[...] fonic enzymes that me[...] are reduced in pasteur[...] makers should be able to understand this critical distinction: fermentable cider retains nutrients and enzymes that pasteurized apple juice loses in processing.

The listed attributes of *Allium sativum* are as an insect repellent, feeding depressant, modest fungicide, and micronutrient foliar spray. Additionally, birds have been reported to leave ripening cherries alone after garlic spraying. Garlic extracts can cause some complex metabolic reactions in plants, namely an increase in foliar and fruit Brix (dissolved sugar levels). The degree to which garlic works in any of these ways is directly dependent on its enzymatic life once in solution. New research suggests garlic also acts as a synergist, enhancing the intended effect of other spray materials. Could the inhibitory mechanism of neem on insect larvae reach curculio inside the fruitlet? Or take Bt: what if it could be temporarily absorbed by plant tissues to up the ante on insect feeding? Could sulfur's "direct-hit" toxicity be transposed into existing scab lesions more effectively?

SYNERGY

The American Heritage Dictionary defines *synergism* as "the action of two or more substances to achieve an effect of which each is individually incapable." Sometimes it's reassuring to realize our Creator works in spheres that reasoned science can't yet imagine.

Garlic grown on the farm could prove the ultimate synergist in a homemade spray.

Garlic extracts can be improved or degraded by certain buffering agents and surfactants. The pH of the spray water should not exceed 6.0 to prevent hydrolysis of the garlic enzymes. One pint of soybean oil per acre substantially increases coverage, yet is light enough to avoid compatibility problems with sulfur. Synergistic effects are increased when spray materials are premixed rather than mixed dilute in the spray tank. Garlic needs to be applied before a pest outbreak occurs in order to work from within the plant tissues (but don't apply between pink bud stage and the end of bloom, to avoid confusing the pollinators). All preventive medicine works best when the patient is well—abundant soil life and tree health are paramount in any organic approach to pest management.

Garlic may well be one of those missing links between our good intentions and an economically viable harvest. The years ahead are the testing grounds for each of us to develop application schedules that fit the reality of our locale. Garlic grown on the farm might provide the ultimate synergistic effect if we could "pickle" its many good qualities ourselves in a homemade garlic beer. And should garlic prove a palatable brew? . . . "Honey, me and the boys are just going out for a taste, uh, I mean, to protect the apple trees."

Horticultural Oils

Superior oils are highly refined to be less phytotoxic to fruit trees. A *dormant oil* is applied before bud break on pears to control pear psylla and blister leaf mites. A *delayed dormant oil* is applied after bud break up to half-inch green tip on apples to smother European red mites and scale insects. Delaying this application to tight cluster increases aphid susceptibility. Northern growers need to be aware that oil applied within twenty-four hours of temperatures below 40°F may increase damage to foliage. Both Sunspray and Omni Supreme are safe for summer use, and research is underway in Oregon on the effectiveness of smothering moth eggs and larvae with these lightweight oils. Female codling moths do not like to lay eggs on an oily surface, so border sprays used in conjunction with mating disruption lessen immigrant damage.

You don't need to apply oil to organic fruit trees where foliar pests are kept in check by beneficials. Skipping a dormant oil spray saves having to wait fourteen days or more (to avoid phytotoxic overlap) to safely apply sulfur. But, like any tool, it's there should end-of-season mite populations or a scale incursion the year before have you worried. Young plantings usually get oil regardless: high aphid pressure early in the growing year can take a toll on shoot vitality before beneficials take command. Oil sprays are also useful in the South to stimulate trees into breaking dormancy in years when there is insufficient winter chill. Summer oils, in conjunction with baking soda, have been successfully used to smother powdery mildew spores.

Mating Disruption

Hanging hundreds of pheromone lures in trees to saturate the orchard air with the sexual attractant of the targeted female can't be considered a spray, but it sure seems gentle. Even if it is frustrating for the guys.

Mating disruption is recommended for orchard blocks four acres or larger where pest pressure is moderate, but some growers report positive results on as little as one acre. Ideally, fruit trees are well isolated from outside sources of impregnated females and air saturation of pheromone isn't diffused by constant wind. Additional lures can be tied outside small blocks (cost per acre would be higher) or border sprays applied, if deemed necessary. Mating disruption is currently available for codling moth, oriental fruit moth, and peach twig borer, with research underway for various leafrollers and tufted apple bud moth. Cost per acre continues to drop as this treatment becomes more widely adapted. Two treatments may be required to protect against second- and third-generation damage, or you can rely on Bt sprays if there is monitored resurgence. A bigger conundrum with a mating disruption strategy lies in a mixed-pest situation. Lesser appleworm, for instance, is active at the same time as codling moth here in Lost Nation. Their pheromone isomers are not the same, thus Isomate-C will not work with the lesser species. Yet ryania and/or Bt applications based on degree-day countdowns give adequate control of both.

Insecticidal Soaps

The potassium salts of naturally occurring fatty acids found in soap dehydrate soft-bodied insects. It's tempting to reach for the soap when a massive aphid infestation suddenly appears in a nonbearing block, but be wary of phytotoxicity. The ladybugs and other beneficials are usually just a week away from getting the situation in hand. Insecticidal soaps rapidly degrade in the soil (having a half-life of less than one day). The M-Pede formulation desiccates the fungal spores of powdery mildew, giving it both fungicidal and insecticidal properties.

Biodynamic Contributions

Horsetail (*Equisetum arvense*) is said to have "a regulatory function of manifestations of the watery element." In other words, a tea made from the plant and applied as a homeopathic dilution acts as a preventative fungicide. Biodynamic practitioners use silica-rich horsetail much as others use sulfur in scab season. Nettle tea is often rhythmically stirred with equisetum for control of summer diseases. A dual canopy/ground spray after harvest is thought to inhibit spore development the following spring.

Tree Paste is a mixture of fine bentonite clay, fresh cow manure, and occasionally sand, mucked in water to equal proportion. It is said to enliven the cambium layer, heal pruning wounds, and smother eggs and insect pupae within bark crevices (much like dormant oil). The paste is brushed on the trunk up to the lower limbs, either following harvest or in spring before bud break. Essentially, it's a mud pack, intended to rejuvenate the bark tissues by applying the healing forces of earth.

Meanwhile Back on the Microbial Front

Other bacteria, fungi, and viruses have been discovered since Bt was first found in diseased flour moths in the German town of Thuringia in 1911. The possibilities of orchard use are suggested here.

Beauveria bassiana has long been recognized as a biological control of many insect pests that spend part of their life cycle in the soil. Troy Biosciences has come out with a spray formulation of this fungus called Naturalis. These fungal spores attach themselves to the insect's covering and then secrete enzymes which dissolve the skin to allow hyphae (kind of like fungal roots) to enter the body of the pest. Robbed of moisture and nutrients, the insect dies. All life stages of the insect are vulnerable, and, unlike Bt, this fungus works by contact alone. Many insects are listed on the label, including weevils (think about curculio possibilities now), which makes for legitimate broad spectrum concerns. Naturalis claims a three- to seven-day residual period on the leaf surface provided fungicides are currently not in use. A soil application offers the potential of naturalizing.

Codling Moth Granulosis Virus was finally approved for nationwide use in 1996 after decades of research work. This baculovirus encapsulates itself until it is eaten by the codling moth larva. Applications are necessary every seven days beginning at first-generation egg hatch until oviposition ceases. Phillip Unterschuetz at Integrated Fertility Management reports granulosis virus is slower to act than ryania—thus expect more entry sting damage—but still kills the majority of such piercing larvae (that would otherwise come again in the next generational wave).

Phytophthora crown rot is a disease experienced by susceptible rootstocks planted in poorly drained soil. If your site is marginal in a wet year, you might want to consider inoculating your trees' root systems with *Streptomyces lydicus*. This soil organism covers the roots with protective mycelia that live in a symbiotic relationship with the tree. Soil diseases are thus outcompeted for living space on the roots. Cost-wise, however, picking a well-drained orchard site in the first place is a far superior strategy.

SPRAY EQUIPMENT FOR THE SMALL COMMERCIAL ORCHARD

I've been given this striking image of my grandparents in their market orchard by my aunts. Pop-Pop has Mom-Mom on the cart hand-pressurizing the barrel sprayer while he directs a hoseline of arsenate spray into the treetops. Neither wears protective clothing or a respirator. It took two working in tandem to drench the trees and move the cart about.

Modern spray equipment has come a long way since the 1920s. One person can cover many more trees in a session and much more thoroughly than my grandparents ever dreamed. The first decision for a small-scale orchardist moving up from a backpack sprayer is whether to invest in an airblast sprayer or opt for the more directed wand. Guy Ames prefers a hand-held, hydraulic spray gun over a mist blower rig in his three acres of Arkansas orchard, but points out that timely coverage for many more acres might necessitate going high-tech. Cost is the major consideration. The smaller airblast units requiring a tractor with sufficient horsepower at the PTO to operate (in the 20 to 35 hp range) start at about $3,500. The SOLO independently powered mist blower costs about the same and is pulled by either an ATV or garden tractor. Lightweight pulling capacity like this limits tank volume to about fifty gallons. A hydraulic sprayer of this capacity, motorized and on trailer wheels, can be purchased for $1,200 and up, but if you want a much larger tank, a tractor with a power take-off is required. Self-made sprayers save money only if you're innovative about reclaiming some of the parts: Don MacLean in Ancram, New York turned a motorized leaf vacuum into an eight-nozzle fan sprayer.

Recommended dilute rates are based on applying a sufficient volume of spray water to wet all foliage surfaces to the point of runoff. Label rates often are given per hundred gallons of water. Airblast concentrations can be adjusted to get the same amount of material on the trees (as if dilute), but with less water. Thus a 6x concentration uses just fifty gallons of water where three hundred

DAVID CRAXTON

Our Lost Nation hydraulic spray rig, applicator included, provides thorough coverage.

might once have been felt necessary. Low-volume mist blowers can apply as little as fifteen gallons of spray to the acre (makes for less tank refilling) on the theory that fine electrostatically-charged particles cling to the leaf. Whatever the concentration, airblast works best when the wind is perfectly still so that spray doesn't drift; sunrise is often dependably calm. Spraying with a hydraulic rig is much simpler, particularly when rates are figured on a per acre basis. I find fifty to seventy-five gallons of spray sufficient to cover an acre of semidwarf trees with my hand-held spray gun. This method can be more precise in everyday orchard conditions when your aim counts for more than total fog immersion. The debate is on which system gets better coverage. Directing a spray gun can tire out your arms by the end of a session, but it is easier to skip varieties in an eclectic planting that don't need a

particular spray. And beat the wind when timing is indeed everything.

Sprayer manuals provide the scoop on calibrating airblast models. Driving at a set speed along the tree row at a specified pump pressure should result in precise coverage at the chosen rate of application (whether concentrate or dilute) if calibration is done correctly. The size of the nozzle affects outflow as well. Worn nozzles end up overapplying spray, which is why large orchard operations replace nozzles yearly as a matter of course. Rates are adjusted for *tree row volume*, which accounts for row spacing and larger trees needing more coverage than dwarfing stock. Hand spraying is calibrated on your own intuitive sense of coverage at the given rate per acre.

Timely spraying depends on good equipment maintenance. All the focus on scab infection periods becomes useless if your sprayer is down when

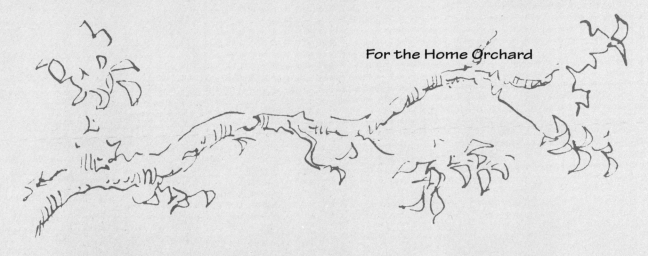

THE BACKPACK SPRAYER

The first time I used a backpack sprayer its value showed immediately. No longer did I have to set the sprayer tank down to work the pump. I could carry more spray per tank, up to five gallons. The wand extension let me reach the top of all but the tallest trees. The hip-high pump handle worked with efficient ease. Choice of a flat fan nozzle or an adjustable brass nozzle for mist spraying allowed a quick switch from row-crop applications to the orchard.

Backpack sprayers come with either a piston pump or a diaphragm pump. Both compress air in a pressure chamber, which allows irregular pump action to result in a steady stream of spray. The piston-type pump can generate a higher pressure than the diaphragm type. Greater pressure results in smaller-sized droplets of spray and thus more coverage per gallon. Abrasive materials like ground botanicals and copper powders shorten the working life of a piston, but are less hard on a diaphragm pump. Still, in the days when I used rotenone on occasion, the sediment in the spray solution often proved too great a weight atop the diaphragm to allow pumping action. A home orchardist using Dipel, liquid seaweed, and garlic extracts on disease-resistant trees (thus obviating the need for sulfur applications) may find a piston-pump sprayer enough for ten or so trees. A quality backpack sprayer will run you on the order of a hundred dollars, with accessories adding to the final price tag. The Ben Meadows catalog offers the SOLO sprayers I've enjoyed using, backed with a full replacement parts listing. Guy Ames is big on the Cooper Pegler model, which he offers through his Ames Nursery catalog.

One quick comment about wand extensions. SOLO offers a sixty-inch brass wand retailing at $17.50. One winter the tiniest bit of wetness accumulated near my wand's tip and froze, splitting the brass. The plastic fittings are epoxied onto the brass, so I was out a wand. The next spring I downgraded to the twenty-inch plastic wand extension for $7.50. I found the floppiness of the plastic option useful, as the wand waved back and forth on its own under pressure. The rigid brass required more wrist action on my part for similar coverage.

Gasoline-powered backpack sprayers provide greater power — and thus a finer mist — without any manual pumping action. Strap one of these onto your back with the motor running and you'll feel prepared to lift off to the moon. There is more of a sense of urgency to get the spray applied when you move about within the drone of a muffled engine. The SOLO Model 422 does get the spray up into the top branches of a standard tree, which is a consideration if your home orchard consists of mostly big trees. Better agitation in the tank prevents the clogging factor from heavy sediment, but this really isn't a problem with most organic spray materials. This move into the Industrial Age will cost you close to $500, an investment maybe only worthwhile if you have an acre of fruit trees. Positioning five-gallon buckets of spray solution throughout the orchard before you begin spraying helps get the job done quicker. A full sprayer weighs in at a hefty sixty pounds, so fill the tank according to your back's capacity.

you need to use it. Stocking critical parts can make all the difference on "one of those days." Roller and piston-type pumps delivering abrasive elemental fungicides should have their seals replaced annually. A shot of Citra-Solv in the rinse water after a spray session is an effective tank cleaner. A spray gun adds one final advantage: you can power-wash the sulfur off your tractor.

PROTECTING THE BODY AS WELL AS THE SOUL

Orchardists are the ones on the front lines of exposure. Food-safety activists often miss this point: those most at risk are the growers putting on the spray materials so consumers can have a fruit finish without flaw. We spray to make a living. And then just barely.

Any spraying has some element of risk, be it from spray inhalation, skin absorption, eye irritation, or prolonged exposure in the orchard. I mean, you don't normally hang out in a cloud of copper or Bt or even liquid kelp. A snug-fitting respirator and proper clothing are a must. It doesn't matter that you're not spraying chemicals or even harsh botanicals. The Gempler's catalog offers all the gear: rubber boots, rain jackets and pants, neoprene gloves, goggles, respirators, and eyewash. It's worth spending extra bucks for a full-face respirator with an internal nose cup (to reduce lens fogging). Lastly, there's that all-important baseball cap with its exposed bill to wear out to dinner after you've finished your spraying chores.

Common sense applies to all contact with spray materials. Be familiar with warnings given on each product label. The restricted-entry interval (REI) is the period immediately after a spray application during which entry back into the orchard is limited to those wearing appropriate gear. Generally, the REI is twelve hours for a Caution label, twenty-four hours for a Warning label, and forty-eight hours for a Danger label. Low-risk materials have a four-hour REI. Wear your respirator to measure out wettable powders—fine dust permeates even the stillest air. Spills need to be cleaned up immediately. Keep all products in their original containers and safely locked away.

I can't imagine dealing with the concerns that come with handling and applying synthetic chemical toxins. What I'm doing in the orchard is relatively safe for me. And the birds. And the beneficials. And my little daughter. I like that a lot.

RECORD KEEPING

You need to track both rates and dates of application of all spray materials, if only to compile a year-end use report with your state's agriculture department. Being a *certified* organic farm entails a slew of additional record-keeping requirements: soil test results, fertilization history, pest-control actions, sources of materials used and copies of all labels, and harvest totals. Similarly, filing a business tax return means a modicum of bookkeeping to categorize expenses, tally sales receipts, and balance the checkbook. If you see all this as so much drudgery, you're missing out on a potent decision-making tool.

Lessons learned in the orchard from year to year are made plain by comparing the results of successive growing seasons. Field notes jotted down in an orchard journal can be just as valuable as empirical data, if not more so. Take my observation from early June one year: "Dipel spray with sulfur at pink seems to have done its job in that visible leaf damage is rarely accompanied by the presence of the leafroller itself." Experience answers my annual question about the compatibility of these materials. I couldn't make decisions about scab infection probability without tracking temperature and wetting periods. Jotting down decision variables in the moment at hand about whether to spray sulfur or

THE FQPA RISK CUP

The Food Quality Protection Act of 1996 revises the standards pesticides must meet to be approved for use by the Environmental Protection Agency (EPA). Previously, each pesticide was evaluated in its own right solely for dietary exposure, whereas now classes of chemicals sharing a common mechanism of toxicity will be judged by aggregate exposure encountered throughout our environment. The acceptable amount of exposure for each chemical grouping over a seventy-year lifespan has been characterized as filling a *risk cup.* I'll be the first to say a more holistic approach to judging these matters is for the good. Unfortunately, like anything human, the evaluation process is not straightforward in prioritizing which pesticide uses will remain, placing all the good IPM work in orchards these past twenty years in jeopardy.

American Fruit Grower magazine estimates current organophosphate and carbamate use on apples alone will fill their respective FQPA risk cups. Enter in the humble flea on your dog Fido and those nasty bugs on the suburban rose bed. Chemical flea collars for pets and home garden "solutions" often feature the same class of chemicals now selectively used for specific orchard pests. Guess which uses make more profit for the chemical companies? Guess which uses will be first in the risk cup?

Orchardists who have been pushing the margins of IPM toward organic practice will have three choices if organophosphate use (including Imidan) on tree fruits is eliminated by August 1999. One, revert back to harsher chemicals — categorized by yet another risk cup — whose broad-spectrum effects will knock beneficial insects on their existential ass. This strategy will necessitate more chemical use to combat pests no longer held in check by beneficials. Two, call it quits. Or three, embrace the organic approach outlined in this book. That last alternative isn't going to work until such time as local markets support local agriculture. And as the bureaucrats in Washington see it, people can always get fruit from the West Coast or Argentina or even China for that matter. Don't you just love global economic ethics?

Under FQPA, the risk cup can include an additional safety factor for children and infants, leaving even less room for pesticides and uses. The Gerber Products Company is extremely sensitive about pesticide residues on their baby foods, and accordingly has begun to give the use of organophosphates "a great deal of scrutiny," according to Nicholas Hether, manager of biochemical research, food purity, and regulatory sciences at Gerber.

"As difficult as this may be for growers, I think it provides a real opportunity," says Charlie Edson, Michigan State University's IPM coordinator. "The opportunity is to look at the broader production system, think in integrated terms and think about alternatives. If the EPA gives us enough time in a suitable transition period, then perhaps some alternatives can be worked out where now there are none."

not—and then going back to review those thoughts in the light of good scab control—can disclose the dropping of a doubtful application as prudent the

following year. Try recording apple maggot fly counts from border traps one year on a schematic of your orchard to reveal the "hot spots" where this migrant enters. Such maps (showing each tree in the block) give occasion to walk through the orchard at the height of summer to rate fruit set, vigor, and observations on a tree-by-tree basis. Fruit damage assessments at harvest are proof positive of how your approach in a given year fared.

Farming for a living is a business as well as a passion. Financial records are just as necessary as horticultural ones to plot a viable course. Each winter we draw up a budget for the orchard year ahead that takes into account soil fertility, critiques changes in pest-management strategy, and makes clear the fiscal reality that *you can't have everything*. It's an occasion to decide upon application rates, look for bulk buys, and inventory stock on hand. Cash flow for new plantings and equipment purchases fits in here as well. We've kept a labor log in the past to track the hours put into each task: organic orcharding is labor-intensive, yet there is a point of diminishing returns for the effort expended that any sound business needs to evaluate. Hours spent cleaning hundreds of unbaited maggot fly traps justifies the purchase of a mere couple dozen Ladd traps to replace the wooden originals. The bottom line for a commercial orchard is how input costs (including labor) tally up on a per bushel basis.

Good records offer the hindsight and the foresight needed to plan a fruitful future.

*Apples in their ripening are much like wine, at first too acid,
and when overkept, tired and tasteless. There is, of course,
a happy moment of perfection when flavor, acid,
and sweetness are at their most grateful balance.*

—E. A. BUNYARD, *The Gardener's Companion* (1950)

CHAPTER 8

Reaping the Harvest

Fall would be nowhere near as glorious without the traditional ritual of bringing in the apple harvest. The rhythm of bushel upon bushel can get downright overwhelming in a bumper crop year. I try to remember two things in particular while picking. One, to thank the tree for the gift of its fruit. And two, to look up every once in awhile at the mountains and sky to take in the beautiful day. Yet by season's end, I find myself echoing Robert Frost's sentiments in his famous poem, "After Apple-Picking":

> For I have had too much
> Of apple-picking: I am overtired
> Of the great harvest I myself desired.

WHEN TO PICK

Tree fruits approaching ripeness go through a period of rapid cell expansion, growing daily by as much as 1 percent. The base skin color of an apple gradually changes from green to light green to yellow; the flesh inside turns from greenish to creamy white. Stone fruits will soften enough to give ever so slightly under pressure from the thumb. The stem of a ripe apple will break easily and cleanly when its calyx end is tipped up towards the spur from which it hangs. Most telling, ripe fruit tastes good.

Some apple varieties ripen unevenly over several weeks. Spot-picking the best-colored fruit on the outside canopy of the tree allows sunlight to enter and color the inner apples for picking a week later. High-value cultivars are worth picking three or even four times to maximize color and size. Fruit picked too early is more subject to shriveling, scald, bitter pit, and brown core. Overmature apples quickly soften and show internal breakdown. Pressure testing for firmness is common in large orchards where prolonged storage quality is more critical than flavor: fruit firmness, however, is not an early gauge of maturity.

Apples for storage and some pear varieties should be picked when they become physiologically mature. Seeds have fully developed at this point, though the flesh is not yet ripe. Pome seeds will be fully enlarged and brown-black in color when ready. European pears left to ripen on the tree become gritty instead and often rot from within. Apples continue to ripen in storage—quality lasts longer when picked a week or two before maximum ripeness—but never taste quite as good as those that ripen on the tree. Winter keepers that get picked before a hearty November freeze eventually reach their peak flavor a month or more down the storage road. Fruit frozen on the tree needs to be allowed to thaw before picking to prevent bruising. Lethal damage occurs at 22°F, but even moderate freezing to the core causes faster deterioration in storage. Stone fruits only go downhill once picked, emphasizing once again why locally grown is the way to go.

Pre-harvest drop gets to be a concern in vast blocks of Gravenstein or McIntosh where even a professional picking crew can "only" muster two thousand bushels of fruit a day. A small orchard with mixed varieties can generally stay on top of bringing in the harvest. Organic fertility begets a denser stem that helps hold the fruit on the tree longer. A lack of foliar pests improves tree vigor, making it better able to clench on to the fruit. Abbot Labs has introduced a natural plant-growth regulator that inhibits the production of ethylene, the gaseous plant hormone that induces fruit maturation and fruit drop. ReTain is expected to be considered acceptable for use in an organic system.

An intuitive sense of fruit set can tell an orchardist what to expect for a harvest yield. Value-added operations with crop budgets (see "Cider Economics" in chapter 9) use this estimate to seek out more profitable avenues for marketing their apples. Dessert-quality fruit is certainly the foremost goal, but what about the rest of the organic crop? A straightforward method of estimating the apple harvest is based on knowing the typical yield of a mature tree in your orchard. Many variables enter in here—rootstock, tree spacing, pruning system, soil fertility, good fruit sizing weather—so *average crop per tree* is best based on actual production records. Our mature Cortlands on M7 rootstock reliably produce four to five bushels of apples per tree. A tree with incredible set in a good sizing year ups this average another bushel. I walk down the tree rows in August and *sense* the crop on each tree: "This is a two-bushel tree, those next four look full, great set on the six Macouns, no fruit on the Pound Sweet. . . ." Each row has its tally, which, added all together, gives us a reasonable estimate of our apple crop. Multiplying this total by last year's combined packout percentage indicates how many bushels of select, processing, and cider-grade fruit to expect.

The return of the kids to school in early September also marks the time when we get our "report cards" as orchardists. Or at least when data needs to

THE SCIENCE OF APPLE COLOR

The shorter days of late summer initiate a growth of cells at the stem where the ripe apple will eventually sever. This *abscission layer* stops production of green chlorophyll in the fruit (thus unmasking yellow pigments already present) and restricts sugars from flowing down to the roots. Cool nights in autumn cause even more sugars to be trapped. Direct sunshine by day promotes the synthesis of these sugars into anthocyanins, which depending on the variety of apple can be red, purple, or maroon. A mild to moderate drought adds to the brilliance of these red hues.

Dr. Alan Eaton, UNH Extension Entomologist, making a pre-harvest assessment on fruit quality at Lost Nation Orchard.

be collected for those invaluable fruit damage assessments (the numbers can be tabulated after the last apple gets picked). These tell you, more or less, what took place in the orchard over the spring and summer as regards insect and disease dynamics under your chosen management approach. Alan Eaton, our Cooperative Extension entomologist in New Hampshire, does this for orchardists throughout the state to record pest patterns from year to year. Ten apples are examined on fifty trees randomly selected throughout the orchard. Different cultivars are included; fruit location in the tree is varied. Each type of injury gets noted: scab, calyx end rot, flyspeck, tarnished plant bug, and on through to hail, branch rubbing, and russeting

from spray. Fruit size, color, and shape are not taken into account. Damage percentages in each category either affirm successful strategies or point out dire concerns. Fruit lost to European apple sawfly or curculio back in June don't get accounted for, however. It's interesting to compare Lost Nation percentages to those of conventional and IPM orchards (identified by code number only on the final ratings chart). We mostly "lose" — organics is nowhere near as controlling as a chemical approach — but our numbers are tolerable taken in context. Perspective can make all the difference in the world.

HARVEST EQUIPMENT

You'll need a harvest bucket, a ladder, and bushel boxes or bins to pick your fruit.

A picking bucket consists of a foam-lined metal frame with a rope-release canvas bottom, which unhooks so the apples can gently slide into the bushel box. Shoulder straps free both hands for apple picking. The smaller-size buckets (one-half, three-quarter, and full bushel are the options) don't allow you to bring as much fruit away from the tree at one time, but then having a fifty-pound weight around your torso when coming down a picking ladder may not be convenient either. Buckets are more effective than sacks at protecting picked fruit from bruising against a tree limb or ladder. A compartmentalized bucket, designed to keep select and cider apples sorted as they get picked, would aid organic growers immensely.

Traditionally, apple ladders are tapered such that the side rails meet at the top, so they can be placed in the crotches of tree limbs. A tripod stepladder works best in younger trees that have been grafted on semidwarf rootstock. A wide base gives more stability on uneven ground, and the tripod leg is swung between and over branches to reach all sides of the tree: keep ladder access somewhat in mind when pruning. Straight aluminum or wooden

This Baldwin tripod ladder is as sturdy as ladders come.

Bushel boxes filled with organic Cortland apples.

ladders cost $8 to $12 per foot of height; shorter tripods cost $12 to $16 per foot of height. The handcrafted wooden orchard ladders from Baldwin Apple Ladders in Maine have a sturdy feel I prefer over cold metal. Particularly in those spots in the orchard where electrical wires loom overhead.

Every picker has a ladder story. From toppling a tripod on a slope to a weathered rung snapping underfoot. Mine illustrates a fundamental precept about gaining weight. Our crew was picking Macs in standard trees. Rain had been falling all morning when I came to a loaded branch towering above empty space. The tip of my eighteen-foot ladder reached the branch crotch with a foot to spare. Up I went and began to pick. Three dynamics were happening: the apples in my bucket increased the

weight on the ladder, the tree limb was rising as it became unladen, and the bottom rails of the ladder were sinking into wet turf. Suddenly I was catapulted into the air to land facing the sky with apples crashing into my chest. Years later, I still watch the point of my ladder in a big tree.

Bushel boxes have their advantages and drawbacks in a small commercial orchard. Certainly fifteen- or twenty-bushel bins are easier to fill and move with equipment back to the packing shed. Each bushel box in the orchard needs to be lifted and carried to a truck or trailer to be hauled away. More handwork is involved in topping off each box so it's full but not overly so. Yet the bushel box is human scale: cider apples can be dumped by hand into the grinder, select fruit can be carried into the

The lift-and-twist picking motion.

walk-in cooler or lifted onto a table for sorting. Handling systems at the packing shed determine which container you get to pick into out in the orchard. Lowboy trailers allow bushel boxes or bins to be filled *on wheels*—just counterbalance the weight as you pick—without the need for immediate mechanical or hand lifting.

THE APPLE PICKER'S REEL

Fruit are picked with the slightest lift-and-twist motion. Reach for the apple so it rests in the curve of your palm. Lift its weight slightly upward and turn your wrist so the stem pivots off the branch. If the fruit hangs onto the branch, use your thumb as a fulcrum point against a woody stem. A straight-away pull often strips off next year's budwood contained in the fruiting spur or rips the stem out of the fruit. Such stem pulls are to be avoided because open wounds cause the fruit to spoil sooner.

Skin punctures result from rough handling in the branches and from the stems of colliding fruit in the picking bucket.

Tender fruit are easily bruised at any point in picking. Fingertip grips leave a recognizable series of marks, as does squeezing fruit against each other in one hand. Apples should be placed carefully into the picking bucket and kept level. Gently release the fruit through the bottom of the picking bucket into the bushel boxes or bins (or onto a blanket if you're opting to finish-grade an odd variety in the orchard). Bend low into the downhill side of a bin to prevent rolling bruises. Apples picked into bins need to be somewhat leveled as you fill to avoid toppling bruises. Tree fruit that gets strip-picked often show a higher percentage of bruises and skin punctures than when spot-picked for color and size.

Bottom branches get picked before treetops. An apple or two inevitably falls—often the most beautiful ones—no matter how slowly and carefully you work. Stripping the bottoms on one side of the tree opens up a ladder placement. Start topwork empty to expend less energy climbing and to allow a partial bucket to get topped off (with low fruit) on the way to the bin. Try to reach as many apples as you can from the ground without having to sacrifice one of your picking hands to hold down a laden branch. *Two hands picking* is the jingle of a fast picker. The nuances are equally important: holding two or three apples "lightly" in each hand; keeping the picking motion inbound (reach out for those first apples); picking as you climb the ladder. A tight row of trees can be worked from either side of the aisle as separate assignments. Picking is a dance, with the movement going round the tree, up and down, round the tree, up and down. Stepping off the ladder onto a stout limb can be effective in clearing a treetop, provided a fully weighted bag doesn't prevent your return. L. H. Bailey always said "nothing answers the purpose so well as a strong, nimble boy who is not afraid to climb."

An organic crop with variable packout should be sorted (to some extent) in the orchard. Handling a cider apple in between picking it and finally dumping it into the grinder hopper doesn't help the cause. Strip-picking a tree into decent and cider categories is an organic form of spot-picking with the parameters reversed: the small and the ugly are sought first over the fruit with good color and size. Cue in primarily to smallness as you begin to pick a tree. Fruit low to the ground and deep within the canopy usually qualify for cider grade as well. Leaving the better fruit till last furthers the opportunity to fine-tune your culling for insect damage. The

apples higher up in the tree tend to have less disease damage, so once up the ladder, you can assume decent fruit the rule and wait to pull any cider apples glimpsed rolling into the box. Sorting fruit while picking slows you down, but handling every apple again in the packing shed is even more time-frustrating.

I got to experience "civilized picking" Down Under. My letter addressed to *Any Orchard in New Zealand* after my first itinerant Vermont apple season brought back an invitation from a farm family there. Tucker Orchard in Motueka overlooks tropical Tasman Bay and the snow-capped mountains of South Island. Fruit picking in the Southern Hemisphere begins in early February and lasts into April: I had no qualms leaving winter behind to go pick Cox's Orange, Sturmer Pippin, and Granny Smith apples. Day one started with an introduction to my picking partner (much more sociable to pick together, don't you think?), who turned out to be a plucky Australian girl named Jack. (Or Vicki, if you wanted to be formal about it.) Three times a day one of the Tucker family would come round the orchard on a motor scooter to call the crew together for a billy of tea. Sometimes there were even freshly baked scones. And all the while I was getting paid to experience this absolutely delightful adventure.

HIRING HELP

Farm families with children and partnerships have an obvious advantage when it comes time to bring in the harvest. There never can be enough willing

"A spirit of loyalty and sympathy among workers should be promoted by all available means.... In one case, where a large small-fruit business was carried on, and girls and boys were chiefly employed for picking, the pickers reported at the office at the stated time, formed into a line and marched to the field to the music of a drum and fife. This is mentioned as one means of fostering the loyal spirit." E. S. Goff, *Lessons in Commercial Fruit Growing* (1902)

hands when apples need picking, grading, and processing. Hiring good help can be difficult at best, especially if your personal wage falls below what's reasonably expected to be paid out. As well, the bureaucracy mandated on an employee/employer relationship can be downright oppressive.

A small farm operation rarely can offer a full-time position. Farmers often depend on people with daytime flexibility to put in limited hours: the parent with kids in school, the kids in school, and odd-jobbers happy with seasonal work. A motivated twelve-year-old (or thereabouts) can be trained over the course of several years before the lures of adolescence call them off the farm. Our "Lost Nation kids" start by labeling jugs and boxing cider apples, bottling cider, and eventually are entrusted to greet customers and give change. Apprentices seek out organic homesteads in exchange for learning about farming and a place to stay, usually receiving a living stipend of $25 to $75 a week. These arrangements thrive on clearly stated expectations, patience, shared humor, and a willingness to learn from each other. Not all farmers are good teachers

nor are all apprentices up for the tasks at hand. Where it works, though, the "good life" finds mutual inspiration.

Varietal planning comes into play at harvest time. Orchardists with substantial blocks of a cultivar prone to drop need help in a big way. Arrangements with a larger grower to share a day crew are fairly common, but availability won't necessarily fit your ideal schedule. Lining up an "independent contractor" to pick on a spot basis might better fit the needs of a small operation. Skilled local pickers aren't easy to find, however. Grading fruit while picking complicates matters. I strip off cider apples ahead of my one-man crew the days we pick Cortlands. Pay in the Northeast has held steady at eighty cents a bushel for a decade. An hourly wage of $6.50 is more appropriate when pickers are also asked to help bring the apples in from the orchard, clean up drops, and repair broken boxes. Such hourly motivation takes the rush out of the piecework-based approach—resulting in less bruised fruit—but the day's output will be less too. Another small farm alternative is to cut a

THE CIDER BARTER DEAL

Swapping apples and cider with farm volunteers offers two advantages: responsible adults quickly learn the nuances of the job at hand; and help from all quarters builds a cooperative community. The Lost Nation rate for an hour of barter time is choice of a gallon of cider or a quarter-peck of organic apples. Any given season finds twenty or so folks offering to pitch in at various tasks. People have labeled caselots of products, joined us in "peeling bees" on apple-butter processing days, dished out apple crisp at our festival, and helped bring in the crop on those frantic evenings when a deep freeze is predicted. Two friends go well beyond the call of duty: Joe serenades foliage crowds with his guitar every Sunday when not helping to press cider, and Calvin comes by so often we're inclined to believe we've found that valued third partner.

Joe regularly serenades the cider mill crowds on Sunday afternoons.

EDITH TUCKER

harvest deal with your buddies: you help bale hay in June, they return the favor come apple-picking time.

We haven't let our customers pick fruit, thinking they wouldn't understand the minor blemishes inherent in an organic orchard. But growers who have pick-your-own blocks report this isn't the case: people will pick anything, including cider apples, to fill their bag. The drawbacks—lots of fallen fruit, next year's spur being yanked off with the stem, and increased liability exposure—need to be weighed against any niche-marketing edge to be gained. It's prudent to keep the public off ladders by offering picking poles instead. Inevitably, should you decide not to allow pick-your-own, families will arrive with every intention of picking. When the little ones look up at you with disappointment in their eyes, tell them, "But you know what? I was just going out to get me a good apple to eat . . . wanna come along and get one for yourselves?" Taking time to chat with customers and explain how fruit gets grown organically is a big part of what brings people back to your farm.

WINDFALLS AND FAT SHEEP

Begin gathering dropped apples four weeks before harvest—the first windfalls are the wormy ones—and feed them to livestock. Finding fallen fruit is easier if you mow or scythe the grass under the trees ahead of time. Weekly drop duty prevents apple maggot flies from reaching the soil to pupate. The final "get-down-on-your-hands-and-knees search" takes place the day of the harvest before the trees get picked. Only fruit subsequently knocked off the trees in picking (lying for only a few short moments on the soft grass beneath) are considered "not drops" and still worthy of the cider bin.

Old-time cidermakers insisted on pressing sound, ripe apples only. It was said that an apple that reached the ground imparted an earthy flavor to the cider. Our standards of what constitutes an acceptable cider apple have undergone quite a decline since the last century. J. M. Trowbridge stated this position emphatically in *The Cider Maker's Handbook* in 1903: "Whoever thinks that any apple is good enough for cider had better not engage in the business." Bruised drops essentially make a bruised cider. Those of us wanting to reintroduce quality back into cider should begin by letting the sheep have their proper share.

Large operations without the option of making cider from drops will no doubt deem the gathering of plentiful windfalls a nonrecoverable expense. This in turn will defeat the IPM goal of limiting in-orchard populations of apple maggot flies and lepidopterous pests. Border-trapping then becomes significantly less effective, and growers will resume making summertime organophosphate sprays . . . interesting, isn't it, to see the connections between cheap cider, E. coli worries, and the chemical rationale of industrial agriculture?

FROM ORCHARD TO PACKING SHED

Getting the field heat out of the fruit as soon as possible bolsters the apple's keeping ability. Boxes of picked fruit need to be kept out of the direct sun until brought to the packing shed. Hot weather during harvest increases susceptibility to storage scald. Ideally, fruit should be cooled to 32°F within twenty-four to thirty-six hours after harvest. Leaving the afternoon's picking effort on the shady side of the row to cool down overnight can reduce peak demand on a refrigeration system.

The three-point hitch on a tractor can be rigged with prongs for lifting bins. Often bins are loaded onto a flatbed truck for a long haul to the packing shed. A loaded tractor moves slowly, and, even with a front fork, can only move two bins. This may be perfectly suitable for a small operation with the trees in sight of harvest headquarters. A lowboy trailer (hydraulic bin trailers are available that ease unloading) can be pulled out of the orchard with a pickup truck. A full bed pickup can hold two fifteen-bushel bins or forty bushel boxes stacked two layers high. We often load a riding mower trailer with up to ten boxes of apples when spot-picking odd varieties. If the turnaround at the end of the row isn't maneuverable, or a breakdown "makes your day," you can always resort to the garden cart. Bins of cider apples—everybody runs out of bushel boxes at the peak of harvest—can be lifted with chains hooked to the front-end bucket of a tractor (with a rear counterweight) to later be dumped into boxes on a ramp for moving into the mill.

This hefting of the apples to the sorting table and cider press is the crux of whether bins can be used instead of bushel boxes. A bin dumping system—complete with a water pool to float the apples—starts off the packing line in large operations. Next comes the brusher washer, followed by sizing screens that direct fruit accordingly to either the cider chute or to actual people who grade out culls. Larger apples end up boxed; utility-size fruit often get bagged. None of this is affordable for a small orchard, of course.

Grading apples one by one is a much slower task and, some might argue, is *asking for a bruising*. Lifting and turning an apple to examine all its sides certainly isn't as protected as watching for culls on a roller belt. Sorting direct out of the bin into loose-pack boxes is hard on the back, even when a top side can be removed as the bin gets emptied. Sorting out of a bushel box into other bushel boxes on a tabletop can be more comfortable, but never quick. Home-built packing lines, made with wood and personal ingenuity, can be patterned after the ten thousand dollar and up "Cadillac" models. Even a loose-pack operation, though, would benefit from having apples floated out of the bushel box and shunted across a rubber sizing belt onto a

Lost Nation cider apples get hand-boxed from the bin to "sweat" a few weeks in the mill. Apples designated for immediate pressing are boxed much quicker by tilting the full bin onto a wooden ramp.

padded table for visual inspection. Tew Manufacturing offers replacement parts for its line of packaging machinery that might help in crafting a small farm system. Minimum acceptable apple diameter is 2¼ inches, though any fruit passing through a 2½-inch hole are best promoted as "lunch box apples." The idea of a smaller bin intrigues me: four bushel lots could be skid-rolled off a trailer, manually tilted onto the press conveyor, and swung by pulleys into a water bath for grading. Forty pounds to the bushel determines reality in the packing shed.

Steve Johnson in Washington opts to loose-pack his organic apples in bushel boxes right out in the orchard. A canvas-top field table allows each box of picks to be gently rolled out for sorting. Select grades are gauged by eye into three sizes: large, medium, and small. Seconds with minor blemishes go in one box, those lacking good color go in another. Several people working together coordinate tasks like sorting a particular category, resupplying packing boxes, and loading the truck. That leaves the cider apples, which make up about 20 percent of the crop at Johnson's Lazy J Tree Farm. Neil van Nostrand in Nova Scotia brings his crop to the barn, but no further: "My customers phone in their order and then pick it up at the barn. If I'm not around, they put their money in a jar. I offer just one grade, and that's salable fruit."

GRADING REVISITED

Most of us are not yet getting 90 percent fancy fruit in an organic orchard except in the drier regions west of the Rockies. Brian Caldwell in West Danby, New York, offers up this representative synopsis of an eastern crop: 40 percent select grade, 25 percent utility (a few minor blemishes), and 35 percent cider grade. Disease and insect pressures vary—even over the next hill—allowing some growers to fare better in their packout. *Select* in the organic grading handbook means "reasonable to eat." A society that calls for safe food and environmental stewardship needs to learn tolerance. A minor scab speck, a curculio dimple, a smidgen of sooty blotch, even some minuscule blotching around the calyx should not downgrade fruit to the cider bin. The choice to rate unmarred skin over flavor and lack of chemical residues is just that—a choice.

The initial purpose behind establishing grades for fruit was to reassure distant buyers that their order was up to snuff. Some of our great-grandparents, apparently, weren't beyond filling a barrel shipment with less appealing fruit and packing the top layer color-cheek up. Apple grades naturally evolved into upper echelons of value. *Extra fancy* has good

color, good size, and not one single iota of insect involvement—we won't mention that a bee pollinated the blossom—and rightfully should be worth top dollar. The overemphasis placed on intermediate grades, however, has helped create not only further distinctions in market value, but also the conception that fruit struck by hail or dimpled by a tarnished plant bug isn't fit for human consumption. Squeamishness should not be encouraged. A sustainable agriculture requires elements of common sense on the receiving end as well as in the orchard.

Yet regulations are set in stone for anyone packing for a wholesale broker. Either you're fancy grade or you're not. A mixed bag of reasonable eating apples merits little more than a utility price. Local natural food stores can emulate organic farm stands by offering loose-pack fruit under the grading banner of *orchard run*. Ostensibly this means "just as it came off the tree." Selecting those orchard run apples allows a reasoned sorting under the current standards that can be valued more fully. The store folks can do their own bagging to abet sales of a known quantity. Don't hesitate to individually wrap your best fruit in fancy gift boxes for maximum return.

Your reputation hinges on being fair about grading. Create standards that make sense to you and stick to them. That means accepting having less select fruit to sell in a scabby year. There's a world of visual difference between a surface crescent and an apple with half of one side sucked into the core, even though both are the work of curculio. Your utility grade should consist of good-sized fruit of reasonable proportion: peeling away surface blemishes is expected; encountering small fruit too lopsided to bother with is not. Never sell fruit where an insect awaits inside . . . the only thing worse than biting into an apple and finding a worm is biting into an apple and finding *half* a worm. Each organic fruit grower is beholden to the others when it comes to upholding sensible standards.

CIDERMAKING

Cider means different things to different people. Its root meaning, from the Old French *sidre*, is "the fermented juice of the apple." Go anywhere in Europe and ask for cider and it will be alcoholic to the last drop. Our colonial forebears here in North America desired nothing less of their first cider than a warming taste to get through a long winter. The term *hard cider* came into vogue as a means of distinguishing the first pressed juice of the apple—today's *sweet cider*—from the fermented brew that once flowed by the barrelful. Changing the term "fermented" to "fermentable" ends this ambiguity, and settles the commercial debate of whether apple juice that has been heat-treated or had chemical preservatives added is honestly cider. Federal regulations somewhat skirt this issue by empowering the word *fresh* to give consumers assurance of purchasing a true apple cider. But be warned: most apple juice sold today as sweet cider isn't necessarily fresh sweet cider.

Even without such linguistic meandering, cider is still far from the rich drink enjoyed a century or more ago. Varietal blends have fallen by the wayside along with a once-vibrant regional agriculture. The best cider is made from a blend of apples that balances sweetness with tang and body with clarity. Many good cider varieties are no longer grown in large orchards because cider is not a profitable venture in and of itself. A cidermaker who is not limited to the culls of a few commercial varieties can press incredible blends once again. But only if the latest fears of E. coli contamination don't push the feds into banning outright what was once our treasured national beverage.

Sweet Cider

Apples are categorized primarily based on their content of sugar, tannin, and acid. American tastes lean toward the sweet side in fresh juice, but a more flavorful hard cider will result from a tart blend. A

(Lost Nation cartoon by Susannah Becker)

handful of crabby cidermakers get very exacting about proper varietal proportions, but my advice is to have fun and trust your intuition. The best cider is made after "sweating" the apples for two to four weeks. Our cider apples are set aside by variety in bushel boxes before pressing. The apples yield their juices more readily after this mellowing, and the flavor of the cider is fuller. When a good firm squeeze leaves finger indentations on the fruit, it's ready for grinding. Some apple varieties—Rome and Jonathan come to mind—are best pressed ripe from the tree, as their juices begin to turn bitter after storage.

The final juice blends all the varietal tastes in a way that the first irresistible gush off the press may not. Sweet cider kept cold is good for fresh drinking one to two weeks after pressing and perhaps two weeks more for those with some fizz tolerance. Cider begins to turn "fizzy" as the natural yeasts in the juice begin to convert the apple sugars to alcohol. We're still a good way from a noticeably alco-

E. COLI 0157:H7

Cider was always thought to be too acidic to harbor *Escherichia coli* bacteria, but the newest strain has caused the death of one little girl and several outbreaks of diarrheal illness across the country. Undercooked meat and lettuce have been indicted along with unpasteurized fruit juice. Apples that have come in contact with "hoofed and horned" animal droppings are thought to introduce E. coli into the cider. A conscientious cidermaker would never use fallen apples gathered in a pasture, but no apple grower can ensure that deer won't find ways into the orchard. Rinsing apples down with a hose is not an effective wash. Quality goes hand in hand with safety if all the apples being pressed have been picked directly from the tree. But even that may not be enough. The Odwalla incident in 1996 involved a juice company that supposedly used only picked fruit and followed all sanitation guidelines.

Large producers soon won't be able to sell sweet cider, regardless of whether the government enacts a ban. Chain stores are going to refuse to accept unpasteurized product, insurance companies won't risk the liability, and concerned parents won't buy cider for their children. Small cidermakers will be left a failing niche that will be foreclosed come the next outbreak of foodborne illness. The onus for such problems belongs to industrial agribusiness as a whole, but sweet cider — and probably the small farmer to boot — will take the hit.

Pathogens continue to evolve and adapt in order to survive: the list of virulent bacteria is completely different from what it was only fifty years ago. The massive doses of antibiotics pumped into beef and dairy cattle these last few decades are highly suspect in light of our current confrontation with E. coli 0157:H7. What happens when this nightmare manifests on the fresh apple itself? Be it from an orchard neighbor spreading raw manure on a windy day or customer hands pawing apples in the supermarket? What then? Food can never be absolutely safe — we are biological beings swimming in a sea of uncompromising micro-organisms. Commonsense answers lie in a human-scale agriculture.

holic cider at this point, though many of the charming ladies who come to our mill after church on Sundays suspect me on this. My own preference is to let cider mellow for a few days in either the refrigerator or a cool cellar to enjoy it at its optimum. Carbon dioxide production—an honest man would admit this to be yeast flatulence—kicks into high gear after several weeks regardless of refrigeration, and then fizzy cider becomes too strong for all but the most obstinate ciderhead.

Press Options

The small commercial cidermaker has three choices in equipment: refurbishing a turn-of-the-century gem; crafting a hydraulic press with a piston jack and purchased grinder unit; or spending more money than you might wish for a new rig. Provision for getting the apples to a grinder located directly above the press are either by paddle elevator or second-story access to the fruit hopper. Sanifeed

CIDER APPLES OF RENOWN

Heading the list of classic cider apples are the Golden Russet, Ribston Pippin, and Roxbury Russet. Each of these cultivars makes a singularly rich cider all by itself, a nonblended distinction that few apple varieties can boast after centuries of opinionated cidermaking. Bill MacKentley of St. Lawrence Nurseries likens a Golden Russet cider to "the nectar of the gods." Russets tend to yield a third less juice by volume than other varieties, but when dealing with ambrosia, who cares?

The North Orchard at Thomas Jefferson's Monticello estate in Virginia was dedicated exclusively to the pursuit of fine cider. Virginia Hewes Crab, Golden Pearmain, and the lost Taliafero were particular favorites. Tom Burford of the nearby Burford Brothers Nursery in Monroe does a cidermaking workshop at Monticello each October: "It's become commonplace to me now to hear people say, 'I didn't know there were so many tastes in apples'." The spicy Grimes Golden gets a Southern commendation for hard cidermakers, with its high sugar content of 18.8 percent fermenting to 9 percent alcohol.

Out in Courtland, Kansas, amongst the wheat and milo fields, Dan and Carla Kuhn are defying the windswept plains with orchard plantings for their Depot Cider Mill. Jonathan apples squeeze out a sprightly, subacid juice that the Kuhns blend in a renaissance spirit with Stayman Winesap, Arkansas Black, and St. George. There are apples for every region and a cider for every taste.

My own cider favorites don't need to withstand tree-leaning winds as much as deep, cold winters. I'll know in the decades to come if these vintage cider apples — Sweet Bough, Peck's Pleasant, Wickson, Ashmead's Kernel, and St. Edmund's Russet, to name a few — continue to pass the winter hardiness test on our sloping mountainside. Equally exciting are bred selections of *Malus domestica* that offer both marketable fruit and tasty juice. Milton adds an aromatic sweetness to our late-September pressings. Tree-ripened Cortlands make a good juice base. Macoun, today's vogue apple, crunches sweetly into the October nectar flowing from our water-powered press. The University of Minnesota has developed a series of Malinda-crossed varieties with wonderful cider qualities — Haralson, Sweet Sixteen, and the nutty-flavored Chestnut Crab among them. Bill MacKentley affirms the worth of this century's selections: "The cardinal rule of a good breeding program," he says, "is to release an apple only if it is superior to its parents." Name recognition aside, the buying public is missing out on the likes of Sharon, Joyce, and Wellington.

Home cidermakers and orchard entrepreneurs will deserve high praise for restoring cider to its former glory and full complexity of flavor by blending apples such as these. Such acclaim doesn't belong only to our era, however. As Mr. Jefferson might aptly remind us through the easy drawl of Tom Burford, "Oh no, we had that a while."

systems pump the squeezed pomace from a free-standing grinder to the press table (ladling the pomace from pots is a "low-tech pump" for some). Rack-and-cloth-type presses utilize slatted wooden racks or grooved plastic to maximize the squeezing pressure between cloth-held layers of ground apples. Nylon press cloths are tightly woven to keep solid fruit particles in the pomace. The cider tray needs to be made of nonreactive stainless steel. Juice is pumped through clear tubing to either a refrigerated stainless-steel holding tank or a cheaper polyethylene tank for immediate bottling.

Even picked cider apples should be washed and ideally brushed before pressing. Running water (have it tested) is preferable to reusing the same bath water, chlorinated or not. Take no shortcuts in keeping your press equipment clean! The walls, ceiling, and floor around the press should be washable surfaces. Cloths should be triple-rinsed after every press day and washed with bleach after every weekend. Rig up laundry lines behind your mill to hold the dripping cloths to air-dry. Use the "sniff test" to direct any vinegary cloths back to the washing machine. Racks need to be vigorously scrubbed with bleach water at the end of every press day. The Cider Equipment Cleaner from Orchard Supply comes highly recommended for removing pectins and tannins from cloths and racks. Rinse, then wipe down, all surfaces on the grinder and press with bleach water, and then rinse them again. Run a tubing brush through all lines monthly in addition to daily flushing the pump system with bleach water. We owe it to our customers—and each other—to keep small commercial presses aboveboard on all accounts.

Custom Pressing

Custom pressing at a cider mill is a good option for area families with lots of apples but no press of their own. Here in Lost Nation, we ask people to call ahead for an appointment to press at least eight

Lost Nation Cider Mill's rack-and-cloth cider press is still a-squishing after one hundred years.

bushels of apples (the minimum pomace height necessary for our piston to achieve a good squeeze). Golfball-size fruit are rejected, as they tend to clog the conveyor leading up to the grinder. Drops are too risky a contaminant source for our cloths and racks, let alone the custom cider. The juice from the apples—whatever the blend—goes into a custom tank outside to be bottled by the family. We charge one dollar per gallon squeezed, and another quarter per jug for folks needing containers. Hard cider makers often have the cider pumped directly into a barrel on the back of a truck. Custom pressing keeps the colonial tradition of a community mill works alive.

THE HANDSCREW PRESS

The handscrew press is the one affordable option for today's home cidermaker. The best handscrew press by far is made by Bill Courtis of the Phoenix Foundry in Marcus, Washington, who crafts his entire line on a custom-order basis. It's worth waiting for one of Bill's presses — you'll have it within the year — and spending the money for a tool you can pass on to your grandchildren.

The single-tub Villager press is his most popular model, a choice generally based on lower cost and acceptance of a one-bushel pace. The double-tub American Harvester (three- or four-leg models are available) allows one family member to continue grinding apples while the alternating tubful is being pressed. A joyous cider crew can expect to crank out one-and-a-half to two-and-a-half gallons of cider per bushel batch, depending on the juiciness of the apple varieties pressed.

JILL BROOKS

A good grinder is integral to any pressing operation. Cidermakers long ago discovered that apples first grated to a juicy pulp yield thrice the juice of whole apples. Flywheel handles, once set in motion, require less effort to keep the grinder turning than a continuous-crank handle. The Phoenix Foundry adds a 1:3 gear ratio on its double-tub models to improve the flywheel conver-sion effort that much again.

The quality of these presses shows through-out. The wood frame is made from either fir and larch or more traditional oak, both laminated for maximum strength and to prevent twisting with age. The tub staves are beveled on all edges for easier cleaning and better juice flow. The one-and-a-half-inch Acme threaded screw passes through a full three-inch cast-iron nut that isn't going to bend when you commence squeezing. The rolled threads on the screw are much more wear-resistant than cheaper machine-cut threads.

Bill feels particularly sure about his work, backing it as only a craftsman can with a five-year war-ranty. His Villager press ranges in price from $418 to $526, depending on options chosen. You can spend as much as $868 for the four-legged American Harvester press with an oak frame and gear handle. Hardware kits are available for those inclined to do their own woodworking.

For more information, contact The Phoenix Foundry, Box 68-L, Marcus, WA 99151, (509) 684–5434.

Frozen Cider

Freshly pressed cider freezes incredibly well. Letting customers know that gives them a reason to stock up for the winter. The taste after the thaw is nearly indistinguishable from that of those glorious fall days when the juice is pressed. The secrets of a good result are but two: don't let the cider sit around for a few days before freezing, and pour out 1½ inches from a full plastic jug before placing it upright in the freezer. The option to freeze cider helps commercially as well, when projected weekend sales fall short of the gallons left in the tank. One or two local outlets for frozen cider over the winter months may justify the energy costs of running a freezer. Or you can process apple jelly at a more convenient time.

THE JUICE OF THE APPLE

Sweet cider marks just the beginning for juice squeezed from the apple. Small farms can be ready with an array of worthy alternatives should federal regulations come to pass that ban the sale of fresh cider. Returning to the root meaning of cider may ultimately prove a boon to local marketing once people discover the full flavor and versatility of organic apple juice.

Apple Juice

Good juice is made from good cider. The varieties of apples and the blend achieved matter just as much. All producers will lose the tangy effervescence of a sweet cider to the pasteurization process, but small farmers will not lose the qualitative edge on flavor. Caveats of the process follow as well: heating fresh juice to 170°F for a few minutes is sufficient to destroy pathogens like E.coli and natural yeasts, but it's a far cry from overcooking the nutrients out of the juice as is of the banal product typically found on the grocer's shelf. Filtering removes pectin and the finer attributes of zest, body, and roughage.

High-tech producers are going to be able to afford flash pasteurization or irradiation units. Adults comparing such treated cider to memories of previous insipid blends won't notice much difference. The conventional market will continue to offer "cider" in the usual plastic jug. While there's no point trying to go head-to-head with "winter tomatoes" that sell at a low price, *real* apple juice, like summer-ripened tomatoes, has merits that industrial agribiz can't comprehend, much less duplicate. Besides, it's more honest to call pasteurized cider apple juice. Tout the real thing for what it is and explain to people that flavor and nutrition has value. Give kids a taste of your finest and they will know the difference. Carbonate your beverage for marketing distinction. With or without the bubbly, isn't it nice to know you've got a (shelf) life?

Consumers expect a premium fruit juice to come in a glass bottle. Cost-effective ways of pasteurizing are a processing hurdle for a small producer. The stainless steam kettle found in a community processing kitchen is one alternative, with the juice pumped to a bottle filler. Bulk transport of juice from the cider mill, however, doesn't make the process any more efficient. Dairy pasteurization equipment starts at around ten thousand dollars for a twenty-five gallon unit. Shallow evaporating pans (for maple syrup) could be covered for much less money provided you had approved processing space. Obviously, costs are going to run high until local economies are thriving and small bottling plants—sensibly set up to refill bottles—are a part of every community.

Hard Cider

Making hard cider is a relatively straightforward process. Oak barrels are the traditional fermenting vessel, but glass carboys are less temperamental for the initiate. A used whiskey keg is a forty-eight-gallon cider commitment, whereas a five-gallon carboy batch allots more attempts at playing around with different juice blends and sugar ratios. The wooden vats used by some British cidermakers have been in continuous use for as long as four hundred years. Enter a pub in the mother country and choose your draft, be it ale or cider. The current American fascination with microbrewed beers also embraces fine ciders. This makes sense, since the alcohol content of hard cider and beer are comparable, and the two satisfy similar tastes. Market sales of hard cider are doubling yearly, so if you've the inclination, get on board. Teaming up with a local winery for serious production can save much investment expense.

Not that we'll ever return to the voluminous days of colonial consumption. One settlement of forty families near Boston put away three thousand barrels of cider for the winter of 1721. Cider was as good as cash in the barter economy of the day. One diary from 1805 records trading a half-barrel of cider for a child's schooling. Cider was considered good for one's constitution, and even President John Quincy Adams started his day with a glass or two. Cider's popularity and moderate alcohol content created a schism in the growing temperance movement in the 19th century. While some groups were out in the countryside attacking cider orchards with hatchets, others were serving cider to aid the discussion on the deleterious effects of rum and other distilled spirits. This societal acceptance of cider carried through the Prohibition years of the 1920s, when a farmer's hard cider was one of the few exemptions to the Volstead Act. Such a loophole still stands in some states: we're allowed to market a natural (no added sugar) cider at our mill without any regulatory hassle.

A culture so strongly tied to its brew readily builds up a collection of tales. Regional cider lore may again garner stories like this one of Bill Lord, Cooperative Extension fruit specialist here in New Hampshire. It seems one fellow from Union Village hadn't been seen for two months one winter. Finally he showed up at the general store for supplies. "What'cha been doing these days, Nathaniel?" asked the shopkeeper. "Working at home," came the taciturn reply. "Not much doing in winter, is there?" "Can't say there is, though you'll have to allow it's hard work hauling thirty gallons of cider up the cellar stairs, two quarts at a time."

Cider Vinegar

Cider vinegar is the end result of hard cider left to sit in the open air. The alcohol converts to an acetic acid in the presence of vinegar bacteria, classified en masse as *acetobacter*. My first attempt at making vinegar was simply setting aside a few jugs of sweet cider that had gone fizzy to "do its thing," in the hopes of producing a few interesting gifts for friends. Many months later one jug was a delightfully clear vinegar, but the other two remained cloudy and off-tasting. There are numerous strains of bacteria that made foul play of the sugars in these latter jugs of partially fermented cider. I was lucky in the one. The surest way to make good vinegar every time is to make hard cider first and then rely on "mother."

A vinegar mother is the gelatinous mass of acetobacter to be found floating on the top of a finished barrel of vinegar. Good mother is akin to the sourdough starter passed down in a baking family. Vinegar is made in a partially filled barrel where a large surface of the hard cider can be exposed to air. The vinegar mother is added as a leavening to further acetobacter growth. Cover the bunghole with several layers of cheesecloth to keep out dust and fruit flies. Vinegar should be made in a warm, dark place, and expect this process to take a year or more (in addition to the time needed to ferment the cider). Time preserves the delicacy of flavor found in a natural cider vinegar that is lost in the forty-eight-hour acetator process of industrial vinegar-

A BASIC HOME BREW

Anyone entertaining commercial notions of a hard cider label should read Annie Proulx and Lew Nichol's *Sweet & Hard Cider* book for the finer points of the art. In the meanwhile, here's some brewing basics to get a carboy started.

The carboy, rubber stopper, and plastic air lock (see photo opposite) should first be sterilized with Campden tablets (16 tablets per quart of water make a 1 percent metabisulfite solution) to kill any unwanted bacteria. A sloshing rinse does the trick. Fill the carboy to the top with freshly pressed cider if making a natural cider — utilizing the natural yeasts and sugars already in the juice — or leave room to add sugar and a champagne yeast before topping off. The potential alcohol of your hard cider is determined by the sugar content of this *unfermented must*. Apple sugars alone generally provide a 5 to 6 percent alcohol content, depending on the varieties used and the influence of weather and soil. Adding a half cup of sugar per gallon of cider pushes this up as

The airlock on this glass carboy prevents vinegar bacteria from spoiling the fermenting cider.

high as 9 percent, provided the fermentation goes completely to the dry side. A couple of handfuls of organic raisins is an old-time alternative to sugar. A sweeter cider results if the yeast stops working before all the sugar is consumed, which is more likely in a cool room or when too much sugar is added. Using a hydrometer to determine the specific gravity of the must takes the guesswork out of targeting sugar content.

Keep your full carboy at room temperature for the primary fermentation. When this boiling-over stage is complete in a few days, wipe down the sides of the carboy and thoroughly rinse the air lock. Utilize some of the Campden tablet solution for the water seal in the now-clean air lock. This prevents vinegar bacteria from getting into the cider, while at the same time allowing carbon dioxide gas to escape during the secondary fermentation. A regular bubbling will continue for six months or more, depending on holding temperature and the vigor of the yeast. A smoother cider results from a slower fermentation at cooler temperatures in the 40° to 60°F range. When the bubbling subsides and the amber liquid clarifies, the cider is ready to be tasted and siphoned into sterilized bottles. A hard cider with a minimum alcohol content of 5.7 percent will keep for years and get mellower with age.

making. You can expect an acid strength equal to the alcohol content of your hard cider; thus the 5 percent alcohol of a natural cider converts to a 5 percent acetic acid vinegar. Stronger vinegar is often diluted with distilled water to reduce its acidic sharpness.

Organic cider vinegar can be marketed to anyone who understands good health. This is the tonic of the ages, the therapeutic buffer of the human circulatory system. Promote the presence of your mother (strands will appear in your bottled vinegar) as proof positive that living vinegar comes unpasteurized. No health claims need be made for natural vinegar (you'd be thwarted by the FDA anyway), as people have held onto the notion of vinegar's worth.

Cider Jelly

Cider can be boiled down much the same as maple sap in the making of maple syrup. The natural pectin found in the apple leads this evaporation to a jellied end, however. A true New England cider jelly comes "fully puckered," with no sugar added to lessen the tangy apple flavor.

Boil down fresh cider in a stainless-steel evaporating pan as rapidly as possible, till it approaches the jelly boiling point of 220°F. Pumping the hot liquid through a syrup filter to a maple finishing pan allows more control of the boil. The hot cider will "sheet" off a testing spoon in a continuous lip when it reaches the jelly stage. Tap it off into sterilized jars and secure with sterilized lids. One gallon of cider will be reduced to just over two 8-ounce jars of jelly. Wild or crab apples (high in pectin) in the cider blend help ensure a good set. Don't be dissapointed with apple molasses—a more syrupy version of boiled cider—as it lends itself wonderfully to Shaker cider pie or as a glaze on roast duck or ham. We label such batches "Cider Glaze" and reap the marketing benefits of an expanded product line.

APPLE STORAGE

Apples continue to live and respire once off the tree. Oxygen is consumed and carbon dioxide, ethylene, and other gases are given off. Starches convert to sugars, acid balances change, and bitter-tasting tannins decline. Winter apples develop their full flavor in storage. Roxbury Russet often picks up a hint of licorice; any Winesap family variety takes on the bouquet of a fine wine; and the distinct tang of pineapple comes out in Newtown Pippin. Each variety has its "season" when flavor and texture are considered optimal. Esopus Spitzenberg makes an aromatic leap to perfection at Christmas. The honeyed sweetness of York Imperial boosts spirits on late-winter days. Arkansas Black goes from too hard to eat at harvest to a crunchy treat in February to positively greasy by May. Apples soften as the pectins binding flesh cells together tire.

The finer points of heirloom apples with good keeping qualities are lost on us today. Controlled atmosphere (CA) storage allows large growers to essentially halt the ripening process by limiting the level of oxygen around the stored fruit, thereby tripling post-harvest life. Calcium chloride and fungicide dips are used to limit bitter pit and fruit rots. Diphenylamine is a common scald-inhibiting chemical that comes with a warning not to feed treated apples to livestock. Think about that one for a minute. The wonders of modern storage are not without chemical ramifications.

Our great-grandparents relied on bermed storage beneath a building or carved into a hillside. Cold air could be vented into such "chill rooms" at night. Blocks of ice, kept through the summer under sawdust in the ice house, also helped temper autumn heat until a freeze settled on the land. Today it still makes sense to utilize the earth's temperature for long-term storage, but now the initial cooling can be aided electrically with refrigeration.

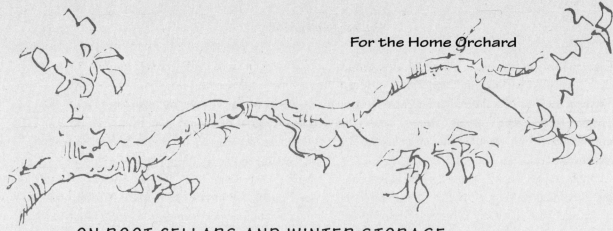

ON ROOT CELLARS AND WINTER STORAGE

Apples keep best if stored at or near 32°F with a relative humidity approaching 90 percent. Our unheated farmhouse cellar works great: the drafty stone foundation keeps things quite cool, and the dirt floor is always damp. Mesh wire cages hold six bushels of apples at a time, safely away from nibbling mice. Covered porches and woodsheds do in a pinch for late fall storage. Just cover the fruit with old blankets and sleeping bags on particularly crisp nights. When the deep cold settles upon the land, you'll need to protect your winter keepers from freezing solid. Sort through those apples one last time, putting the best in perforated bags in the fridge, and all the rest into that apple butter you never quite got made over the busy holidays.

Apples and potatoes should be stored separately. The ethylene gas given off by the ripening apples causes the potatoes to sprout sooner. An ideal storage arrangement would be a two-bay root cellar built into a hillside, but most of us will need to work out a more practical compromise. Our potatoes are kept on the far side of the cellar from the apples. Two pits in the backyard — some people bury a lidless chest freezer — covered with a thick straw mulch and then protected with a piece of sheet-metal roofing is another option. In the old days, apples were often wrapped in paper, then packed in barrels that were covered with straw and kept in the barn.

The length of time apples can be stored depends on the variety, their maturity and soundness at harvest, and the storage temperature. In general, apples ripen about four times faster at 50°F than at 32°F. Late-maturing varieties such as Yellow Newton, Winesap, Arkansas Black, Northern Spy, Baldwin, and York Imperial are best for home storage. Pick apples when they are mature but still hard: fruit harvested on the green side tends to shrivel in storage and is more affected by diseases like scald and bitter pit. Sort through your fruit monthly to remove any proverbial bad apples, which can indeed spoil the whole lot. When apples become softer than you like for fresh eating, bake 'em up in a pie or make sauce.

Our walk-in cooler runs on hydroelectric power; Bear Well Orchard in Maine relies on the sun to similarly get its apples chilled. But it's okay to be on the grid: what's critical is getting the field heat out of the fruit so the ambient temperature of the earth and the cold night air can maintain a uniform ideal. All walls and the ceiling of storage rooms should be properly insulated. A chimney flue works well for removing warm, impure air above the respiring fruit throughout the winter, provided a cold air inlet is located down low to create a natural draft.

Picked apples left out in the orchard at 70°F ripen as much in three days as they would in one month of cold storage at 30°F. Some varieties shouldn't be kept quite this cold: McIntosh and Newtown Pippin develop an internal browning at slightly below-freezing temperatures. Stacking slotted containers on spacer sticks increases airflow around the ripening fruit to cool it down quicker. Humidity rates equally high in effective storage: set pans of water or frequently sprinkle down a cement floor if moisture levels are less than 90 percent. Cold air let into the storage room is dry and will take up moisture as it warms. Golden Russet keeps well into April provided humidity is adequate; otherwise this thin-skinned ambrosian pome transpires away. Storing shrivel-sensitive varieties in perforated plastic bags can help. Only well-colored, mature (but not fully ripe) fruit should go into storage. Strict grading out of minor scab and any sign of bitter pit in the field makes sense. A final packout is requisite when the apples come out of cold storage, to inspect for storage disorders like water core and Jonathan spot. Scald, a superficial browning of the apple's skin which does not extend deep into the flesh, is attributable to poor aeration in storage.

The ability to grow and store good keeping apples goes hand in hand with neighborhood markets wanting that fruit. When winter's crispness is finally lost to the warming breezes of early spring, people need to remember the apple butter and sauces and dried apple rings that will tide us over till Yellow Transparent beckons harvest time again.

Source: The Principles of Fruit Growing, *L. H. Bailey, 1897, 1926.*

One grows fruit either for a special or personal market,
in which case he looks for his own customer and is independent
of general trade; or he grows what the market demands,
and allows the machinery of trade to handle the product.

—LIBERTY HYDE BAILEY, *The Principles of Fruit Growing* (1897)

CHAPTER 9

Marketing in the Local Economy

A small organic apple orchard is not going to compete in the big leagues of brokers and supermarket chains. Rather, your chance for a fair economic return and customer appreciation lies in the direct sale. Farm stands, farmers' markets, the local natural foods store, neighborhood food co-ops, the growing CSA movement, a Mom-and-Pop grocery are your markets. Here customers can know you as a friend and hard-working farmer, and the nonconformity of your fruit offerings are an asset. Apples grown without chemical sprays, picked at the peak of ripeness, with varietal names and flavors that astound—check off marketing advantage number one. Fancy gift packs of dessert fruit and a line of processed butters and syrups can launch a grassroots mail-order venture. Educating palates to the high art of cidermaking (both sweet and hard) can establish a market niche that willingly pays a premium for juice as good as it gets.

Marketing is half the work of a small farmer, and frankly I don't believe there's any way around it. Yes, you can size, grade, and box your apples to sell to a regional natural foods distributor. It'll take just a few phone calls to sell a quality crop. But will your packout be high enough to compete against the unblemished organic fruit coming from the West coast to justify the costs incurred? Is the distributor willing to handle a small volume? And, at the heart of the matter, can you afford not to make that retail markup after all those hours of hand-thinning, insect trapping, and shoveling compost? Possibly, too, you can locate a juice processor or maker of organic baby foods to take your cider-grade fruit. But now the value of those apples drops to a tonnage price that barely covers the cost of harvesting the crop. It's a whole other ball game when you ask "the machinery of trade" to handle your product. A larger orchard pulls this off by gaining equipment efficiency over a hundred or so acres of fruit trees *and* by achieving that all-critical packout of 90 percent or more dessert-quality fruit. Organic agriculture needs to reclaim its niche in the local economy by other means.

Liberty Hyde Bailey pointed out the attributes of the personal fruit market at the turn of the century just before apple growing lost its eminence in our culture. His words still ring true for those of us who value that Jeffersonian vision of many working small farms. "The narrowness of the enterprises, the competition in restricted areas, the respect for traditional methods and varieties, conserve the very elements that appeal to the discriminating consumer, while, at the same time, they develop great skill in the fruit-grower. The care bestowed on individual plants, the niceties of exposure and of training, the patient handwork, may almost be said to develop special traits in the fruits themselves. Such fruits may not find a place in the open market, but for that very reason they may have a higher commercial value."

Smaller growers need to resort to a grassroots marketing approach—one that's innovative, goes that extra step to assure customer satisfaction, and is fun for all involved. A major thrust of any marketing approach needs to be educational. People need to understand food safety concerns, to upgrade their taste expectations, and, most importantly, to willingly pay the full worth of nutritious food to local growers, who in turn circulate their fruit dollars back into a vibrant local economy. People can't just be told these things, particularly where it affects their wallet. Shopping for the lowest price is a sacrosanct tenet of our consumer society. It's a gradual process to get people to fully think through all the implications of their economic choices. Such must be done if we're going to live in a balanced world.

Farm profitability is marginal in the context of these economic times. There's a deliberate governmental policy to keep food relatively cheap in this country, a policy that places the value of our nourishment beyond the influence of correcting market forces. Crop surplus sales, irrigation and transport subsidies, a regulatory process on agricultural chemicals that doesn't safeguard our health, and marketing grants to large corporations are the reasons local agriculture continues to decline. Otherwise, we could easily compete on the proverbial level playing field. All of us have grown up with an expectation that we pay only so much for basic commodities. Take those dozen chicken eggs, for instance, and the horrid factory-farm conditions that have kept egg prices hovering on either side of a dollar a dozen for decades. Free-range birds fed an organic grain produce a much richer egg, yet the costs of offering such eggs aren't met by going market rates unless there's an enlightened consumer willing to pay more. And therein lies our salvation.

GETTING A FAIR PRICE

I expect someday to be accused of consumer heresy. These are very materialistic times, and the emphasis of life seems to be on *more, more, more*. That's achieved, of course, by having things cheaply priced at the cost of ignoring social, environmental, and spiritual values. Our plunge into the industrial age more than a century ago remains very much in need of some Amish rumination.

How much we spend on the necessities of life—food, clothing (to a non-Calvin Klein degree), and shelter—determines what is left for nonessentials and conveniences. I've often been struck by the percentage of income the average American pays for food, 11 percent, being less than half what most Europeans pay. This percentage jumps that much higher again in the subsistence economies of Africa and the Indian subcontinent. There's something telling here, for despite the domineering thrust of the so-called global economy, a locally oriented agriculture can exist in societies that double their food bill. What might we gain for a $2.59 carton of fresh eggs and a $6.00 gallon of cider? Perhaps groundwater that is uncontaminated by herbicide runoff? Local economies that once again see local dollars recirculating as much as seven times before leaving the area? A cancer rate in decline? A happier people in touch with the land that feeds them and each other? A few less plastic things to take to the dump?

These are tough times for enlightenment. The best we can do today as growers is tell our stories and suggest the possibilities. Most people won't listen, but a few will. Life is a gradual process that is constantly unfolding. So is the quest to getting a fair price that would put farm income on a parity with the incomes of others in today's society.

Basic commodity prices are suggested first in the nearby supermarket where your community shops for its food. Some states publish weekly retail price lists based on the range other growers are asking for their produce and specialty items. The newsletter *Growing for Market* adapts the latest USDA Market News Service information to print wholesale produce prices in each monthly issue. Regional variables come into play in assessing your target markets: people tend to have more discretionary income in populated areas or when they are away on holiday. Nearby competitors also determine the going value of locally grown produce to a degree, as bargain deals attract customers in droves. You'll need a loyal clientele that appreciates both quality and the organic alternative in order to ask a higher price to cover production costs.

Rule number one in obtaining a fair price is not to sell yourself short. It's always easier to adjust prices downward if your production process gets more efficient or you need to boost sales. Emphasize high quality and live up to it. A good reputation is worth far more than a low price. Repeat customers are vital to a sustainable farm effort, and they won't come back if what they bought the first time wasn't up to snuff.

Don't view yourself as selling *just apples* or *just cider*. Customers coming direct to the farm are purchasing more than food. Both you and your orchard are a living experience of the source of food. That translates into added value that the plugged-in supergrocer can't replicate. We'll talk more on enhancing the farm experience in a bit.

Costs must be covered unless you're a financially independent idealist. Your own labor is a legitimate but too often overlooked cost. What is a grower's time and skill worth? Ten dollars an hour without benefits and the hope of a better tomorrow? That's been our goal in Lost Nation, though admittedly we haven't yet achieved it. Our first year in business we paid ourselves zero. The next year we figured fifty cents an hour a modest gain. First business years often require such wage sacrifice to get off the ground, making infrastructure investments and building a reputation. These last few seasons we've held steady at $3.50 an hour while making investments in expanding our plantings, purchasing

WAGE SHARING FROM PAST LOST NATION NEWSLETTERS

"The most pleasant surprise of the season was David and Michael both being able to take an annual salary of $500. Though this amounts to less than fifty cents an hour, we feel confident of surpassing the entry-level McDonald's worker by the time the 1998 season rolls around."

"Expenses were up, so we have yet to achieve a minimum hourly wage for Michael and David. We'll get there . . . now if only we can talk President Clinton out of raising the national minimum wage."

"Our partnership earnings held steady at $3.50 an hour. This compares to a New England average wage of $7 per hour for hired farm workers. Looks like all we need to do is hire ourselves!"

equipment, and initiating a mail-order catalog. Farmers need to keep rough track of their hours to divide into the profit left at the year's end and thus to get an understanding of their hourly wage. We let our customers know how we're doing through a cider mill newsletter but don't belabor the point. Customers need to understand the realities of farming, but at the same time your analysis needs to be light and upbeat. Hope draws good energy to itself; pessimism makes for a drowned rat.

Marketers figure the difference between retail and wholesale pricing in one of two ways. We give a suggested retail price that is 40 to 50 percent higher than the wholesale price charged, using the lower percentage for perishable products like apples and cider, the higher percentage for the processed products more often sold in tourist venues and natural foods stores. Our fresh cider (without preservatives, thank you) is backed by an unconditional guarantee that we'll replace any unsold jugs weekly with new product. A gallon of Lost Nation organic cider wholesales for $3.95, retails in town at a suggested $5.50, and can be bought freshly pressed at the mill for $4.95. The lower mill price is intended as a purchasing incentive for folks to make the drive "out on the Nation" to buy direct from us.

It was in a large supermarket (before I knew better) that I experienced the other approach to figuring retail profit or margin. Here "50 percent" meant what I would call a 100 percent markup in the first approach: the retailer views half the selling price as the store's share. Today's $3.95 wholesale jug of cider would sell for a full eight dollars, and would turn fizzy long before any price-conscious consumer picked your product. This kind of "keystone" pricing is more common in gift shops and is not unworkable in an upscale market with value-added products preserved in a sealed jar. Remembering that a 33 percent margin on the higher retail price is exactly the same as a 50 percent markup on

the lower wholesale price helps if and when you choose to get involved with commission sales.

Surplus production with no planned market in sight is often a grower's biggest nemesis. It's easy to panic and drop prices when you're sitting atop a perishable harvest. A good storage facility gives you a longer selling opportunity for dessert-quality fruit. Still, a marketing plan is imperative, and arrangements made ahead of time with natural foods stores ensure such a plan. Great-tasting winter keepers are a good niche for growers where a regular early-October freeze doesn't jeopardize the crop. A sense of your orchard's production capacity and knowledge of each variety's packout percentage allows you to plan how to disperse the harvest. Our current processed production is based on past sales and projected growth for each Lost Nation product: cider jelly, Yankee apple butter, cider glaze, apple jelly, and cider syrup. Case output for a fifty-bushel batch of each product according to recipe and process method is known. For instance, we can make seventy case lots of our apple butter out of that amount of apples. This knowledge lets me draw up a crop budget to meet all our anticipated marketing plans, from fresh apple sales at the mill to the last drop of cider (see chart on p. 201).

CIDER ECONOMICS

A few years back we set another financial goal to work towards, that being to sell our crop in the way that returns the most value for our growing efforts. Such a concept is all the more critical for a labor-intensive organic farm. Squeezing a bushel of juicy apples into cider yields three gallons, which, after jugging and pressing costs are deducted, places a mill value of $12 on that organic bushel. Organic cooking apples are hand-graded for size from the slightly blemished apples, so our mill price on that bushel is $15. Utility-grade fruit from a chemical orchard sells for $5 to $8 a bushel around here,

A handscrew cider press, as discussed in chapter 8.

leaving us at a competitive disadvantage, but what's the point of selling these apples for less than we'd make for the cider? It's still a real deal for customers who consider flavor, nutritional content, environmental safety, and their own health.

Our potential for making a living wage at this farm effort, however, will only be reached by selling select-grade apples by the half-peck bag or through a value-added product line. Our dessert-quality fruit retails at the mill for $4.50 a half-peck and on up to $29.50 a bushel. Eight half-pecks make up a bushel, so this divided sale reaches a bushel value of $36, considerably up from the cider value of $12. One gallon of cider boiled down yields two-and-a-third 8-ounce jars of cider jelly, which, at the wholesale price of $3.50 a jar, results in a wholesale

bushel value of almost $17. The retail markup gained by a direct sale at the mill is allotted to overhead expenses. Each wholesale product has a bushel value (based on a uniform processing wage of $6.50 an hour) which allows us to determine our most profitable product lines and plan our crop budget accordingly.

Numbers like these are never set in stone, but certain conclusions do stand out. Our apple butter is a bestseller despite a suggested retail price of $5.95 for a twelve-ounce jar. It's quite labor-intensive to make since we manually peel the apples, but we can put up 164 jars in three hours of cooking and filling time at the commercial processing facility in our town. Apple jelly looks to be the way to go, but at a $3.25 retail price, we're not looking to compete

CROP BUDGET FOR EACH 500 BUSHELS OF APPLES

Select fruit	100 bu @ $29	Utility fruit	20 bu @ $15
Mill cider	180 bu @ $12	Wholesale cider	40 bu @ $10
Apple butter	35 bu @ $32	Cider jelly	75 bu @ $17
Apple jelly	5 bu @ $69	Cider syrup	10 bu @ $72
Mill hard cider	17.5 bu @ $22	Organic vinegar	17.5 bu @ $19

The packout figured here is a minimal 20 percent. The budget is adjusted to sell apples in the highest value category if the requisite quality is there. This budget yields approximately forty-eight caselots of each processed product and a barrel each of hard cider and vinegar, which correlates directly to our marketing plans.

with Smuckers. We have not gotten into bottling organic apple juice, as the projected bushel value is the same as for wholesale cider. We do this to gain name recognition in area stores despite it being the least cost-effective way to sell our apples. Producing dessert-quality fruit remains a foremost goal on the path to profitability.

NICHE MARKETING

It's essential to understand to whom you're marketing your organic apples, cider, and value-added products. Equally important, understand that not everyone is going to seek out your offerings no matter where you advertise or how innovative your promotions. Targeting your efforts to specific market segments is the first order of the day.

What is the market for the organic apple? It's honest to say maybe as little as 5 percent or so of the people in a given place are willing to pay a premium price for fresh, organic food. Another 30 percent might say they'd purchase organic if they could get it, but when push comes to shove—say a tarnished plant bug dimple on the apple's skin—these people will generally choose the lower-priced fruit grown via chemical means. This leaves a whole lot of folks who haven't thought about food safety

issues and a few diehards (literally) who don't want to even hear about it. Marketers who are adept at fitting some educational snippets into their promotions to challenge and inspire people's way of thinking might only improve these percentages by a few points. Such is the power of the notion to shop for the lowest price.

All is not lost, however. Other target markets exist for a small-orchard effort that focuses on quality and varietal selection. The easiest sell in the world ought to be anything other than Red Delicious. There are some people who still heed the need to support local ventures. Others yearn for the authenticity of real people growing real food, for that quintessential country experience. A trip to the orchard and cider mill becomes as much a quest to fill an emotional hunger as a physical one. Our cider mill is not just a place to buy apples and homemade pickles. People come here to see apples squeezed and juice flowing, to walk in the orchards and ask about insect traps, to get a taste of the "hard stuff" back by the walk-in cooler with the guys who barreled the cider the year before. We're sharing a way of life missed by far too many today. It's the main virtue a small farm has over high-volume price competitors that refer to farming as an industry.

Farming—the stewardship of land, plants, and animals from which we draw our sustenance—is meant to be a shared culture, not an industry. The root meanings of *agriculture* suggest this human bond, that of tilling (the Latin *cultura*) the land (the Latin *ager*) together. This we are no longer doing. But imprinted deep in all our memories is this bond to the earth, to good soil, to sunshine and growing things. Bringing out these attributes in a marketing package and right on down to the smile on your face is how local agriculture is going to reclaim its rightful place in local economy.

Finding your niche begins with identifying potential markets. Farmstands allow your customers to come to the farm for that all-important direct sale. A water-powered cider mill like ours is a tourist draw. Locals bring out-of-town family and friends for the experience; innkeepers and guides at state information booths direct travelers out our way for terrific views and terrific cider. Foliage peaks during the course of the apple season, and we do our best to ride the tourist swell while the leaves are still on the trees. Farm stands need to offer consistent hours, and given that small farms often can't afford to pay outside help, such consistency means you need to commit to time away from bringing in the harvest and processing product. Our solution has been an extended weekend schedule, with cider pressed Fridays, Saturdays, and Sundays and the mill open 9 to 5 on those days. We fit in school tours on Friday mornings, and wholesale deliveries that afternoon. It's a schedule that best fits our being off the beaten track (not many people travel out Lost Nation Road during the middle of the week) and leaves days for all the other work of farming to prepare for the weekends. Don't be afraid to condense your selling window to fit the reality of your life. Customers will learn your hours and respond accordingly. Burning yourself out to be open seven days a week defeats the whole notion of a sustainable agriculture: you, too, need to be sustained.

EDITH TUCKER

Chatting with cider mill customers encourages ardent small-farm supporters.

Direct sales with that all-important retail premium can also be made on market day. Anne de Cosson and Larry Berg grow apples on Denman Island off the coast of British Columbia. "We bring fruit to a large Farmers' Market in Vancouver, which is two ferries and about sixty miles away. The market in Vancouver is upscale, and we get a fairly good price for most apples, ranging from $1.39 to $1.69 per pound. Because we have a wide range of varieties—including old ones and English and French varieties—we find they almost self-market. We always provide taste samples. Some customers come because we're organic, but at this time, the range of varieties is more important."

Good farmers' markets can make up the difference for isolated farms. The basic rules of high

Label artwork by SUSANNAH BECKER

"Tap into the flavor of a New Hampshire apple tree! This tasty pancake syrup touts the delicious sweetness of our organic apple cider. The sugar maple is no longer the only tree on the block," reads our back label for cider syrup.

quality and an inviting display apply as much at market as at the home farm stand. Be lavish in display, stacking jar upon jar to create abundance, letting produce cascade from crafted baskets. Offer tastes of cider to show the mettle of your blend. Apple tastings will sell uncommon varieties. Or try a bit of humor—our varietal sign on the Rambo apple reads, "An old French variety that has absolutely nothing to do with Sylvester Stallone." Sampling cider jelly, apple butter, and the like on bite-size crackers can help introduce your products to new customers. Farmer chit-chat and informative signs like "Cider syrup is an apple-flavored treat for your pancakes" help people realize how to

TRADITIONAL CIDER PIE

Friends invited to our Wassail party each winter are served a slice of cider pie when we come in from the orchard ceremonies. You might want to try baking it for Thanksgiving or your own special occasions.

Pastry for a two-crust 9-inch pie
3/4 cup sugar
3 tablespoons cornstarch
Pinch of salt
8-ounce jar cider glaze (or cider jelly)

1/2 cup boiling water
1 egg, beaten
1 tablespoon melted butter
2 cups sliced apples

Combine sugar, cornstarch, and salt in a bowl. Add cider glaze and water and mix. Add egg and butter. Lay out apples atop bottom crust in pie plate and add filling. Place top crust on pie, slashing cuts in top. Bake at 425°F for 40 minutes.

fully enjoy your products. Provide the family recipe for boiled cider pie to enhance cider glaze sales. Customers literally feed on new ideas.

The local wholesale market shouldn't necessarily be overlooked. Natural foods stores in our area always sell several bushels of our select organic apples each season and a small but steady amount of fresh cider each week. Sales of our processed products always go up over the holiday season. The supermarket chains have proven off-limits to us, because regional sales managers nix the idea of a small farmer dealing with just one store. One good argument for the old-fashioned general store in a revived local economy is to circumvent the central distribution system of the big guys. The greatest merit of doing some wholesale business is keeping your name out in the public eye. However, finding time to make deliveries at a lesser price than you'll get at home on the farm makes the wholesale market less attractive.

One marketing niche that holds great promise for the organic apple grower is mail order. That statement is offered advisedly, as the specialty foods market is extremely competitive and printing and mailing costs can add up. Yet a grassroots mail-order catalog doesn't need to be big-time to be effective. People who want organic food but can rarely find organic apples other than Delicious from the West Coast will be repeat customers. Ned Whitlock in Arkansas lists a bushel-tray pack of select-grade fruit for $50 postpaid and mixed-variety gift tray packs of twenty apples for $22 postpaid. A bulk bushel of sound eating apples (but not quite as select) gets shipped for $36.

Our Lost Nation catalog features our processed products, such as Yankee apple butter and cider jelly, along with other northern New Hampshire specialties like maple candy and beeswax candles. This part of the state is known as the North Country, and being the only commercial orchard up this way allows us to seek out everyone with family or senti-

mental ties to the region. We've identified a dual niche: organic apple products to be offered New England-wide, and North Country delights for the folks who either often visit or who grew up here but left the region for more promising opportunities. Our cider mill mailing list was built check by check, having recorded each address after payment. A season-long raffle would provide all kinds of names if a lavish gift basket of all farm products was offered as the prize. Mailing lists can be bought as well, and here our thoughts have turned to state organic gardening associations (the New Hampshire group charged us ten cents a name) and publications like *Organic Gardening* magazine. Classified ads in such national magazines may come in future years, but for now we opt for a low-cost display ad in *The Natural Farmer,* a publication put out by the Northeast Organic Farming Association (NOFA). We're beginning this venture tentatively so as to have enough stock to cover orders and to see whether our estimated shipping and handling fees actually cover costs. Our mail-order markup was deliberately kept at the level of suggested retail prices with our mill customer base in mind. Don't overlook contacting local businesses that annually send Christmas presents to their best clients. An order for thirty-four gift boxes at $14 each (plus shipping) certainly launched our hopeful start.

A last niche to consider are the specialty foods trade shows, particularly state- or community-sponsored events where consumers can make purchases directly. I don't overly enjoy hawking our wares at such "marketing opportunities." Depending on the buying mood of the crowd, these specialty food fairs can turn out to be a farmer's nightmare. Samples of cider jelly become a free lunch to the guy who's brought his girl on a really cheap date. Or try holding your tongue on hearing this: "Hmmm, how tasty . . . what brand of crackers are these?" My friend, Bob, figures he'll lose his sales savvy one day when, after offering a taste sample

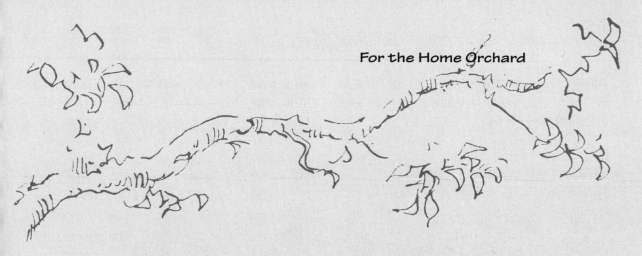

BARTERING WITH THE NEIGHBORHOOD

Orchard economics can be even more direct than the passing of a
few dollar bills for a peck of apples. Nor do you need an advertising
budget and regular farm stand hours to bring in customers. The
home orchardist can have crop aplenty, perhaps even jugs of freshly
pressed cider, to offer neighbors in trade.

   The possibilities are endless. Food for food is a straightforward
trade: several loaves of whole-grain bread and a hot apple pie to
boot for a bushel of Wealthy apples is a bargain both ways. How
about a jug of hard cider to the local handyman for sealing that leak
around the chimney? The babysitter is a bit shrewder — two gallons
of apple juice gets you some time away. Perhaps your pies are the
blue-ribbon winners at the county fair. Might the shoe repairman
consider two Saturday pies to resole those boots? Once you've got
the apples, it never hurts to ask!

   Growing advice has value too. A confident pruner can always find
some willing trading partners who haven't a clue where to begin.
Offer a timely spray or two in the next yard over for help with that
deck project. Perhaps plum curculio has gotten the upper hand
(some would say upper *snout*) in your young trees; there are still a
few eight-year-olds around who would delight in receiving a choco-
late chip cookie for every curc they collect. Bartering is all about
matching each other's needs and surpluses in delightful ways.

and hearing, "No thanks, I just ate," he'll quickly retort, "Look, buddy, I'm not offering you a meal; just taste the mustard." Certain shows accept a wider range of vendors, leading to days spent looking askance at a woman giving her "miracle cloth" demonstration over and over and over again. This kind of sales pitch engages the first person's attention, draws in an intrigued crowd, and makes whatever seem a deal that can't be lived without. I never got very far adapting her particular style: "Hello, ma'am, would you like to see me eat some apple butter?" Your food might taste good, but who has a hundred-and-one uses for apple jelly? I've learned that merely recovering the booth fee at such ventures can be considered a modest success if advertising goals like handing out catalogs and promoting good times at the cider mill are the prime motive. Agricultural fairs can be a better opportunity to set up your fruit offerings, with Maine's honest-to-goodness all-organic Common Ground Fair in late September being the ideal in our neck of the woods.

We've gone the route of many niches, juggling our mix as it best suits lessons learned and net return. Foliage season is boon time at the mill. Our regular customers from the surrounding towns are the greatest folks but too few in number to carry us far beyond the tourist influx. We're six miles out of the nearest town and easily forgotten on a rainy November weekend. Mail order, given the North Country loyalty factor and the uniqueness of being an organic apple farm, holds great promise for the holiday season and beyond. Everyone has a natural niche upon which no big operation can lay better claim.

VALUE-ADDED PRODUCTS

Fresh cider turns fizzy. Apples lose their crispness. Farm earnings don't necessarily come when expenditures mount and some personal cash is vital.

Putting the cider and apples into a jar—or freezing or drying—gives shelf life to your perishable harvest. Income becomes possible year-round. The value of that bushel of fruit is increased. An organic orchardist needs to give strong consideration to adding value to the apples that don't make select grade to have a shot at making a viable living. The organic premium in most parts of the country (where cider apples are a significant portion of the crop) is no guarantee of such a living.

Value-added is not without its cost and bureaucratic hurdles, however. A licensed processing kitchen can be expensive to set up—spending ten thousand dollars for used equipment and to renovate an existing space is not unusual—and as unjustified economically for small acreage as are the large orchard sprayers and flail choppers. Product liability insurance is a must. The market needs to be tested, eye-catching labels designed, and recipes developed. Nutritional labeling isn't required until your gross sales top $500,000. Analytical tests required for food-safety purposes include pH acidity, water activity (linked to microbial growth prospects), and shelf life. Admittedly, most growers will find all this more frustrating than any orchard pest.

Fortunately, finding an already approved kitchen to use as a startup facility isn't as daunting as it may sound. We initially relied on the licensed restaurant facilities of a small inn which serves meals only on weekends. While a restaurant kitchen is not a full-fledged processing kitchen with a steam kettle and filling machines, it is equipped to make bushel batches of product that you can then trial-market. Finding a cost-justified price, the right-size container, and creating a label that does more than just say what's in the jar takes a year or two of adjustments.

Some states have begun to make community processing kitchens available to encourage specialty foods entrepreneurs. The NH Cooks program has

Value-added-product display at Lost Nation Cider Mill.

opened such kitchens in Epping and our home-town of Lancaster. The facility is inspected down to the hairs on your chinny-chin-chin (I'm talking beard nets here, mate). Our $50 membership fee and $100 food-processing license allows us full use of the facilities for every product we've had properly food-tested. The kitchen area is rented at $10 an hour, the canning room at $26. Yes, these are more costs to figure into the pricing equation, but now we're able to fill 480 jars of apple jelly in an hour. This is a kitchen we could never have capitalized ourselves, but it makes sense for many area farms, bakers, and mustard makers to come together and share. It will also allow us to test-market more basic apple products like sauce and juice without further equipment investment. Best of all for a common-sense guy like myself, there's a kitchen coordinator available to help growers wade through all the bureaucratic mire.

Dried apple rings may be the simplest option for small orchards. David Gill in Clifton Springs, New York, dries two bushels in five hours time in a film cabinet rigged with sixteen screens and the guts of a propane stove. "Dead-ripe apples with a waxy finish have better flavor and dry quicker," he says. "You need to turn the heat down near the end of drying, as the nearly dehydrated apples will scorch at 190°F." The key to this kind of production is the commercial corer/peeler available from the F. B. Pease Company. Gill's Oven-Dried Apples are wholesaled to area supermarkets at a net profit of $25 per bushel. "The secret to making sustainable agriculture work is processing something for sale at home to get more of the sale price," as David has aptly shown.

Whatever the product, analyzing costs and setting a wholesale price accordingly is integral to success. Direct costs are easy to assess once you know batch size: jar, label, non-apple ingredients, special equipment (amortize five years' worth of product at so many cases per year), utilities, and kitchen rental. Work back from your suggested retail price by dividing by 1.5 to get the wholesale price for a non-perishable product. Knowing the time it takes to make a batch, and establishing a common processing wage, you can figure a bushel value for each apple product at the wholesale level. Allow a 15 percent sales factor into the wholesale price to cover either a sales rep's commission or your own wholesaling efforts. Such numbers are invaluable in determining where your farm profitability lies. Overhead costs like property tax, insurance, and advertising are assumed covered by our retail markup on direct sales. Mill prices are marked up 33 percent from wholesale to give us a producer's competitive advantage over area stores that carry Lost Nation products at suggested retail prices.

There are a few bootstrap approaches to getting your value-added products out on the market beyond your farm stand. Commercial bartering works between small producers. Try swapping a few cases of your product with the mustard maker for her product. She in turn can sell your cider jelly at the country fair while you're busy on the home front with sales that include her mustard. Catalog offerings can be mutually shared as well: trade listings of each other's product on a drop-ship basis. Local stores may be more open to consignment sales rather than an outright purchase until repeat sales are assured. I'm inclined to have a consignment price just slightly higher than the wholesale price in this situation, giving the store a 33 percent markup to get to suggested retail price.

QUALITY AND APPEARANCE

Quality is everything in building a small business. The apples you sell need to be crisp and firm. Organic aesthetics are different from chemically induced perfection, but that doesn't mean bruised fruit qualifies for select grade. Our cider is never more than a week old—otherwise it's identified and the price marked down a dollar a gallon. We replace wholesale cider each week so only our freshest product is available on the grocer's shelf. We don't want to lose a customer who comes to think that Lost Nation stuff goes fizzy a day or two after it's bought. The return policy works, as we swap back very little cider. Our "fizzy customers" readily scoop the week-old cider up at the mill, where we recoup the wholesale price in full. The vinegar barrel is always another option for cider that's close to fermenting. Sometimes cider jelly doesn't jell to our standard. Such loose jelly first got used in the apple butter, but then we saved the jarring effort by offering cider glaze.

Organic growers are beholden to each other in putting their best stuff forward. We have the taste advantage. The produce we grow is safe for our children and good for the earth. There's no reason any potential customer should be turned off by poor appearance or fruit picked green. Apple growers

---

PRICING EQUATION FOR ORGANIC CIDER JELLY

$0.72 Product Cost = 42¢ jar + 12¢ labels + cider (only ingredient) + 8¢ gas + 10¢ evaporator

$0.45 Labor Cost = 5 hours (includes clean-up) x $6.50 wage ÷ 72 jars (from 30 gallon batch)

$2.33 Apple Value per Jar = $3.50 Wholesale Price − $1.17 Total Costs

$16.78 Wholesale Bushel Value* = $2.33 x 72 jars ÷ 10 bushels of cider apples

*$13.00 if deducting sales expenses.

with mixed offerings can easily cover the quality gamut of organic aesthetics given the value-added and cider options. Utility-grade fruit at our mill is perhaps the best organic buy—some nonworrisome surface blemishes, but just as sound for fresh eating if the customer so wishes.

This same appearance standard applies to your advertising, display, and farm newsletters. This doesn't mean brochures can't be funky or the message not hilarious. It doesn't mean you have to spend umpteen bucks at the printers—but do spend some. A typed mailing label on a jar of pickles is nothing compared to a farm artwork sticker with *Dill Pickles* calligraphied in green ink at less than five cents a label. We spent outrageous money for our four-color cider label, but it was a big factor in the beginning in telling people something new was happening in Lost Nation. That same artwork is featured on the brochure that attracts tourists to the cider mill and has become the label for cider vinegar, hard cider, and apple juice by simply changing the printed type. Displays of crafted baskets, pine shelves to catch the vertical eye, and deep-hued tablecloths can set off your fruit and jarred products at practically no cost. Appearance matters because it's the first point of introduction of you to your customers.

ORGANIC CERTIFICATION

There are marketing advantages to identifying apples as organic, provided quality is good and the price premium not outrageous. Today, more people are aware of food safety issues, though often that awareness doesn't include greater tolerance for blemished fruit. Organic fruit growers generally opt for certification, and reasonably so, given their intensive management effort and higher labor costs.

Which isn't to say debate on organic certification shouldn't be encouraged. "Certification works against the small grower," says Frank Foltz of Northwind Nursery in Princeton, Minnesota. "A close consumer/producer relationship—trusting one another—is far better than government fees and remote standards." We have Lost Nation apples and cider certified by the New Hampshire Department of Agriculture (the current annual fee being a moderate $100). Certification isn't needed for direct sales at the cider mill, as I'm on hand to promote our apples and answer questions. It's more for when I'm not present: certifying our cider as organic in natural foods stores and substantiating our mail-order promotions.

Apple growers who clearly can't call their fruit organic are also wrapped up in a debate of terms to distinguish their apples in the consumer's eye. Friends I consider equally committed to growing healthy food on healthy soil have had to face the reality of a plum curculio infestation that devastates as much as 90 percent of their orchard. John Bemis at Hutchins Farm in Concord, Massachusetts, calls

IN TRANSITION

Organic certification standards require a three-year transition period between the last application of chemical inputs and the harvesting of a certified organic crop. Ecosystems always react to change: any grower contemplating such a conversion should be prepared for a lowered packout and a probable loss in farm income. There's no outright marketing advantage to offering "transition fruit." However, the learning that takes place during these years — coupled with an organic premium — can eventually produce an equivalent return. Large operations are best advised to undertake a switch over to organic methods one block at a time.

his apples *not quite organic*. Guy and Carolyn Ames of Ames Orchard in Fayetteville, Arkansas, have decided upon the term *ecological*. Both farms use one or two sprays of Imidan, a selective chemical easy on beneficial insects, to get beyond curculio. Their marketing emphasis is on getting customers to first taste the apples and then to talk aesthetics. As Carolyn explains, "It would take many additional sprays of a mixture of pesticides to produce blemish-free, supermarket-type fruit. We hope that the newly educated palates of our customers will lead to an appreciation of the true worth of a good apple . . . flavor, wholesomeness, and vitality!"

The term *low-spray* can communicate a positive image to most consumers. The problem here lies in the ambiguity: ecological growers fall right beside conventional spray growers using more persistent chemical options who can now honestly claim to be spraying fewer times. Fruit labeled *certified IPM* can be equivocal as well, for, despite the good intentions of its promoters, the checklist of production guidelines need only be met partway.

Ultimately, the customer's best bet in finding safe and great-tasting apples lies in knowing the orchardist. This is more an argument for local agriculture than it is for organic certification, I think. The day is coming when national standards may only work for the big growers and then, as Eliot Coleman has suggested, we'll have to find a new word to express ourselves. How does *apples with integrity* grab you?

ADVERTISING

There are appropriate times to spend money on advertising. Target your local market, find venues that reach the tourists, and use the broadest sweep of all to inform organic-minded families in your region that, indeed, organic apples are available. Another maxim in getting the attention you need is to repeat your core message over and over in different

yet consistent ways. Figure that people will need to hear something as much as twenty-seven times before it penetrates their primordial consciousness and they make it part of themselves.

Spending hard-earned farm dollars on advertising brings most of us a feeling of "damned if we do, damned if we don't." Our first-year ads were too crammed with print to distinguish themselves on the printed page. Since then, we've caught the reader's eye with pictures of silent film stars making some inane apple quip. The ad format remains the same from week to week, with Lost Nation Cider Mill in bold print followed by our product offerings and mill hours, but we often change the photo and quote. My favorite is Marie Dressler, wagging her finger in the air and saying, "There's only one cider for the North Country, and those boys in Lost Nation make it." A smaller, business-card ad is rotated in some weeks to remind customers that we're still pressing cider like fiends, even though traditional apple season winds down after peak fall foliage.

We have a defined budget to keep this advertising effort from going overboard. Rules of thumb on advertising recommend spending anywhere from 2 to 8 percent of your gross receipts. We've settled in at a 4 percent budget, which includes printing costs of brochures and inclusion in statewide apple maps. Amazingly, we're still reaching people in nearby towns who just didn't know we were here.

Rotating the mediums in which you place advertising can be effective for reaching such folks. We've hooked up with a local radio station, which in exchange for our providing free cider for a live broadcast event, promotes our Lost Nation Cider Mill a few days ahead and throughout the event itself. I've a feeling the next step will be putting voices to those silent film stars used in our print ads.

You need to be persistent and audaciously creative to catch people's attention. Word-of-mouth appreciation remains a marketer's best drawing card. Yet you need the mix advertising and other market innovations provide, as each avenue only reaches some of the people some of the time.

MARKETING INNOVATIONS

We market the Lost Nation experience and our friendliness in all our brochures and ads, at our annual Harvest Festival, on Friday school tours, and in a series of educational pamphlets we've the gumption to call Lost Nation Trading Cards. It's a marketing package that has evolved with experience and commonsense insights. Those necessary sparks of creativity seem to come at just the right moments when you love and believe in what you're doing.

A Bold New Look

Our first marketing step was to create a cider label to boldly state our presence on local store shelves. None of the stock cider labels available expressed what we intended to revive in a full-bodied cider, so we bit the bullet and printed Lost Nation cider labels at triple the cost of a generic label. The artwork we chose, of a hand-picking an apple, is printed in four colors at a cost of $950 for ten thousand labels.

Was it worth it? I think so. It caught the eye of the local market and told people that something new was happening in Lost Nation. It was a quality presentation that encouraged consumers to expect equally high quality in the cider. And it made us all the more excited about our business and what we intended to achieve. Good energy draws energy to itself, and this was just the beginning.

Press Releases

We write press releases occasionally to attract newspaper interest in our farm effort. Think up interesting angles to promote yourselves anew, provide

(artwork by Susannah Becker)

a few quotes for a reporter to integrate into the final story, and offer a photograph if appropriate. Try these approaches for press releases to keep your name in the public eye: launching a new venture like a mail-order catalog, hosting apple tastings or harvest festivals; announcing your official certification as an organic farm; or providing early-season growing tips for backyard growers. A photo opportunity can serve the same end, be it the apple-growers posed with a lively bunch of second-graders or a visiting group of Eastern Europeans interested in sustainable agriculture. Our best coup yet was getting a cider-pressing picture of David on the cover of a statewide tourist weekly when the fall foliage season was at its peak.

Lost Nation Trading Cards

People who understand what makes for a good

cider—and the impassioned work that goes into it —are going to be your best customers. Efforts at consumer education need to be brief and fun. Thus was born our Lost Nation Trading Cards. Not that anyone in the world is going to collect the whole set or even look for a checklist to mark off the cards in their collection. (Can you tell I collected baseball cards as a kid?) Yet the cards do serve several functions.

We started off with "Cider Facts." Then came "The Organic Apple," followed the next year by the lore of "Hard Cider." Trading Card No. 4 was an out-and-out marketing pitch for "Cider Bonds." The educating part comes in snippets, like this gem: "Old-time cidermakers insisted on pressing sound, ripe apples only. It was said that an apple that reached the ground imparted an earthy flavor to the cider. Our premium organic cider is made exclusively with hand-picked apples." Then there's this plug for organics: "Organic food will cost more until the marketplace fully recognizes the environmental and health costs of chemically grown food. You, the consumer, help the cause by seeking out locally grown food, asking questions about how your food is grown, and being more appreciative of organic perfection."

We hand out the new season's card with each purchase, usually with a statement along the lines of, "and here's a little something to read while you drink your cider." Past cards are available in a card rack on the wall. We also offer up the trading cards in mail-order gift boxes as an attractive bonus.

Newsletters and Cider Bonds

We've encouraged community involvement in our apple vision from the start. Newsletters are written twice a year as a way of sharing our orcharding sagas, financial hopes, events, and apple offerings. Originally the newsletter was offered primarily to farm members, these being folks who made a one-time investment donation of $25 or more to help capitalize our new plantings in exchange for a future return of sweet cider from those baby trees. This idea evolved into the sale of cider bonds, through which we have raised $4,000 so far. Cider bonds are our customers' opportunity to participate in the long-term success of Lost Nation Orchard. Four actual bonds (a spoof version of U.S. Savings Bonds), redeemable in the year 2000 for a gallon of cider each, are issued now to farm members. Such shared investment is a concept not readily grasped in our competitive society. For us, it's yet

LOST NATION CIDER BOND

One Gallon

LOST NATION CIDER MILL
LANCASTER, NEW HAMPSHIRE

SERIES LN
CiDER TURNS FIZZY
30 DAYS AFTER ISSUE

REDEEMABLE IN
THE YEAR 2000

To _____

Farm member as of _____

Those boys in Lost Nation

0009007.1 701280937

One Gallon

Lost Nation Cider Bond.

WHAT DO CIDER BONDS OFFER YOU?

- Providing an agricultural legacy to future generations of this community.
- Four gallons of the best cider you'll ever taste.
- Or, if you prefer, keep your four cider bonds into perpetuity until some collector finally offers your asking price.
- Being a valued partner on the last organic frontier as we discover the nuances of growing apples organically.
- Knowing you helped two good guys do a good thing on this earth.

another innovation intended to overcome the challenges facing small farms today. Like any good marketing copy, the bonds are pitched in self-valued terms.

Cider bond investors have given us a lot more than their money. Sharing belief in a mutual vision does more to strengthen our hearts than mere dollars will ever be worth. Visions are built by getting through the struggles. There are times when the underlying economics behind a commercial organic apple venture seem so impossible: these are the times we recall the people who believe so much in what we are trying to achieve. And then we keep on keeping on.

School Tours

School tours have proved an incredible avenue for reaching new customers. We have some five hundred children visit the mill over the course of several Friday mornings. A tour group consists of two classes at a time. I take the kids into the orchard to explain how apples grow, show them how to pick, and make a plug for organics using a sticky trap with a large rubber bug stuck to it as a way of getting their attention. Meanwhile, David has the other class in the mill to see how our water-powered press grinds the apples and squeezes out the juice. The kids all get free samples of cider afterwards and their parents get the chance to buy big-time (we hope). The greatest part of this experience for us is finding the kids bringing the rest of their families back, and observing the parents on the tour itself nodding their heads in appreciation of what we do to grow organic fruit. Again, we're reaching some of the people some of the time.

Festivals

We began hosting an annual harvest festival in 1994. We rent a festival tent and hire two fiddlers to call a contradance all afternoon long. A whole-grain baker comes to sell delicious calzones and tempting desserts. My wife, Nancy, leads the kids in bobbing for apples and to see who can achieve the longest apple peel. We sell apples and cider and more cider, but rarely get to dance ourselves. I fit in an organic-growing workshop in the late morning. David keeps the press a'squishing and repeats an-

Bobbing for apples at the Lost Nation Harvest Festival.

JILL BROOKS

School classes love coming for tours of Lost Nation Orchard.

swers to the usual questions with enthusiasm. His wife, Andrea, serves out hot apple crisp and ice cream. Several hundred people come to enjoy a glorious fall day. It's our way of returning to the community that sense of sharing that local agriculture draws from the bounty of the land. Such a festival is worth every penny and all the extra effort we expend in making the day possible.

CSA Shares

Our orchard is one of several CSA or *community-supported agriculture* farms in the area that put out a cooperative marketing brochure each spring offering share packages for sale. An apple share consists of four gallons of cider and four half-peck bags of apples, to be picked up over the course of the cider mill season. The price is $35, which represents a 15 percent savings over our regular fall prices.

Both the farm budget and our customers gain from this offering. The twenty or so shares sold each year represent $700 to be put toward spring expenses at a time when our cash intake is virtually at a standstill. It also serves as an impetus to get shareholders out to the mill several times each fall, and often they find something more to buy.

Apple Tastings

Apple-tasting parties are a great way to share the many flavors of the apple with people who might otherwise never try them. The idea here is to bring your wares to town, perhaps to the library or a church hall or the natural foods store, to attract people who haven't yet been to the farm stand. Make it a free event. Get people to rate their favorites and describe the flavor and texture of each fruit. You'll all be participating in a shared feast dating back to the Persian Empire, when fresh fruit was first served in the closing stages of a meal. The grand finale of the organic apple is as good now as it was then.

LONG-TERM VISION

Small farmers are visionaries. It takes vision to believe your agricultural efforts will come to fruition. Such hope is based upon hard work and willing trial and error. Trees grow over the course of years, and in the same way we must grow with them. Perhaps one of the greatest delights of apples is this understanding of the long haul.

Marketing the fruits of one's organic labor in the context of 20th-century economics also calls for long-term vision. A similar patience to cultivate an appreciative customer base goes with the nurturing of the trees. A homestead orchard requires thought enough as to what to do with a full harvest. A small commercial planting of an acre or more of fruit needs to be backed up with a sound marketing plan.

We started out in Lost Nation with two-plus acres of bearing orchard, an existing (though much depleted) cider mill business, and a lot of unknowns. Still, our initial five-year plan turned out to be on target. The second year we grafted enough rootstock to satisfy a perceived need for a full organic harvest, based on replacing the percentage of low-spray apples we currently "import" from an orchard in Maine. In the next years we planted five additional acres of apples. We began to make processed product and learn the lessons of pricing. A gift box offering expanded into a more extensive catalog sent to a rapidly growing mailing list gathered over the past seasons. Advertising found its stride, and we learned to reach a broader audience for less cost. We cut out aspects of the business that weren't time-effective and became more aware of personal needs. All wasn't necessarily planned, nor did it evolve overnight, but in retrospect, we got here from there.

Now it is time for the next five-year plan. The new plantings call for better equipment to enable us to manage more orchard. The mill facilities need to be expanded to handle additional crop. The mail-order business and wholesaling of caselots is a more competitive arena, but we have confidence in our organic apple niche and grassroots approach. It's legitimate to ask, what if these ideas fail? Perhaps even more daunting, what if they actually succeed? Planning goes both ways.

There's one last aspect to this "vision thing" that shouldn't be forgotten. Are you doing something that gives you great joy and pleasure in life? The dance of the apple trees is but one dance of many.

It is much desired that the fruit garden shall return to men's minds, with its personal appeal and its collections of many choice varieties, even the names of which are now unknown to the fruit-loving public. The discriminating admiration of fruits for odor, good form and color, and for choice quality is little known amongst us today. Our desire for fruits is mostly uncritical, easily contented, and confined within narrow and uninteresting limits . . . The commercial market ideals have come to be controlling, and most fruit-eaters have never eaten a first-class apple or pear or peach, and do not know what such fruits are; and the names of choice varieties have mostly dropped from the lists of nurserymen. All this is as much to be deplored as a loss of standards of excellence in literature and music, for it is an expression of a lack of resources and a failure of sensitiveness.

—LIBERTY HYDE BAILEY, *The Principles of Fruit Growing* (1897)

CHAPTER 10

The Last Organic Frontier

We each live where our communities need us to grow such choice fruit. Small farm orchards that can please apple lovers will find a local following. And that success will be the impetus by which organic promise can become sustainable reality.

THE SUSTAINABLE ORCHARD

An agriculture that integrates human needs with ecological sanity is sustainable. Inherent in this kind of farming is a continuing ability to produce food from the land century after century. Our destiny begins and ends in good stewardship of the soil. Each generation is accountable to the next for its methods of farming. Our current dependence on fossil fuels, petrochemical fertilizers, and organophosphate poisons leaves much to be desired. Chemical residues are accumulating in our atmosphere, our soil, and our bodies. Even if this were not the case, the little gas that's left in the tank will

soon be drained. Changes are afoot regardless of our organic (or not) inclinations.

This book has attempted to take a first step—a beginning but necessary one—towards sustainable orchard practice. We've picked up the trail where our great-grandparents left it a century ago. Valid elements of their agriculture have been too long overlooked in the rush to grasp more convenient and, in the immediate scheme of things, more profitable technologies. Integrated pest management discoveries equally suit our purpose. We are poised to make use of the best of both eras as we move ahead into the final organic frontier.

A market expectation of surface perfection in every apple—aptly dubbed "pestophobia" by Ron Prokopy—must be changed if we desire to tackle issues of sustainability head-on. Organic fruit practices (other than on the West Coast) are not likely to control insect and disease damage to the same degree as "conventional methods" anytime soon.

Beautiful organic apples.

lars locally to support broader values? Orcharding does not happen outside the world around it. Fruit growers cannot begin to truly change until society as a whole embraces a lifestyle that can sustain us all.

We're moving towards an organic agriculture regardless. The bankruptcy of the chemical approach becomes even clearer as the years pass. The gasoline that fuels the big machines is going to run out. Horses are due for a noble comeback. More people are going to need to be involved in farming again. This is a good thing, whether these people return directly to the land as growers themselves, or engage in interactive, revitalized local economies that makes neighborly farming possible. So many imponderables get answered when we turn from the *big and naughty* to the *small and beautiful*.

ORGANIC PERSEVERANCE

All winter long we waited. Orchard sanitation couldn't have been better. Pollination was good, fruit set is heavy. But what's this? Traps indicated very minimal sawfly activity compared to years past. Yet now the apples on the end six feet of almost every branch show the telltale frass hole. It's a significant crop loss despite our good efforts. A couple of chemical sprays might have made a full harvest possible. The apples would be cosmetically beautiful . . . so why do we even try to grow fruit organically?

Growing a reasonable proportion of beautiful fruit without synthetic chemicals is doable. Still, it is rarely enough for a dependable living in the economic context of these times. The onus for change is on our culture: have we the will to spend our dol-

---

AN ORGANIC APPLE GROWER'S WISH LIST

- A solution to curculio, whatever the combination of trapping, beneficials, and repellents
- Round-headed appletree borer to be effectively kept from our trunks
- Grower-coordinated research trials that point to conclusive answers based on fewer farm inputs
- Consumers to realize that minor blemishes on fruit represent a better value than excessive chemical residues
- A sustainable agriculture fully restored as the mainstay of vibrant local economies

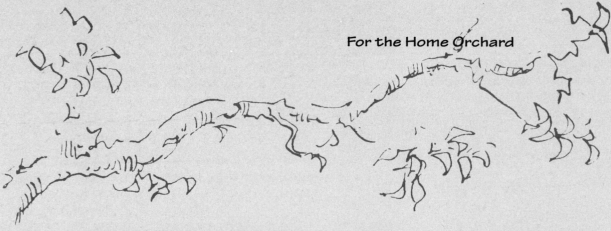

THREE-TREE SIMPLICITY

Nurturing apple trees is an earthly pleasure not to be missed. Obviously the home orchard won't be near the scale of even a modest commercial planting. But that simplifies things in terms of insect and disease control. Choose rootstock according to the space available and an anticipated harvest that won't overwhelm you. Varieties should be family favorites appropriate to your hardiness zone. Summer apples go by quickly, but a winter's supply of Red Astrachan applesauce may be one of your goals. Spreading the harvest season out with an early-fall variety, a midseason apple, and a good winter keeper may be the best choice. Home cidermakers may want to double such a planting to have a wider selection of varieties to blend.

- Pollination will be readily achieved by the wild pollinators found in a diverse garden setting (bumblebees, orchard mason bees, etc.). The blooms of three different apple varieties suited to your area will likely overlap enough to ensure cross-pollination, and don't rule out neighboring trees on this account either.

- Removing all alternate-host trees (plum, hawthorn, cedars, etc.) within a hundred yards of your trees will reduce insect damage as most apple pests won't migrate this far in search of your apples. You can always offer to care for a neighbor's fruit tree that's been too long neglected.

- Scab control can be achieved by raking up all the fallen apple leaves in late fall. Either compost these in a general humus mix or take them to a nearby woods where apples aren't growing. The fungal spores of apple scab might blow in from as much as two miles away, but the greater disease source is always the inoculum from the year before on the fallen leaves and fruit beneath your trees.

- Choosing scab-resistant or scab-tolerant varieties will insure you never need get into a sulfur spray regimen. Apples like William's Pride, Redfree, and Liberty are

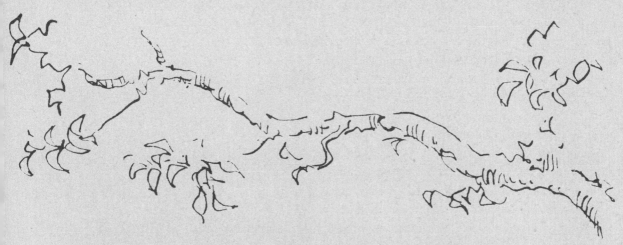

immune to the scab fungus. Tolerant varieties like Burgundy, Sweet Sixteen, and Tompkins King can get scab, but damage will be minor in a normal season.

- The home orchardist's greatest advantage may lie in being relieved from the economic pressure of growing dessert-quality fruit. Which isn't to say you won't have your share of winners at the county fair. The blemished fruit is just as much a boon when making preserves, juice, or applesauce. Sort the best-looking apples for fresh eating and storage.

- Hand-thinning is as vital in the backyard as on any apple farm. Fruit should be left every six inches along the branch. Always make the effort to remove insect-stung fruit. Raking up June drops for this very purpose is doable with just a few trees in a mown yard.

- Curculio is likely to be the greatest insect problem. Jarring the little buggers daily onto ground sheets is a viable option during the two weeks or so of egg-laying activity. Apple maggot fly can be effectively trapped out with red spheres (four traps per standard tree or one per dwarf). Codling moth pressure can be reduced by hanging cut-open milk jugs containing several inches of vinegar-molasses solution spiced with a few drops of sassafras oil. Bt is a very safe spray alternative for any caterpillar pest.

- Borers destroy young trees. One old-time repellent worth noting was a wood-ash slurry with onion juice used to coat the trunk thickly at the soil line in late June. Any egg slits brazenly made by the adult beetle need to be gouged in September to prevent the grubs from doing greater damage.

- Your local Cooperative Extension office can help identify any unknown insect or disease that might be plaguing your fruit trees. Organic solutions may not be forthcoming from the Extension agent, but then, that's why you bought this book.

It seems inevitable that such moments come up each season. At these times we need to be able to look at the broader picture of what happens in the orchard. Birds nest in our trees and rear their young to flighthood. One little boy never ate an apple till he had an organic Cortland: no doubt youthful intuition about the long-term concerns of pesticides in our food. Another man has been buying a winter supply of our apples to make fresh juice a part of his cancer cure: we're glad to report Bernie is still with us, alive and kicking. There's our own disinclination to ride the chemical cloud to economic prosperity at the cost of our health. And you know, on second thought, we are quite blessed with a beautiful crop of apples despite that early-season letdown.

Struggle is a vital part of what we do. Our learning curve is often slow and haphazard when it comes to discovering Nature's ways. No matter what our approach to growing fruit, we're never as in control as we like to think. The economics of orcharding certainly make it tempting to apply a few judicious sprays. It takes significantly more labor to grow organic apples well. Chemicals could eliminate the need to spend many days hand-thinning, trapping out insects, cultivating young trees, and completing orchard sanitation. All orchardists work long hours and take tremendous risks with their farm investments. It can be hard not to cash in on the chemical guarantee.

Down in our farmhouse cellar is an unopened bottle of Ortho's Lindane Borer & Leaf Miner Spray. I bought it at a home garden center the winter after we lost about twenty young trees to severe borer infestation. Two years before, I had smugly wrapped window screening around those trees as "permanent protection." Whether borers were already beneath the bark or adult beetles crawled behind the screening to lay their eggs is irrelevant. *Orcharding without trees* didn't appear promising, so in my frustration I reached for the then-recommended spray remedy. That next spring I replanted. Come July it

Hope begins anew every spring when the apple trees bloom.

was time to spray . . . but I couldn't do it. I knew in my heart I needed to outwit this pest and persevere; that, for me, having the trees by chemical means was not a desire. No doubt the Lindane would have done its stuff, but whether or not I would have suffered any bodily harm, an essential part of my hopes would have been altered. It's important to add here that these trees are thriving today, provided each season I meticulously probe out the bug that apparently won't go away.

How we orchard is a question of personal conviction, one that each individual needs to answer. There's no place for a "holier than thou" attitude in organic farming. If anything, I sometimes feel "stupider than thou" when I look at the monetary result of my nonchemical efforts. Growers deserve decent earnings, but even those using chemical means come up short some years. The magnitude of investment ultimately determines our options for us. Lost Nation Orchards will always be comparatively small for several reasons. Our family income comes from that typical Yankee mix of *a little bit of everything*. David and I—and our "Holediggers in the Sky"—can only cover so much ground. We're learning something of value here to pass on to other growers. And at this scale, it's simply a joy to be doing what we're doing.

Ted and Beth Schlapfer of Sunshower Orchard in Oregon offer one final perspective on organic perseverance. "First we sent our children out—now it's the grandkids—to pick and eat apples right from the tree. Not having to worry about what might be on that fruit is reward aplenty."

ESOPUS SPITZENBERG AND A BETTER TOMORROW

Many small diversified farms—each with an orchard!—nourishes us as a people on a spiritual level. Food grown organically enhances our vitality. Life is not a mere combination of chemicals manipulated for the greatest yields. Those orchardists attempting to transcend the economic goals of first-level IPM have a richer intimacy with their trees to which industrial agriculture can lay no claim. Small-scale growers and the enlightened communities that support their efforts are leading us towards a better tomorrow.

These are the words of Lynn Miller in the twentieth anniversary edition of the *Small Farmer's Journal*:

We believe in small farms. Not just casually because they are worth having or saving. Not because the family farm (read small farm) is as American as apple pie and tortillas. We believe in small farms in a BIG way. We know that human society needs small farms for food security. We know that most humans need small

farms for the right livelihood they offer. W̶ rural communities die without small farms̶ makeup. We know that human culture bec̶ annihilating without a significant base of p̶ are true craftsmen at farming. We know that anyone who has a burning desire to be a farmer CAN, and SHOULD, be a farmer. We know that we can never have enough farmers. We know that the reservoir of human experience and knowledge as it pertains to farming is as valuable and fragile as any gene pool.

Esopus Spitzenberg symbolizes the small farm orchards we've left behind. Thomas Jefferson chose this brilliant orange-red apple as his favorite over the many others grown at Monticello in the early nineteenth century. Orcharding embodies the well-rounded approach to life Jefferson expressed in his writings and achievements. A fruit grower needs to comprehend some of botany, entomology, microbiology, agronomy, organic chemistry, and even humanistic philosophy. The broader our understanding, the more likely we can perceive answers to the challenges facing us. The appeal of orcharding knows no bounds: growing beautiful fruit is satisfying whether in the home orchard or on a commercial scale. Those looking for the "one spray that grows all" won't find anywhere near the fulfillment that Jefferson found in his beloved orchard or you will in yours. Embracing challenges is what makes life real.

We share a spiritual bond with our trees. More is going on out in the orchard than the mere growing of fruit or the harvesting of dollars. Miracles unfold every day before our eyes; songs we can't quite hear intone the glories of Creation. Our recognition of our spiritual nature—and that of our trees—is where the true journey begins. Someday we are meant to understand that it was never intended we leave the Garden of Eden. And then we can go home.

The final organic frontier is a journey of both the soul and good science. The answers to growing marketable organic fruit are within our reach. Like

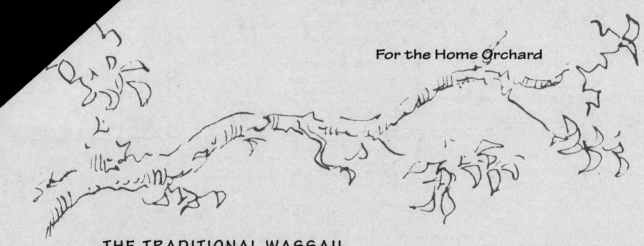

THE TRADITIONAL WASSAIL

The most delightful party we host at our snowbound farm takes place on the Saturday evening following January 17. Our apple friends and neighbors are past the rush of the holidays and the beckoning call of distant families. With a bow to the modern weekend, we go out to wassail the apple trees about the time of Old Twelfth Night.

Wassailing the apple orchards with cider and song is an English custom going back centuries. The ceremony awakens the spirit of the tree in the depths of winter to our hopes for a plentiful fruit crop in the coming season. A calendar adjustment of twelve days in 1752 (leap years now keep our position around the sun more incrementally dated) met with stubborn resistance: farmers knew not even the king could move Christmas. Accordingly, the country folk kept what would have been the holidays that year — celebrating Old Christmas on January 5 and wassailing the wheat fields and orchards on the eve of Old Epiphany twelve days later — which in turn became part of the tradition.

Our Lost Nation tradition has its own wry twist, in that our gathering often occurs on the coldest night of the winter. There's certainly an almost mystical power in sharing apple custom with forty dear friends as you dance around the selected tree at thirty degrees below zero! Under the glow of hundreds of miniature lights strung in its boughs, I begin by telling of this ancient earth rite. Then comes a proper toast: the "butler" brings forth a piece of toasted bread, ceremoniously pours cider over it, whereupon the "master" hangs it on a fruiting spur. The entire company then lifts their glasses high, and shouting a hearty "Here's to you, oh apple tree," drinks the health of the tree. Our guest of honor shares in the toast through cider poured atop its roots. Then we bow to the tree, rising three times as if laden with the biggest box of apples ever harvested . . . leaving no doubt what it is we wish as a blessing in return. The wassail song brings the circling entourage to a clamorous finale: bottle rockets are fired and pots banged to drive away any "evil spirits" that would limit the desired harvest. A slice of cider pie and the warmth of the fire awaits the returning revelers back inside.

the solutions to all our earth-shattering problems, they are human in scale and will be found on small farms and in vibrant local economies. Many of the links need to be made by us, as university research remains tied to industrial agriculture, despite an admirable emphasis on reducing chemical use. As in life, we all have a piece of the truth in front of our eyes. Learning the intricacies of the natural orchard is one step. Revitalizing local markets and consumer tolerance, another. The organic apple is a simple but ever-so-eloquent expression of where we need to go.

THE WASSAIL SONG

Oh apple tree, we'll wassail thee in hope that thou will bear.
The Lord does know where we shall be to be merry another year.
To blow well and to bear well, and so merry let us be:
Let every man drink up his cup, here's health to the old apple tree.
To blow well and to bear well, and so merry let us be:
Let every man drink up his cup, here's health to the old apple tree.

(repeat all twice more)

Apples now —
Hats full,
Caps full,
Barrels full,
Three bushel bags full,
Barn floors full,
And even a little heap under the stairs.
Hip, Hip, Hooray! Hip, Hip, Hooray! Hip, Hip, Hooray!

APPENDIX I

Compendium of Orchard Tasks

Each orchard will have ever-evolving spray schedules and task checklists to account for a unique pest complex and other regional variables. Some of the basics will be the same as ours here in Lost Nation, New Hampshire. Primary scab season, for instance, occurs ten to fourteen days either side of pink no matter where you roam. Other concerns vary. Oriental fruit moth doesn't live this far north, though its cycles and control are quite like our lesser appleworm and codling moth. We have two generations of these pests, whereas orchards with longer growing seasons might experience three or four generations. Bud moths and leafroller pressures vary by region, though well-timed applications of Bt based on trap monitoring are the principal means of control. Different tree fruits have their own particulars.

Our Lost Nation task compendium doesn't tell you so much what to do in your orchard as provide an example. Writing down your orchard's schedule will deepen your understanding both of what needs to be done and what can be improved. We act because we perceive a reason to act, not because a book tells us we should act.

Dormant Season

- Check for deer incursions at least weekly
- Ski through orchard to pack down vole tunnels
- Collect scions for grafting
- Prune all bearing trees
- Burn brush pile of previous year's prunings while snow is still on the ground
- Complete routine maintenance on all orchard equipment
- Order orchard supplies for the coming season

Bud Break

- Remove all prunings from orchard
- Finish any compost spreading not completed in late fall
- Remove all trunk guards

- Spray copper for fire blight (if necessary) before quarter-inch green
- Spray 2 percent oil emulsion on young trees for aphid control at tight cluster on a warm day
- Plant new trees as early as possible

Pink

- Apply organic fertilizer blend to nonbearing trees
- Cultivate around gravel mulch on nonbearing trees
- Spray bearing blocks with Dipel, seaweed, Solubor, garlic extracts
- Hang white sticky traps for European apple sawfly
- Primary scab season has begun . . . spray sulfur before next predicted rain

Bloom

- Cut down wild apple trees spotted in bloom within a hundred yards of orchard
- Move in honeybee hives
- Scythe down competing bloom
- Hang pheromone wing traps for codling moth monitoring
- Train young trees with limb spreaders

Petal Fall and First Cover

- Spray garlic/neem to repel curculio
- Gather EAS traps
- Primary scab season ends with next daytime rain after 760 degree days . . . drop the "sulfur vigil"
- Complete round one of borer detail
- Spray for first-generation codling moth according to degree day tracking
- Follow through on curculio trap-tree strategy
- Include Solubor in a spray mix
- Thin crop and dispose of infested fruitlets
- Prune out fire blight strikes

- Cultivate around trees and renew gravel mulch
- Till new row edges and cover crop with annual legume
- Mow green hay and distribute mulch under trees

Midsummer

- Whitewash tree trunks for borer visibility and potential southwest scald protection
- Hang out Ladd traps for apple maggot fly and renew sticky every two weeks
- Summer-prune all young trees and watersprouts on bearing trees
- Spray foliar calcium at monthly intervals
- Spray for summer "leps" control if necessary
- Order custom-budded stock for future plantings
- Cruise through orchard and record tree observations
- Collect leaf samples and send to lab for tissue analysis
- Mow aisleways for better harvest access

Harvest

- Record data for harvest assessments
- Complete Round Two of borer detail
- Mow-mulch row edges in new plantings and cover crop with oats or winter rye
- Gather AMF traps and clean
- Gather all drops weekly
- Oh yeah . . . pick an amazingly high percentage of beautiful fruit

Winter Preparation

- Spread lime on fallen leaves, flail-mow, then spread compost
- Replace tree guards
- Take soil samples every few years to monitor cation needs
- Fork mulch back from tree trunks
- Hang peanut butter strips on electric deer fence

Grower's Source List

The future of agriculture lives in those people who develop low-input integrated systems. Economics won't have it any other way, nor will the planet. Still, growers need what they need when they need it. Buy wisely!

ORCHARD EQUIPMENT

Ben Meadows Company
3589 Broad Street
Atlanta, GA 30341
1–800–241–6401

A. M. Leonard
P.O. Box 816
Piqua, OH 45356
1–800–543–8955

Friend Manufacturing Corp.
Prospect Street
Gasport, NY 14067
(716) 772–2622

Millcreek Manufacturing Co.
2617 Stumptown Road
Bird-in-Hand, PA 17505
1–800–311–1323

Baldwin Apple Ladders
P.O. Box 221
Brooks, ME 04921
(207) 722–3654

King Machine Company
P.O. Drawer K
Scottsburg, IN 47170
1–800–365–2467

Orchard Supply and Equipment
P.O. Box 540
Conway, MA 01341
1–800–634–5557

Michigan Orchard Supply
07078 73½ Street
South Haven, MI 49090
(616) 637–1111

Forestry Suppliers, Inc.
P.O. Box 8397
Jackson, MS 39284
1–800–647–5368

Wilson Orchard Supply
1902 S. 11th Street
Yakima, WA 98903
1–800–232–1174

Occupational Services
17 Redwood Street
Chambersburg, PA 17201
1–800–745–8189

Alamo Flail Mowers
P.O. Box 549
Sequin, TX 78156
(210) 372–3551

Pike Agri-Lab Supplies
RR2 Box 710
Strong, ME 04983
(207) 684–5131

Best Angle Tree Stakes
RR2 Box 85
Muncy, PA 17756
(717) 546–5571

ORGANIC NURSERIES

Fedco Trees
P.O. Box 520
Waterville, ME 04903
(207) 873–7333

Northwind Nursery
7910 335th Avenue NW
Princeton, MN 55371
(612) 389–4920

Bear Creek Nursery
P.O. Box 411
Northport, WA 99157
Shipments from Washington must be chemically treated by state law for Apple Ermine Moth larvae.

St. Lawrence Nurseries
325 State Highway 345
Potsdam, NY 13676
(315) 265–6739

OTHER GOOD NURSERIES

Ames Orchard and Nursery
18292 Wildlife Road
Fayetteville, AR 72701
(501) 443–0282

Amberg's Nursery
3164 Whitney Road
Stanley, NY 14561
(716) 526–5405

Classical Fruits
8831 AL Highway 157
Moulton, AL 35650
(205) 974–8813

Hilltop Nurseries
P.O. Box 578
Hartford, MI 49057
1–800–253–2911

Lawyer's Rootstock Nursery
950 Highway 200 West
Plains, MT 59859
(406) 826–3881

Cummins Nursery
18 Glass Factory Bay Road
Geneva, NY 14456
(315) 789–7083

Rocky Meadows Orchard & Nursery
360 Rocky Meadow Road NW
New Salisbury, IN 47161
(812) 347–2213

Burford Brothers Nursery
Route 1
Monroe, VA 24574
(804) 929–4950

Adams County Nursery
P.O. Box 108
Aspers, PA 17304
(717) 677–8105

TRECO Rootstock Company
10906 Monitor-Mckee Road NE
Woodburn, OR 97071
(503) 634–2209

ORGANIC ORCHARD SUPPLIES

Peaceful Valley Farm Supply
P.O. Box 2209
Grass Valley, CA 95945
(916) 272–4769

North Country Organics
Depot Street
Bradford, VT 05033
(802) 222–4277

Integrated Fertility Management
333 Ohme Gardens Road
Wenatchee, WA 98801
1–800–332–3179

Bio-Gard Agronomics
P.O. Box 4477
Falls Church, VA 22044
1–800–673–8502

JP Institute for Applied Biodynamics
P.O. Box 133
Woolwine, VA 24185
(540) 930–2463

Harmony Farm Supply
P.O. Box 460
Graton, CA 95444
(707) 823–9125

Snow Pond Farm Supply
RR 2, Box 1009
Belgrade, ME 04917
1–800–768–9998

Fertrell Fertilizers
P.O. Box 265
Bainbridge, PA 17502
(717) 367–1566

Cal Crop USA
2245 Micro Place
Escondido, CA 92029
1–800–440–2767

Nuthin' But Rock
20 Electro Road
Scarborough, Ontario
(416) 752–6542

Midwestern Bio-Ag
Box 160
Blue Mounds, WI 53516
1–800–327–6012

CIDER MILL SUPPLIES

Day Equipment Corporation
1402 E. Monroe
Goshen, IN 46526
(219) 534–3491

Orchard Supply and Equipment
(see listing on p. 226)

F. B. Pease Company
1450 Henrietta Road
Rochester, NY 14623
(716) 475–1870

Goodnature Products
P.O. Box 866
Buffalo, NY 14240
(716) 855–3325

Michigan Orchard Supply
(see listing on p. 226)

Tew Manufacturing Corporation
P.O. Box 87
Penfield, NY 14526
1–800–380–5839

GOOD BUGS AND TRAPS FOR NOT-SO-GOOD BUGS

The Green Spot
93 Priest Road
Nottingham, NH 03290
(603) 942–8925

Gempler's IPM Supply
P.O. Box 270
Mt. Horeb, WI 53572
1–800–382–8473

Great Lakes IPM
10220 Church Road NE
Vestaburg, MI 48891
(517) 268–5911

Ladd Research Industries
P.O. Box 1005
Burlington, VT 05402
(802) 878–6711

DEER FENCING AND REPELLENTS

Premier Fence Systems
P.O. Box 89
Washington, IA 52353
1–800–282–6631

Green Screen Deterrents
P.O. Box 238-B
Benzonia, MI 49616
1–800–968–9453

Langley Wire Industries
P.O. Box 312379
New Braunfels, TX 78131
1–800–733–7012

Off Limits Crop Protection Systems
355 Phoenixville Pike
Malvern, PA 19355
1–800–923–7378

POLLINATION

Torchio Enterprises
PO Box 6054
North Logan, UT 84341

Bee Research Lab, ARS-USDA
Building 46, BARC-East
Beltsville, MD 20705
(301) 504–8384

Antles Pollen Supplies
P.O. Box 1243
Wenatchee, WA 98807
(509) 662–2905

MEMBER ORGANIZATIONS

North American Fruit Explorers
1716 Apples Road
Chapin, IL 61704

Northeast Organic Farming Association
411 Sheldon Road
Barre, MA 01005
(508) 355–2853

Organic Trade Association
P.O. Box 1078
Greenfield, MA 01302
(413) 774–7511

Home Orchard Society
P.O. Box 230192
Tigard, OR 97281
(503) 639–6250

Tilth Producers
P.O. Box 85056
Seattle, WA 98145
1–800–731–1143

Canadian Organic Growers
Box 6408, Station J
Ottawa, ON, K2A 3Y6 Canada

PUBLICATIONS

Growing for Market
P.O. Box 3747
Lawrence, KS 66046
(913) 841–2559

American Fruit Grower
37733 Euclid Avenue
Willoughby, OH 44094
(216) 942–2000

Fruit Varieties Journal
American Pomological Society
102 Tyson Building
University Park, PA 16802

Fruit Gardener's Quarterly
18292 Wildlife Road
Fayetteville, AR 72701
(501) 443–0282

Good Fruit Grower
105 South 18th Street #217
Yakima, WA 98901
1–800–487–9946

Fresh from the Cider Press
BC Fruit Tester's Association
2618 Sooke River Road
Sooke, BC V0S 1N0 Canada

The Fruit Growers News
P.O. Box 128
Sparta, MI 49345
(616) 887-9008

INTERNET SITES

Tree Fruit Research Center
http://www.tfrl.ars.usda.gov

The Virtual Orchard
http://orchard.uvm.edu

Sustainable Farming Connection
http://sunsite.unc.edu/farming-connection

Cider Space
http://www.teleport.com/~incider

North American Fruit Explorers
http://www.nafex.org

Backyard Fruit Growers
http://www.sas.upenn.edu/~dailey/byfg.html

The Organic Apple
http://www.nofa.org
(coming in 1999)

Comments to author:
mphil@together.net

Great Books—Old & New

The Apple Culturist, Sereno Edwards Todd, 1871. Here's a guy who put a lifetime of apple-growing experience into a classic treatise. The cultural approaches to insect pests are still the jumping-off point for organic methods today.

The Commercial Apple Industry of North America, J. C. Folger and S. M. Thomson, 1921. Take an apple exporter and a USDA fruit crop specialist, put the editing auspices of L. H. Bailey behind them, and you get a good look at that point in time when large apple operations began to avail over the integrated farm orchard. The useful information comes in snippets, like the fact that it takes sixty hours of labor to thin an acre of trees.

The Principles of Fruit-Growing, L. H. Bailey (Macmillan Company, 1897, 20th edition 1926). No one spoke with more insightfulness than Cornell's Liberty Hyde Bailey on all aspects of horticulture. Apples were perhaps his greatest love.

Textbook of Pomology, J. H. Gourley, 1922. A college text on the physiological side of fruit growing. It's a good synopsis of research done earlier this century, particularly on cover-cropping to build orchard soils.

The Orchard Almanac: A Spraysaver Guide, Stephen Page and Joseph Smillie (Spraysaver Publications, 1986). This is the book that got me started with growing apples organically. The monthly layout of orchard needs and concerns is particularly helpful in understanding what to do next.

Temperate Zone Pomology, Melvin N. Westwood (Timber Press, 1993). The science of apples as best understood to date. The many details provided can jell inquisitive minds to higher levels of understanding. And sometimes to astoundingly simple organic realizations.

Training and Pruning Apple and Pear Trees, C. Forshey, D. Elfving, and R. Stebbins (American Society for Horticultural Science, 1992). Here is the in-depth understanding of pruning from the tree's perspective, with a how-to presentation of seven management systems.

Soil and Health, Sir Albert Howard (Devin-Adair Company, 1947). A good farmer understands and reveres soil health. This book remains a clarion wake-up call to Western agriculture. Brace yourself for a profound discourse.

Eco-Farm: An Acres U.S.A. Primer, Charles Walters and C. J. Fenzau (Acres U.S.A., 1996). A must-read for any orchardist wishing to understand the soil-based tenets of eco-farming.

Edaphos, Paul Sachs (Edaphic Press, 1993). The science of soil dynamics has never been better explained. And while Paul may have an interest in selling natural fertilizers through North Country Organics, he'll never steer you wrong.

The Biodynamic Treatment of Fruit Trees, Ehrenfried E. Pfeiffer (Biodynamic Farming and Gardening Association, 1957). This small booklet from the Biodynamic Farming Association introduces the preparations.

Culture and Horticulture, Wolf D. Storl (Biodynamic Literature, 1979). Appropriately subtitled "A Philosophy of Gardening," this is the book that demystifies Biodynamics and broadens our understanding of Nature.

Apples for the 21st Century, Warren Manhart (North American Tree Company, 1995). Pollination, blossom time, growth characteristics of the tree as well as the fruit, rootstock selection, picking dates, and storability of fifty apple cultivars are covered in appreciative detail.

Sweet & Hard Cider: Making It, Using It, and Enjoying It, Annie Proulx and Lew Nichols (Garden Way Publishing, 1980). The art of cidermaking is not forgotten in this book!

Processed Apple Products, Donald L. Downing (Van Nostrand Reinhold, 1989). This comprehensive reference covers everything from apple cultivars through various types of processing, the nutritional value of apple products, and apple microbiology and preservation. Available from The Haworth Press, 10 Alice Street, Binghamton, NY 13904.

State Universities, the USDA and Cooperative Extension offer regional guides and bulletins on orchard management. Some of these date from the past and might still be found on a dusty university shelf; more recent titles include a telephone number you can call for ordering information:

"The Plum Curculio"—by A. L. Quaintance, USDA Bulletin 103, 1912

"The Roundheaded Appletree Borer"—USDA Bulletin 675, 1919

"Orchard Nutrition Management"—Cornell University, (607) 255–2080

"Organic and Low Spray Apple Production"—ATTRA, 1–800–346–9140

"Common Tree Fruit Pests"—Michigan State University, (517) 335–0240

"Apple Tree Fact Sheets"—Cornell University, (607) 255–2080

"Compendium of Apple and Pear Diseases"—APS Press, 1–800–328–7560

"IPM for Apples & Pears"—University of California, (510) 642–2431

Grower Survey Form

Name: _____

Orchard name: _____

Address: _____

_____

Telephone number: _____

- Farm description and goals: _____

_____

_____

- Personal growing experience: _____

_____

_____

- No. of trees (or acres) in production: _____

- No. of trees (or acres) not yet bearing: _____

- Are you happy with size of your orchard? _____

- Favorite apple varieties: _____

_____

- Comments about choice of rootstocks: _____

_____

_____

- Comments about tree spacing: _____

_____

_____

- Other fruits being grown: _____

_____

- Overall yield (bushels) this last growing season: _____

- What are your grading standards, if any? _____

_____

- Percentage use of crop: home use, direct sale, wholesale, processing, cider _____

MARKETING STRATEGIES

- Where do you sell your fruit? _____

- How do you raise consciousness about organics and/or local agriculture? _____

- What price do you charge for select fruit? Utility grade? A gallon of cider? _____

- What processed products do you make, if any? _____

- Do you feel you make a fair return on your orchard work? _____

SOIL BUILDING PRACTICES

- Do you have any notable site advantages or deficiencies? _____

- What do you add to your orchard soils? _____

- How are these materials applied? _____

- Comments about soil testing or leaf analysis? _____

PEST MANAGEMENT PRACTICES

- Noteworthy insects in your orchard? _____

- Sprays and/or preventative controls (be specific): _____

- Disease strategy: _____

- Equipment systems used to manage orchard? _____
  _____
  _____

- Any suppliers to recommend?_____
  _____

- Most vexing problem and ideas to better the situation? _____
  _____
  _____
  _____

- What is most rewarding to you about orcharding? _____
  _____

- Comments about *The Apple Grower*? _____
  _____
  _____

Please return to Michael Phillips, Lost Nation Orchard, RFD 1 Box 275, Groveton, NH 03582.

Index

The Apple Grower

242 *The Apple Grower*